Sociology of Entrepreneurship in India

Sociology of Entrepreneurship in India

Gurpreet Bal

RAWAT PUBLICATIONS
Jaipur • New Delhi • Bengaluru • Guwahati • Kolkata

ISBN 978-81-316-1317-7

Published by
Prem Rawat for **Rawat Publications**
Satyam Apts, Sector 3, Jawahar Nagar, Jaipur 302 004 (India)
Phone: 0141 265 1748 / 265 7006
E-mail: info@rawatbooks.com
Website: www.rawatbooks.com

New Delhi Office
4858/24, Ansari Road, Daryaganj, New Delhi 110 002
Phone: 011-23263290

Also at *Bengaluru, Guwahati* and *Kolkata*

Typeset by Rawat Computers, Jaipur
Printed and bound in India

Dedicated to

Late Professor Kiran Preet Kaur

Contents

Section III
Entrepreneurship across Gender, Caste and Class

Section IV
Emerging Trends in Entrepreneurship

Section V
Role of State in Entrepreneurship Development

Preface

My journey to the study of entrepreneurship began when I joined the Department of Sociology, Panjab University, Chandigarh, in 1979. Being a little more enthusiastic to explore new aspects of sociology, I opted to study sociology of organizations, and entrepreneurship in addition to other compulsory courses which later on expanded to sociology of work and ultimately culminating into economic sociology. During my journey through academics – study, teaching and research – I feel privileged and honoured to have found sincere friends, mentors, teachers and supervisors, Professor Victor D'Souza for MPhil and Professor P.N. Pimpley for PhD. One amongst all, who in fact is my inspiration to bring out this work, is Late Kiran Preet Kaur (Aneja), who was Professor in the Department of Sociology at Panjab University, Chandigarh, and to whom I dedicate this work. She was my friend for the longest time beginning from class eleventh (Pre-University) at GCW, Amritsar. I started knowing her as a gymnast who very sincerely would do the practice of her favourite game each day and when final exams were approaching, she would be so committed to her studies, running around, taking time from teachers, classmates, and friends. Both of us studied together completing MA, MPhil and PhD from Panjab University. Besides treading the academic path together, particularly in the field of entrepreneurship, I owe a lot to her as a person, who was trustworthy, extremely helpful, reliable and compassionate.

Having participated, presented papers and chaired sessions in biennial conferences of entrepreneurship organized by the apex institute Entrepreneurship Development Institute of India (EDII), Ahmedabad, since early 1990s and a constant enriching learning experience through my interaction with conference chairs Professor Dwijendra Tripathi, Professor Dinesh Awashti, Professor Sasi Misra and Professor Sunil Shukla for which I am grateful, I have discerned that the concept of entrepreneurship for long has become multidisciplinary covering sociology, psychology, economics, management, commerce, the financial and business studies. Thus, the canvas of entrepreneurship studies has widened from the earlier who, when, why and how regarding the ventures to the total ecosystem of entrepreneurship. A big hype has been attached to entrepreneurship in India in recent times.

An analysis of themes of publications in *The Journal of Entrepreneurship* from 1992 to 2011, a publication of EDII, Ahmedabad, in which I have the honour to publish four articles, carried out by Batthini, Bhatt and Joshi, show 14 thought-provoking and research-driven keywords which show certain trends in entrepreneurship studies and these are, banking, clusters, entrepreneurial motivation, human resource management, small, medium enterprises/businesses, social capital, women entrepreneurship, microenterprises, social entrepreneurship, rural entrepreneurship, economic development, and innovation. These themes suggest that the entrepreneurship studies have consistently and continuously been progressing to explore recent challenging issues. At present 64 journals throughout the world, including nine from India, are publishing entrepreneurship research. On the basis of 254 research publications in 50 issues of *The Journal of Entrepreneurship*, Ganapathi Batthini and Kavita Saxena have identified emerging areas of research in entrepreneurship. These have broadly been clubbed in the domain of rural entrepreneurship, micro, small and medium enterprises (MSMEs), entrepreneurial education and research, women entrepreneurship, innovation, and social entrepreneurship. I have made an attempt to touch upon these areas of research from sociological perspective in the book along with a focus on entrepreneurship as an effective strategy for empowering the underprivileged with an inclusive and sustainable approach.

I will be failing in my duty if I do not acknowledge and thank my teacher late Professor K.L. Sharma, formerly Professor, Department of Sociology, Panjab University, Chandigarh for initiating me into entrepreneurship studies. Later, at Guru Nanak Dev University in 1987, Professor Jaspal Singh, the then Head and Professor, Department of Sociology, asked me to introduce the paper on entrepreneurship both at MA and MPhil levels. I feel proud of teaching this paper regularly and consistently to nearly 30 batches. I thank all my students for bearing with me. I wish and hope that all my students and scholars take the sociological understanding of the subject to newer heights.

My research in the field of entrepreneurship has greatly been encouraged and stimulated by my husband, Professor Paramjit Singh Judge. His versatility and inquisitive mind would always be ready to give me ideas for the next project. He has always been forthcoming to provide unconditional support in all my academic pursuits, though I often lagged to carry them forward. I take this opportunity to thank him profusely.

I would like to acknowledge the contribution of one and all in my understanding of entrepreneurship. I am grateful to you all!

Gurpreet Bal

Introduction

Economy and Society: An Interrelationship

To argue that there are social bases of economic behaviour implies that it is significant to understand the nature of economy as well as the society over a period of time to understand how both of them have been influencing each other. Throughout history the economic life of the people has been embedded with their social conditions and, in turn, the nature and quality of social life was closely affected by their economic conditions. A change in economic status generally transforms the social life of the people. It is evident that major changes occurred with the emergence of capitalism in 16th century in England and later on in Europe. Capitalism emerged with the collapse of feudalism. In the famous Dobb-Sweezy debate (Hilton,1978) on what led to the emergence of capitalism and collapse of feudalism, Dobb (1946) argues that feudalism almost collapsed in 14th century while capitalism emerged in 16th century in Western Europe. What happened in between? He says that it was in transition mode. For Dobb, it were the internal factors prevailing in the feudal system, that is production relations and production for self-consumption, local market, besides the people's orientation towards customs, traditions, religion, and above all the growth of population that pushed out the serfs to towns and feudal production suffered. In view of Sweezy (1976), there were external factors to pull out the serfs, disintegrating the feudalism. He argues that the long distance trade and the growth of towns accelerated the process of social differentiation. The townsmen encouraged the rural people to escape, as they needed labour. The serfs were the most exploited lot and they were willing to leave villages to become workers in the factories. The growth of trade and commerce led to the change in the consumption pattern and new articles like oils, perfumes, fine clothes led to the desire to produce more for the market and for profit.

The period between 14th and 16th centuries is generally christened as the first phase of capitalism. The second phase is from 16th century onwards when, between 1540 and 1640, England experienced industrial revolution. In capitalism, the system of production and distribution changed to fulfil the needs of the people. The industrial system emerged where the techniques of work improved and rational system of production, division of labour and specialization became the basis of working. Hence relations with other people and within the social institutions also changed. Factory-made goods were more durable, efficient and were produced in bulk resulting into the generation of surplus produce for monetary exchange in the market. A worker was shifted from home to factory where working hours and days were fixed and he was selling his labour for which he was getting wages in cash. These developments clearly address the interplay of the economic system with social structure. Moving the debate further, Dobb argues that the guild masters or small artisans transformed themselves into small capitalists, but Sweezy does not agree with him and opines that it is the merchant class which had the money to start the new industry. Both the processes might have gone side by side, but there is no doubt that the earlier developments were marked by the merchants and traders bringing in the skilled labour to the cities for putting them under one roof to produce commodities. The skills of artisans were utilized in the factory mode of production. Their skills had not gone wasted, rather they contributed significantly to the growth of capitalism in Western Europe. Entrepreneurs in urban craft guilds took to trade and employed artisans on putting-out system.

The emergence of capitalism in England and subsequently Europe has been well studied and recorded by many scholars, but when dealing with its emergence in countries like India one has to take cognisance of their colonial context. The seeds of capitalism in India were sown with the setting up of English East India Company in Calcutta in 1600 with its head office in England. The company is significant in many ways as it pioneered the shareholder model of corporate ownership and built the foundations of modern business administration. The company was far ahead of time in business acumen, but it also engaged in executive malpractices, stock market excess, and human exploitation (Robins, 2006). The East India Company illustrates how an economic system can entangle the lives of the common people, particularly in this case the Bengal society and its people. The artisans were producing best quality muslin, cotton and calico, but when the mechanization of yarn production was first introduced in Dhaka in 1821, there were stories about the thumb and index finger of some of the renowned artisans being chopped off in order to disable them from twisting finer yarns. The change in economic system led them into misery, famines and poverty, though as per records the artisans of Bengal had a better standard of living than their counterparts in England. The gradual economic development of India during the past, more than 420 years, has had a very intimate relationship with various social parameters, which we are going to examine.

Historically, there has been no uniformity and simultaneity in the emergence of capitalist economy in the world. In the countries where capitalism emerged late, the nature and character of capitalism were quite different from each other. Each country has its unique history as well as the history of emergence of capitalism. By 1800, the factory system had been developed in England. While, England took nearly 250 years to reach at maximum level, Japan took only 50 years and India is taking still longer. The extent and speed of industrial development remained slower in some countries than others resulting in the co-existence and simultaneity of feudalism, pre-capitalist and semi-capitalist production systems. The transition from feudalism to capitalism was complete by 18th century in Western Europe, but the nature and character of capitalism did not remain the same. Over the last five centuries, capitalism has been changing its forms and so has the transformation in the society. However, the change in normative structure or non-material conditions has been taking place slowly in comparison to that in material factors.

In Marxian view, human beings have needs and to fulfil their needs they act upon nature by cooperating with each other, but at the same time, they enter into social relationships by forming the relations of production. Together they develop forces of production, while the tools and techniques of work develop continuously and consistently, and hence they begin to produce more than the subsistence to generate surplus resulting into contradictions. This is the time to reset the relations of production. Once it is achieved, there is further development in the means of production, once again a gap between the means of production and relations of production emerges. This is how the societies have developed over the time. It shows the economic factor as a determinant and society is determined as a result of it. Whenever there is disequilibrium in the economic base, social contradictions emerge. The contradictions result from the increasing specialization of the production process, on the one hand, and the increasing concentration of ownership of productive resources, on the other. This leads to class-based division of society that is, property owning classes and property less classes (Suresh, 2010).

Weber rejects the primacy of the economic factor by arguing that there has been role of ideas in influencing the economic structure. All social actions are not economically influenced, and not all groups are economically relevant. Culturally important groups, however, have some kind of relationship with economic elements; all persistent groups must in some way meet their wants (Weber, 1978, p. LXX). Weber in his study, *The Religion of India* (1958), clearly shows the sociocultural factors as determinants. In his famous thesis 'Protestant Ethics and the Spirit of Capitalism' (1976), he establishes the relationship between Protestant ethic and the spirit of capitalism. He argues that wherever there are Protestants, they have fared much better economically than the Catholics. The emergence of capitalism in number of countries of Western Europe is due to its peoples' ethical value system. These ethical values emanated from Protestantism. He argues that the common element in both Protestantism, particularly Calvinism, and capitalism is rationality. However, he overlooks the fact, as pointed out earlier in this chapter, capitalism developed in the 14th century Europe, whereas Protestantism emerged in the 16th century.

The main argument presented here is that both the classical sociologists, Karl Marx and Max Weber, have emphasized the inter-relationship of economy and society. Both economy and society are indispensable for each other. For Marx, economy is base and society is dependent on it, while for Weber society or social values of the people are significant which lead to the emergence of a particular type of economy. Both these sociologists take one factor as independent and other as dependent or in other words they explore the relationship between the economy and the society. What is important in the case of both the thinkers is that economy and society are inseparable in terms of two important aspects: social relations are marked by an element of economic formations in a society where people do not simply interact as economic agents but also develop relations in consonance with the position they hold in society marked by wealth and traditions.

Functionalism has its roots in the early revolutions in biological sciences in which Herbert Spencer (1969) played a significant role by giving the concept of survival of the fittest. Spencer and, later on, Radcliffe-Brown (1952) used living organism as analogy to explain society. Both society and the organisms grow, show interdependence of parts, integration and differentiation of parts, but the life of the organism is longer than the life of the parts. Talcott Parsons (1972) depicts that the economic system and social system are subsystems, having their autonomy as well as interdependence. But they also have internal system of regulation of tensions and maintain integration. Emile Durkheim's (1964) concept of organic solidarity acts as a force in economic life. Interestingly, Malinowski (1978) gives the example of canoe making of Melanesian community. The collective work of boat making gives them a sense of solidarity, an honour to the chief, but, at the same time, new boat will give them more opportunities of catching fish, hence enhancing economic activity. Though both economy and society are two sides of the same coin but the difference is drawn largely due to the subject matter. Within the economic system, the instrumental rational action prevails, where as society is characterized by both rational and non-rational actions, rather more of non-rational actions (Pareto, 1935). Economists study economic phenomena independent of social phenomenon. Many sociologists have criticized the pure economists and predict that economics will become the sub-discipline of sociology.

Within the academics, economy and society have been treated separately for long. Economy falls in the purview of economists and society is the field of sociologists. The sociologists from classical period to the present have treated society as a whole and economy is one part or an adaptive subsystem of the whole. However, when there is a change in the part, it affects the whole and the continuity of the whole depends upon the contribution of the parts. Just consider one illustration from the present times: pandemic. Covid-19 makes this relationship so clear that how a break in everyday life of the people has ruined the economy and the collapse of the economy has affected the social life, relationships and its interactions – the festivals, celebrations, tourism, and religious practices of the people. During the Great Depression of 1929–1933, it was observed that social and political factors constantly acted upon economic life. The whole world fear the economic backlash of the Russia-Ukraine war. It clearly depicts how economic and non-economic factors overlap and how they influence each other.

The famous Hawthorne experiments carried out by Elton Mayo from 1927–1932 in Chicago brings out that human relations are above the economic incentives. In the initial experiments, the effects of light, rest periods, shorter week were seen on the work performance and it was found that non-economic rewards and sanctions significantly affect the behaviour of the workers. The affection and respect of the workers and friends were more significant than the material rewards, i.e. more wages, bonus, etc. Workers preferred maintaining amicable relations with their friends to making more money. The study pointed out that the workers have many needs other than the economic ones. By paying attention to the non-economic, social and cultural needs of the workers, there would be increase in workers' satisfaction and productivity. As a result of this understanding, the emergence of industrial sociology took place and remained the basis of understanding the capitalist development and social life for the subsequent five decades.

The isolation of the economic from social has been overcome with the emergence of economic sociology. The term economic sociology was coined by William Stanley Jevons in 1879. Economists treat economic sociology as social economy or sociological economics as a branch of economics. Sociologists say it is sociological discipline. Some sociologists and economists treat economic sociology as 'no man's land' or 'everyman's land'. The relationship between the two involves cooperation and complementarity rather than competition and substitution. Often pure economic analysis needs to be supplemented by a sociological perspective. It is the sociological perspective which is applied to the understanding of an economic phenomena. The relationship between the two is dualistic in nature. It is sociology of economics and economics of sociology. Economic sociology is generally explained as the study of the social causes and also the effects of any economic phenomena. Smelser (1988, p. 43) defines, 'Economic sociology is the application of the general frame of reference, variables, and explanatory models of sociology to that complex of activities concerned with the production, distribution, exchange, and consumption of scarce goods and services'. The development of economic sociology may be divided into two phases – classical period through the works of Emile Durkheim, Max Weber and Georg Simmel (for details see Smelser and Swedberg, *Introducing Economic Sociology*, 2005, pp. 8–11), and a contemporary phase when there is a revival of economic sociology, designated as new economic sociology. New economic sociology was consolidated with the works of sociologists, namely Mark Granovetter, Richard Swedberg and Howard Aldrich.

For Weber, bureaucracy is the most rational form of social organization for further development of capitalist economic system. Durkheim maintained that the economic factors depend upon social phenomena, because it is embedded in institutions, norms and values. The works of Weber, Marx and Durkheim suggest three propositions as described by Swedberg and Granovetter (1992, p. 6), which are: (a) Economic action is a form of social action; (b) Economic action is socially situated; and (c) Economic institutions are social constructions. As a matter of fact, the understanding of socio-structural basis of economic behaviour has rejuvenated the economics with flesh and blood, which was becoming progressively mathematical science. In a study (Feldmann, 2007), it has been found that countries in which the largest portion of the population practices Protestant religion have substantially higher labour force participation and employment rates, particularly among women. Protestant ethic that stresses hard and diligent work appears to have an enduring impact on people's involvement in labour market. Results also suggest that the Protestant ethics is likely to be influential even in today's modern societies. Among the industrialized OECD countries, the cultural system probably had a stronger effect on the economic system than the reverse. An examination of the impact of the level of economic development suggests that those parts of the cultural system, which are related to the political/social values, are mostly influenced by particular aspects of the economy. In 1990s when American economy resurged from depression, the economic sociology also made great strides. Amartya Sen won the Nobel Prize in economics as he interpreted economic phenomena as a result of social factors. Presently, the sociological perspective on the economy is experiencing a revival.

In the context, the major contribution came with the work of Mark Granovetter (1992), *Economic Action and Social Structure: The Problem of Embeddedness*, which consolidated the new economic sociology in the middle of 1980s. He gave the concept of 'embeddedness of economic behaviour' by which he means trust and malfeasance, embeddedness of economic behaviour with social relations – more specifically social and kinship network. Social relations are responsible for the production of trust in economic life. He has argued that most of our behaviour is closely entrenched in networks of interpersonal relations. Economists take economic behaviour as instrumental rational, but such behaviour also aims at sociability, approval, status and power. The publication in 1994 of the *Handbook of Economic Sociology*, edited by Neil J. Smelser and Richard Swedberg, consolidated the field of economic sociology with 30 contributions on the diverse issues and intersections of economy and society. The gender and economic sociology, economy and environment, and ethnic economy, along with state, law, education and religion in the context of economy have been explored by them. Swedberg developed a sociology of markets and propounds that sociology of money should not only examine the impact of money on social relations, but must pay attention to money as a dynamic and ever changing instrument used to acquire economic power. Howard Aldrich's (2005) work on entrepreneurs is significant; particularly his entrepreneurial strategies show a relationship between the size of population and entry of a firm.

After liberalization of Indian economy, the foreign capitalists saw India's size of population as viable consumers.

During these two phases under the ambient of economic sociology, a number of sub fields or specialities in sociology emerged, such as the study of organizations, work, labour, occupations, professions, industrial sociology and entrepreneurship. We may also add development studies, which cover economic processes as a result of industrialization, social stratification and political system. In recent times, studies on social construction of markets, consumption, consumer behaviour, leisure, shopping, fashion, beauty and tastes are being sociologically mapped in social background even covering the domain of popular culture. With the revival of economic sociology, Gullien et al. (2002, pp. 8–9) have compiled four theoretical sociological insights into economic phenomena which depict the social basis of economic behaviour. These insights are also the underlying thread of the arguments put in different chapters of the book:

1. *Culture:* Economic action cannot proceed without shared understandings about appropriate behaviour in a given social setting, as it helps the actors in making sense of the situation, develop strategies for action, and adjust their expectations and behaviour when they interact with others. Economic sociologists invoke values and norms, network structures, the state, and ideologies as factors creating shared understandings among participants in various arena in which economic activity takes place, including markets, groups, organizations and households.
2. *Networks and Social Capital:* Economic action can be facilitated or hindered by the actors' position in a network of relationships. Many economic sociologists, including Coleman (1988), invoke the concept of social capital to explain why some actors are more successful than others at mobilizing resources or attaining their goals. Therefore, social network analysis has been the primary methodology for studying the economic phenomenon.
3. *Trust:* Economic action is often based on trust, which is historically developed and culturally specific. Trust helps to explain the observed order, stability and continuity in social life that

occurs because of emotional caring or norms of obligation that bind various actors.

4. *Effort and Motivation:* Economic sociologists have pointed out several key factors that shape commitment and effort at work. Good faith and initiative are required if complex organizations are to respond to unforeseen circumstances and opportunities; subordinates must comply with general rules as well as specific orders and these qualities are guided by culture, ideology, or ethic of work and effort. More recently, economic sociologists have revisited social-psychological processes, group dynamics and complexity of human motivation to work hard.

To sum up the context of the interplay of economy and society leading to the development of economic sociology, it is relevant to recognize the complexity and interdependence of social and economic elements. The central figure between the two is an entrepreneur, who is an economic man or individual combining business acumen with social networks. Entrepreneur being a creative and innovative actor takes initiative in commercial/business or manufacturing activity. He has an eye on market and accordingly organizes his/her strategies and tactics to look for profit opportunities. Overall, an entrepreneur is a productive, wealth-generating person, he is a true capitalist who is always looking forward to new opportunities to exploit, his primary objective as an entrepreneur is the enhancement of capitalism and subsequent socio-economic development. Precisely, the significance of social capital to create economic capital is the thrust of the argument.

Gopakumar (1995, pp. 14–15) informs that the position of entrepreneur remained at best on the outskirts of an integrated economic theory. The classical economists assigned practically no operative place for him in the development process, and the neo-classicists accorded to him only a grudging and ambivalent acknowledgement. It is only Schumpeter who brought entrepreneur to the centre stage in the theory of economic development, but that was also for a brief period and as a matter of fact, the entrepreneur practically disappeared from microeconomic theory. Though during the mid-1950s economists did recognize the entrepreneurial capabilities for economic development, but they could not harness his capabilities to solve economic problems. Soon the entrepreneur entered the domain of social scientists, particularly, the sociologists and social psychologists like Amitai Etzioni and McClelland when they emphasized training/capacity building for solving many of the problems. Thus, entrepreneur entered the theoretical framework of economic action as a powerful connection between economy and society.

The present work is aimed at keeping the entrepreneur in middle of the interrelationship between economy and society and it attempts to establish this close bond in the context of Indian society and Indian economy. We will analyse diverse economic activities carried out by entrepreneurs by using sociological variables, concepts, methods, techniques, models, ideologies, frames of reference and perspectives. Economic action is, after all, a form of social action. Weber says that even the rational instrumental action is socially oriented as it is oriented towards others. It takes into account the behaviour of others. An entrepreneur is a product of society and Aldrich (Smelser and Swedberg, 2005) argues that entrepreneur can both reproduce and challenge the existing social order. During the last four decades in India, the entrepreneur and entrepreneurship have treaded an unfamiliar path to reach and become a common idiom in the present times. But still both entrepreneur and entrepreneurship are taken as a product that is, the end-result when not much attention has been paid on entrepreneur and entrepreneurship as a process. The present book aims at examining the process of becoming an entrepreneur and various sociological dimensions of entrepreneurship.

About the Book

After establishing an interrelationship of economy and society in the introduction to develop a context to make the social basis of economic action significant, the book has been divided into five sections consisting of 14 chapters. Section I takes account of theoretical understanding of entrepreneur and entrepreneurship. Chapter one focuses on the concepts of entrepreneur and entrepreneurship, the characteristics and types of entrepreneurs alongside the social profile of Indian entrepreneurs, and also raises some sociological concerns. Chapter two takes account of the sociologically-oriented theoretical perspectives to examine the entrepreneurship. It is not that only sociologists have contributed to theoretical understanding but rather economists, historians, social psychologists also provide great insights into the complex issues and help in addressing the question that why some people tend to become successful entrepreneurs than others. In the second half of the 20th century, an economist turned sociologist Joseph Schumpeter and management expert Peter Drucker became extremely popular with their ideas on innovation and entrepreneurship. Chapter three brings out in detail the contributions of these two scholars towards the understanding of entrepreneurship. The theoretical understanding of various dimensions of entrepreneurship leads us to explore the development of Indian entrepreneurship over time, originating from 1600 with the establishing of East India Company to post independent India following the socialist, welfare model. In chapter four a few enabling and a large number of hampering factors have been explored which in fact delayed the growth of Indian entrepreneurship primarily based on the research of historians.

Since the recognition of the social context of entrepreneurship, a huge stock of knowledge has been created. This broad canvas of research has been divided into two dichotomous categories. One set of argument is that entrepreneurs are born, which means they are natural entrepreneurs who happened to take birth in certain families and hence they are reared to be entrepreneurs and the other argument is that they can be created, nurtured, or made through training and skill formation. Any person from any type of family background can be a successful entrepreneur. These two standpoints have been examined in sections II and III consisting of four chapters by taking the context of social capital vis-à-vis the human capital. In chapters five and six the role of social capital has been examined by taking the cases of traditional business communities, viz. Marwari, Gujarati, Parsi and Sindhi entrepreneurs. Indian business is primarily owned and managed by families. Chapter six also presents the contribution of family businesses and business houses, which has particularly been examined in the competitive global scenario.

Section III explores the emergence, process and pattern of entrepreneurship among various underprivileged groups. This section brings out how entrepreneurs by negotiating gender, caste and class have empowered themselves through the display of their agency.

The gender-based entrepreneurship has great significance, as women, who earlier were almost out of the business domain due to prevalent patriarchy, cultural ethos and gendered roles, have now proved their traits of decision-making, problem solving and leadership qualities. The business and trade has been the realm of the traditional trading castes who from *bazaar* economy moved to the industrial entrepreneurship. The other castes, particularly at the grassroots level, were always looked down upon whenever they tried to shift from their hereditary caste occupations. A number of studies suggest that by becoming entrepreneurs they have not only removed the stigma attached to them but have also achieved excellence in diverse types of entrepreneurial pursuits, be it fashion, e-commerce, entertainment or wellness. Chapters seven and eight elaborate the entrepreneurship amongst women, Dalits and tribals with the basic argument that entrepreneurs can be created on the basis of their personality traits, achievement motivation, education, and skill formation. These entrepreneurs have empowered themselves through self-motivation, hard work and perseverance.

Moving away from starting an enterprise or venturing into entrepreneurship, an attempt has also been made to examine the overall ecosystem of entrepreneurship. In the recent times a new breed of entrepreneurs are emerging who besides earning profits are also sensitive to issues of social concern. The contribution of entrepreneurs in rural setting and social entrepreneurs to address the issues of environment, social problems, and human rights in Indian society is overwhelming. The Indian immigrant entrepreneurs have a special significance who could set up business and run those successfully in an alien environment. They have not just economically contributed to their adopted countries but the contribution is also significant in terms of their remittances sent back home. The chapters nine, ten and eleven in section IV deliberates on such emerging trends in entrepreneurship in India.

Besides individual initiatives, the state also has recognized the role of entrepreneurship as the prime mover of economic development, hence it has been taking a number of initiatives to develop entrepreneurship amongst its people. The last, section V, examines the interventions of Indian government to turnaround the social, economic conditions of the people through entrepreneurship in the country. Comprehensive review of government policies and training programmes to promote entrepreneurship starting from the Independence of the country to June 1991 has been discussed in chapter twelve. In July 1991, the Government of India took a historic decision on the liberalization of the Indian economy with a view to enhance its development. Chapter thirteen critically examines the process of globalization and its impact on entrepreneurship development in India. Keeping in view the plans and strategies launched by the present government to promote entrepreneurship, an attempt has also been made to make an assessment of the Indian entrepreneurship on the basis of Global Entrepreneurship Monitor, India Reports (2010–2020), in the last chapter, that is fourteen of the book. It also makes an evaluation of the challenges and emerging opportunities in the development of Indian entrepreneurship, followed by major conclusions drawn in the context of entrepreneurship in India at the end of the book.

Suggested Readings

Granovetter, Mark and Swedberg, Richard (eds) (1992). *The Sociology of Economic Life*. Boulder, Colorado: Westview Press.

Guillen, M.F., Collins, R., England, P. and Meyer, M. (2002). *The New Economic Sociology: Developments in an Emerging Field*. New York: Russell Sage Foundation.

Hilton, Rodney (ed.) (1976). *The Transition from Feudalism to Capitalism*. Verso: London.

Smelser Neil J. and Swedberg, Richard (eds) (2005). *Handbook of Economic Sociology*. Princeton and New York: Princeton University Press and Russell Sage Foundation.

Suresh, R.R. (2010). *Economy and Society: Evolution of Capitalism*. New Delhi: Sage Publications.

Swedberg, Richard (ed.) (2000). *Entrepreneurship: The Social Science View*. New Delhi: Oxford University Press.

Weber, Max (1978). *Economy and Society: An Outline of Interpretative Sociology*. Vol. 1. (Guenther Roth and Claus Wittich, eds) Berkeley: University of California Press (first published by Bedminster Press Inc. New York, 1968.

Section I

Theorizing Entrepreneurship

1

Conceptualizing Entrepreneur and Entrepreneurship

An attempt has been made in this chapter to take cognizance of various concepts of entrepreneur and entrepreneurship available in the existing and representative literature. Like concepts in social science, these two concepts are contested, in the sense that various conceptual categories have been added to make it more comprehensive, the purpose of which is to cover all kinds of economic activities from which the actors not only earn livelihood, but also make profit. In this regard, it seems reasonable to begin with relevant explanation and definition of the economic man called entrepreneur by asking questions. Who is he and what he does? And how is he distinctive? The meaning of entrepreneur has been undergoing a change with time depending upon the nature of the development of the societies. Since society tends to change in terms of its various aspects, the nature and character of an entrepreneur are expected to change to fulfil the needs and requirements of the people. The understanding of the entrepreneur is multifaceted requiring multidisciplinary approach to comprehend its true meanings.

The discussion in the present chapter has been divided into three parts. The first part explicates various concepts of entrepreneur and entrepreneurship in terms of how these concepts have evolved over a period of time to make a comprehensive view of what it means to be an entrepreneur in particular. The second part offers a social profile of entrepreneurs in India with the underlying assumption that despite certain common characteristics, there could be certain specific features in every social setting. The third part takes cognisance of certain sociological concerns in terms of multidisciplinary nature of the concepts and its social landscape. It may also be informed that most of the discussion is precise, because the subsequent chapters would comprehensively deal with various aspects stated here.

Evolution of the Concepts of Entrepreneur and Entrepreneurship

The word 'entrepreneur' has been taken from a French word, *entreprendre*, which means 'to undertake or to endeavour', 'to take initiative', or 'to do something'. Roughly speaking, an entrepreneur undertakes any commercial or business activity, that is, the one who performs an economic role. He may also be the one to venture into the production and manufacturing of some products, such as an industrialist or a businessman may be called as an entrepreneur. Entrepreneurship is an action or an activity of the entrepreneur in terms of what he actually does, which may be understood as the role or function of an entrepreneur. Entrepreneurship may also be regarded as a process of initiating, coordinating and managing any business activity and while doing so an entrepreneur takes risk, makes decision, bears the uncertainty of the market, provides leadership, and above all, innovates. He is not like a traditional businessman, but he attempts to create something new, different and appealing. An enterprise is an economic organization and in the words of Weber (1978, p. 52), 'Continuous rational activity of a specified kind will be called an enterprise'. The rational economic action requires instrumental rationality, that is, deliberate planning, a means and goals relationship by rationally setting the goals and rationally selecting the means to achieve them. Therefore, economic organizations are all permanent economic establishments involving the activities of a plurality of persons, all the way from a workshop run by two artisans to a business corporation, cooperative associations, partnerships and so on (p. 74).

The concept of entrepreneurship has been dynamic and its meanings have kept on changing with the dominant system of production throughout the history of development. In the early 16th century, adventurers as well as the ones who were carrying military expeditions were referred as entrepreneurs. In the 17th century, the French applied the word entrepreneur to road, bridge, harbour and fortification contractors, later on covering even the architects. The first economic understanding of entrepreneurship is found in the works of Richard Cantillon (1680–1734) who first identified the unique risk-bearing function of the entrepreneur, he also coined the term 'entrepreneur', one who bears uncertainty in the exchange of goods implying that anyone engaged in an economic activity is an entrepreneur (Kilby, 1971; Gopakumar, 1995). By the middle of the 18th century new forms of production, social relations, governance and social thought began to emerge. Adam Smith made references to entrepreneur's decision-making ability, whereas J.B. Say emphasized the role of entrepreneur, the one who carries out the work of application that is the coordination. Thus, the entrepreneur is an agent who unites all means of production and finds the value of products in them. In the later period of this century, the economists also referred agricultural cultivators as entrepreneurs. In the beginning of the 19th century, in an era of industrialization, entrepreneur was the one who had the ability to take risk, and the one who buys the material at a contracted price and sells the produce at a fixed price.

Schumpeter (2000), the 20th century well-known economist, provided a sort of synthesis of differing notions of entrepreneurship propounded before him such as risk taking, uncertainty, superintendence and coordination. If we take his development of thought on the topic, he begins to argue that some people have a capacity for being entrepreneurial. Beside other qualities, he predominantly shows leadership traits. Then he moves to emphasize on the entrepreneurial functions. What he has stressed is that these attributes unaccompanied by the ability to innovate through the creation of a new combination of already existing material and forces would not be sufficient to invest a person with dignity of entrepreneurship. For him the defining characteristic is doing new things or doing the things that are already being done in a new way. Schumpeter observed that entrepreneurial activity is cyclical: period of innovative boom, which is called swarm-like, are followed by assimilation. Innovation is swarm-like in which the appearance of one or a few entrepreneurs facilitate the appearance of others. Over the time, however, innovation declines under capitalism. Entrepreneurs reinvest their profits and retire, thus liquidating their enterprise or consolidating their enterprise or consolidating it with others. In his view, no one is an entrepreneur forever; for, as long as he is actually carrying out innovative activity, he is an entrepreneur, otherwise he ceases to be an entrepreneur and become a usual traditional businessman. Thus, he equated entrepreneurship with innovation which definitely became an industrial religion of the late 20th century.

Though the term entrepreneurship has been in use for well over 200 years, there remains considerable disagreement over its meaning. People hold disparate views regarding definition of an entrepreneur and the nature of his activities. Peter Kilby (1971) informs that an entrepreneur is Heffalump – a large four footed animal hunted by many people, all unable to capture him, but all claim they have seen him and describe him differently. Morris and Lewis (1993) performed a content analysis of key words found in definitions of entrepreneurship appearing in literature and they found that 18 key terms appear at least five times in the sample. The most common terms include starting or creating a new venture, innovating or creating new combinations of resources, risk taking, profit seeking, and creating value. Despite the considerable disagreement existing in its definition, it became quite clear in the last century that anyone engaged in trade, business, or industry could be called an entrepreneur and while carrying on such activities he shows certain entrepreneurial behaviour.

A clear conceptual distinction among entrepreneur, capitalist, and manager existed in the last century in the literature. Capitalist is the one who invests his capital to earn profits, the manager organizes, coordinates and manages the activities of all the employees as his focus is more on the management of the enterprise, that is, getting things done through other people. The role of a manager is of a planner, strategist, organizer, evaluator, coordinator, supervisor and motivator. The entrepreneur, on the other hand, envisions the future, invests his capital, takes calculated risk, and also coordinates the activities of all his employees. Therefore, a capitalist or a manager cannot be an entrepreneur, but an entrepreneur can be a manager as well as a capitalist – he is all in one. The entrepreneurs are the best as performers than being managers/venture capitalists/planners. By combining the roles of entrepreneurs and professionals/managers, there can be entrepreneurial professionals leading the companies. An entrepreneur with an idea can take the financial assistance from venture capitalist to set up his enterprise.

Hisrich (1985) clarifies that entrepreneurship could be practised in all walks of life and not just by individuals but also by groups, communities and societies. Drucker (1985) adds that entrepreneurship was not the preserve of a few gifted individuals; rather it could be practised systematically by large corporations. The head of a corporation may be the owner or the manager/bureaucrat, but he/she can still perform entrepreneurial functions.

The concept of entrepreneur and entrepreneurship has remained dynamic and got refined in the due course of time. Taking the above definitions, it is clear that it is a multidisciplinary field of knowledge. Entrepreneurial concepts and explanatory principles have thus found their way into entrepreneurship research by scholars in many disciplines. Psychologists, historians, anthropologists, political scientists and others, besides sociologists have had a keen interest in entrepreneurship. Aldrich (2005, p. 452) illustrates that political scientists have used the label entrepreneur as a term for individuals who change the direction and flow of politics. Anthropologists studying the economic adaptation of immigrants to their host society have viewed entrepreneurship as a response to the blocked opportunities. Towards the end of the last century with much emphasis on managerial skills in business administration and industrial management, the field of entrepreneurship has moved more towards business, commerce and management studies. However, in recent times, the entrepreneurship development studies have acquired its distinct identity. Swedberg (2000, p. 7) argues, 'The Social Sciences, can provide new and fresh ideas about the theory and practice of entrepreneurship, by looking at innovative business behaviour in other times, in other societies, and in other cultures-and also by looking at entrepreneurship from novel angles and from the perspective of a much wider range of actors'.

It is interesting to note that in most of the available literature, an entrepreneur is defined in terms of the personality traits of the individual which makes him an entrepreneur. Social psychology emphasize environment or social setting in shaping the personality of an individual. Thus, such an understanding of an entrepreneur is social psychological and has limitations in terms of generalizing it in all cases. Meredith et al. (1982) in 1977 prepared a list of six characteristics and 19 traits[1] of successful entrepreneurs on the basis of 64 seminars conducted over four years. The six characteristics are self-confidence, task-result-oriented, risk taker, leadership, originality, and future-oriented. A person having these characteristics has a probability of success in proportion to the degree to which these are present. One need not to have all the characteristics but the more one has, the greater chance is of him being an entrepreneur. All entrepreneurs are not alike; they differ noticeably from each other, but they would be at variance markedly from non-entrepreneurs. In terms of certain personality traits, some are aloof and arrogant, whereas others are withdrawn, shy, introvert and still some are dynamic. Individuals are viewed as having varying degrees of these characteristics. It is also argued that in addition to the above mentioned characteristics, good health, which indicates emotional stability, is the core feature of an entrepreneur. We have many instances of successful entrepreneurs, such as Aditya Birla of Birla group and Parminder Singh of Ranbaxy who could not sustain due to health crisis and their untimely death left a big void. The entrepreneurial role behaviour, depicting six characteristics, namely risk taking, innovative/novel activity, individual responsibility, knowledge of results of decisions, long range planning and organizational abilities, has been the primary interest of McClelland (1961).

Though entrepreneurship by definition means taking risk of some kind, yet McClelland (ibid.) is the one who clearly states how much risk is to be taken by an entrepreneur. He calls for making calculated or moderate risk, neither too high nor too low. High risk taker is like a gambler and the actions of a low risk taker are prescribed by tradition. On the continuum of risk taking, running from low risk to high risk, entrepreneur falls somewhere in the middle. As a corollary to this view, Gartner (1988) argues that entrepreneurship should be studied by focusing on the behaviour and activities of people trying to create businesses, rather than on their psychological states and personality characteristics. Drucker

(1985) also opines that it is not a personality trait, but a learnable set of behaviour. Somewhat differently Schumpeter (2000) emphasizes that an entrepreneur is the one who has the ability to make new combinations.

With the steady development in the field of entrepreneurship, the concept has also broadened to include a variety of entrepreneurs according to their areas of specialization. Scholars have categorized the entrepreneurs by using varied criteria, such as in terms of size (big/medium/small), location (rural/urban), duration (I/II/III generation), level of technology used (low/medium/modern), extent of production, gender (men/women), and degree of innovativeness. Yale Brozen's typology of different categories of entrepreneurs includes innovating, imitating, fabian and drone in terms of the degree of innovative zeal, propensity to introduce change, and qualities of leadership displayed. Innovative entrepreneurs are the ones who see the opportunities for introducing a new technique or a new commodity or a new market, who may raise money, choose top managers and assemble various factors to launch an enterprise. Schumpeter's entrepreneur is of this kind. The imitating entrepreneurs are ready to adopt successful innovations done by innovating entrepreneurs. They do not innovate but just imitate techniques and technologies invented by others. Such entrepreneurs are an asset for developing countries, for they contribute to the development of that country, who on the basis of their sheer observation, practical bent of mind, traditional skills and on-the-job experience can recreate almost identical goods at a low cost to meet the local demand. In developing countries, like India, more and more numbers of imitating entrepreneurs are found, whereas in the developed countries innovating entrepreneurs are numerous, because these countries can allocate much more funds for research and development. Fabian entrepreneurs act with great caution and scepticism in introducing any change. They neither have will nor desire to adopt new methods innovated by others. The change is introduced only when they know that by not doing so they may lose the business. They are more governed by religion, customs, traditions and past practices. Such entrepreneurs are shy and lazy and are not interested in taking a risk. Drone type of entrepreneurs actually cease to be entrepreneurs, as they refuse to adopt and use opportunities to make changes in production even at the risk of loss (c.f. Singh, 1985).

In recent times, it is common to use words such as intrapreneurs, who earlier were working as experts for others and then they started their own business. Infopreneur is the one who is involved in the business of information. The concept of infopreneur was coined by Harold Skip Weitzen in 1985 to include the entire process of selecting, collecting, organizing, repackaging and selling of information for profit, e.g. online searching, outsourcing, library research, etc. Agripreneurs are the farmers who have turned to agribusiness such as horticulture, floriculture, organic farming. Ecopreneurs are engaged in business or producing goods which tackle environmental issues. Finally, there are edupreneurs engaged in teaching and research in entrepreneurship education and so on. Despite all this typology of entrepreneurs, we may broadly classify them into two categories in the Indian context. These are: (a) Natural or born entrepreneurs; (b) Created or trained to be entrepreneurs.

In this book the entrepreneurs and entrepreneurship in India have been examined by using these two broad categories. After having a brief overview of the entrepreneurs in general, it becomes significant to precisely peep into the social background of Indian entrepreneurs.

Social Profile of Indian Entrepreneurs

Conceptualizing the Indian entrepreneur is an exercise carried along two variables, namely the communitarian and individual. The Western concepts of entrepreneur tend to construct an individual in terms of certain personality traits and a structure of orientation towards the goal. The underlying assumption is that a successful enterprise depends upon the ability of the leader to act upon a set of variables and this action is facilitated by the personality and achievement orientation of an actor. Such a theoretical assumption could be seen as a plausible variable only in the context of certain cultures created by a particular kind of socio-economic system which we identify as capitalism. When we examine the Indian landscape, it seems that the Western notions might be little overemphasized as a result of which the role of social structural variables gets ignored or side-lined. For example, it is not informed how many enterprises in the West belong to families who have been controlling certain businesses and industries for centuries.

A large chunk of enterprises belong to specific communities in India. More than half of the total assets are with Marwari community only. Other prominent communities amongst them in northern and western parts of the country are Parsi, Gujarati, Sindhi, and Punjabi, whereas the southern part has enterprising communities like Chettiars, Nadars, Gounders, and Naidus who have almost become synonymous with business and trade. Amongst them there are certain traditionally trading caste groups, such as Bania, Khatri, Arora, and Bohras. They have family enterprises, which are owned, run and managed by families. Dutta (1997) argues that family businesses constitute 99 per cent of the total businesses in India, which, in fact, is true for all countries. Even America, the most developed country of the world, has nearly 80 per cent family enterprises. Families provide the required capital, resources, networks and primordial ties which are found to be the most conducive to start, manage and run the business. Most of them have been entrepreneurs for three or more generations born in business families and brought up in such an environment. We may say that in India, entrepreneurship is predominantly characterized by caste, family, and community.

Entrepreneurs usually are married persons and interestingly marriages are arranged within the community as a result of which most of the entrepreneurs are related through marriage creating a secured environment and providing the ability to take some risks. Dorin (2003) has given illustration of Mittal[2], Bajaj[3] and many more entrepreneurs living in joint family system. Entrepreneurship, however, is spread across all prominent religious groups – Hindus, Jains, Sikhs, Muslims, Christians, besides a few Jews settled in Kerala state of India owing to which it is not plausible to argue that there is a relationship between religious ethic and running an enterprise. Aditya Birla would always go to *Puja* room, say prayers and then would eat and start his work. Whether office or factory, the premises are decorated with statues and pictures of gods, saints and gurus. Their day begins by offering prayers, flowers, incense to them. Many of the big cities, namely, Delhi, Mumbai, Hyderabad, and Jaipur, have Birla Mandir, constructed by the Birlas, on the tourist list and we often hear about them holding religious events like *bhoomipujan*, Laxmi *puja*, Vishavkarma *puja*. Amongst them, we also have great philanthropists like Birlas and Tatas.

Majority of the Indian entrepreneurs, till the turn of the 20th century, were not well educated and lacked technical education. The scenario of Indian entrepreneurship depicts that the entrepreneurs are the most mobile persons and among them the Parsis are the most mobile, constituting a global community. Similarly, the Gujaratis, despite being conservative, have a history of migration to African countries, England, the USA and Canada. The Marwaris though are an exception by not going to foreign countries to do business, but they are found virtually in all parts of the country. It is interesting to find that none of the community has progressed in its own homeland. The Marwaris had migrated to Calcutta, Bombay, Ahmedabad and then to all over the country from Rajasthan. The Parsis had come from Persia (Iran) to India and similarly, the Gujaratis also flourished in foreign lands, the Sindhis had come from Sindh province of Pakistan at the time of the Partition. Even the Punjabis have performed better outside of Punjab. One of the major reasons for their continuous success is that they followed business ethics, practices and values seriously. They practice, as Dorin (ibid.) highlights, a complete compartmentalization of office work and family. Most of them have vegetarian food and wear simple clothes. Till very recently, the Marwaris were identified with *dhoti* and *topi*, and the Gujaratis also led an ascetic life. Though the women of the present generation have entered into entrepreneurship but excepting a few like Maurine Wadia from Godrej family, and Neeta Ambani from Reliance group, we do not find enough cases of women from traditional communities doing business in the existing literature.

The above social profile of the Indian entrepreneur may not be taken as the exclusive characteristic of India. I have already mentioned that such instances abound in the developed world. The success of Jews in the US in this regard underlines the fact that communities and families have a history of entrepreneurship. At the same time, India is not a land of families and communities in entrepreneurship, for such a view would be regarded as a construction orientalism. If we do not look into percentages, then we shall have innumerable examples of individuals establishing their enterprises with innovativeness, determinations and vision. It is, therefore, important to keep in mind that it is quite possible and probable to construct a set of characteristics in a capitalist society which contribute towards the making of a successful entrepreneur.

Sociological Concerns

Aldrich (2005, p. 451) raised three broad themes of sociological concern for entrepreneurship. First, entrepreneurs can both reproduce and challenge the existing social order. Second, entrepreneurship ensures the reproduction of existing organizational populations and lays a foundation for the creation of new populations. Whether a new business simply replicates an existing form or moves into novel territory depends upon the extent to which its founding members possess diverse outlooks and skills as well as the socio-political context in which it is created. Third, entrepreneurship affects levels of stratification and inequality in a society by shaping the life chances of founders and their employees. In this context we find that in Indian scenario, alongside the community-caste dominant entrepreneurs, a new breed of entrepreneurs has emerged in the 21st century as a result of globalization in India. These entrepreneurs have successfully emerged in ICT, IT and service sectors. Earlier the entrepreneurs were either business or manufacturing entrepreneurs, but now service sector entrepreneurship has evolved significantly. India has become a major source for supplying technical professionals. Jain (1998) argues that companies want high flying, inflexible, arrogant business graduates and, as a result, we have now more intrapreneurs who are professionals or technocrats in contrast to earlier artisans or craftsmen. Educated entrepreneurs have acquired prominence, as new knowledge, new technology, and different management practices are required. The manager in demand will not be the one who possesses the same knowledge and skill like ten thousand others, but the one who has a right kind of attitude, creativity, initiative, commitment and adaptability.

India's entrepreneurial landscape has been changing with the entry of non-traditional business communities, castes and groups of people. To begin with, the entry of Brahmins in manufacturing, followed by other castes such as Kammas, Naidus, Reddys, Nadars, Ezhavas, Patidars, Ramgarhias, and Chamars, has given a different dynamics to the nature and culture of entrepreneurship by modifying and diversifying their traditional items of production. The Indian market is also an attraction for many multinational companies to start manufacturing of goods of mass consumption. With the opening up of new export opportunities, interaction with foreign entrepreneurs has benefitted in terms of doing business.

The technological development and the fastest growing ICT sector has taken the entrepreneurship to newer heights.

Emergence of social entrepreneurs is a new beginning towards social welfare with capacity building as an alternative to charity or philanthropy. They aim at bringing social change and sustainable development with human rights perspective. They may opt for-profit or not-for profit model for innovative activities. In recent times, women entrepreneurship has become a cliché, largely engaged in providing various services and a few among them are also in manufacturing. The functional entrepreneurship catering to the needs of local people, particularly of women, has led to their empowerment. The demand for certain products has increased internationally. Various textile, leather, jewellery, beauty products, and foods have tremendously increased and, thus, the rise in their exports. All these are mainly contributed by women, Dalits, and tribal. Environment issues are being increasingly taken care of by the entrepreneurs. Even human rights perspective has entered in a big way into entrepreneurship development.

To end the discussion, it may be pointed out that the concept of entrepreneurship has become multidisciplinary, covering disciplines such as sociology, psychology, economics, management, commerce, and financial and business studies. Thus, the scope of entrepreneurship studies has widened and grown from the earlier narrower understanding to much comprehensive view. In the recent years, entrepreneur and entrepreneurship has got much engagement from the Government of India. A number of interventions, programmes and action plans have been launched with much fanfare. Over the time, studies have shown that handholding, encouraging people to take up entrepreneurial activities can transform the lives of the people. Thus, a number of NGOs and voluntary organizations have been organizing capacity building and motivational programmes primarily at the grassroots.

Trends in entrepreneurship studies in India over the time depict that women entrepreneurship, entrepreneurial motivation, human resource management, social capital, microenterprises, social entrepreneurship, rural entrepreneurship have remained the most researched topics (Batthini, Bhatt and Joshi, 2014). These themes have been examined critically with appropriate methodology pointing towards the consistent and continuous development of entrepreneurship studies.

There is a tremendous growth of entrepreneurship research and dissemination of knowledge in the recent years. Batthini and Saxena (2017) provides a list of 64 journals published largely from the developed world on various dimensions of entrepreneurship, out of which nine pertain to India. Except for three journals, most of these academic journals devoted to entrepreneurship research started in 1990s and 2000 onwards, though the process was initiated in the 1980s. On the basis of research publications[4] it has been found that the emerging areas of research in entrepreneurship may broadly be clubbed under rural entrepreneurship, micro, small and medium enterprises (MSMEs), entrepreneurial education and entrepreneurial success, women entrepreneurship, innovation and social entrepreneurship. It would be worthwhile to explore these areas of research from sociological perspective in the forthcoming chapters, which also focus on entrepreneurship as an effective empowering strategy for the people on the margins of the society. However, the next chapter will undertake an exhaustive delineation of various theories of entrepreneurship.

Notes

1. The traits of an entrepreneur are: 1. Confidence, 2. Independence, individuality, 3. Optimism, 4. Need for achievement, 5. Profit oriented, 6. Persistence, perseverance, determination, 7. Hard work, drive, energy, 8. Initiative, 9. Risk-taking ability, 10. Like challenges, 11. Leadership behaviour, 12. Gets along well with others, 13. Responsive to suggestions/criticism, 14. Innovative, creative, 15. Flexible/openness of mind, 16. Resourceful, 17. Versatile, knowledgeable, 18. Foresight, 19. Perceptive. These traits lead individuals towards success, while others would be confused and disillusioned and would give up and quit.
2. In case of Mittals, the Ispat baron, 69 members of the family were living in 21 apartments of 3 towers in Mumbai till 1984 and were having food cooked in common kitchen.
3. Bajajs, the third largest producers of motorized vehicles in the world.
4. *The Journal of Entrepreneurship* is the publication of Entrepreneurship Development Institute of India, Ahmedabad, and is being

published by Sage bi-annually without disruption since 1992. Researchers from across the globe publish articles in this well-reputed journal.

Suggested Readings

Aldrich, Howard E. (2005). Entrepreneurship. In Neil J. Smelser and Richard Swedberg (eds), *The Handbook of Economic Sociology* (pp. 451–477). New York: Russell Sage Foundation.

Dorin, B. (2003). *The Indian Entrepreneur: A Sociological Profile of Businessmen and Their Practices*. New Delhi: Manohar & Centre De Sciences Humaines.

Gartner, W.B. (1988). Who is an entrepreneur? Is the wrong question. *American Journal of Small Business*, 12(4), 11–32.

Gopakumar, K. (1995). The entrepreneur in economic thought. *The Journal of Entrepreneurship*, Vol. 4, No. 1, 1–17.

Kilby, Peter (ed.) (1971). *Entrepreneurship and Economic Development*. New York: The Free Press.

Meredith, G.G., Nelson, R.F. and Neck, P.A. (1982). *The Practice of Entrepreneurship*. Geneva: ILO.

Swedberg, Richard (ed.) (2000). *Entrepreneurship: The Social Science View*. New Delhi: Oxford University Press.

2

Theoretical Foundations of Entrepreneurship

Sociologists have always maintained that there has been an inseparable connection between social and economic lives of the members of any society. However, entrepreneurship as a universal phenomenon has a lot to do with the advent of capitalism. Merchants, traders and businessmen carried out their exchange of commodities, but in most cases these took the form of an established way of life shaped by centuries of carved-out paths. Right from the beginning, when the exchange of commodities began in the early human history, some people, groups, communities and societies excelled more than others in these activities. It is an intriguing question to answer, for there are different explanations, perspectives and viewpoints existing which hold one or the other factor responsible for difference in behaviour, practices and motivational levels. Interestingly, the same pattern could be seen even when capitalism emerged with its gigantic abilities to produce commodities through a new form of production known as manufacturing. It was the time for the birth of a new economic actor, who had markedly different traits in comparison to the earlier businessmen. And he was christened as entrepreneur and the process through which he operated was called entrepreneurship.

It all begins with Max Weber, who raises the question why economic growth had taken off in 18th and 19th centuries in Europe but not elsewhere when the material conditions were equally favourable in other parts of the world. There may be varied answers to this question in terms of sociocultural, economic, psychological and political factors accelerating or hindering the process of development. Entrepreneurship is a process covering many stages of growth before it reaches the wholesome success. First step is becoming entrepreneur, second is venturing into business activity, third is accelerating the growth, and the fourth is sustaining the business success. Therefore, different factors may operate at each stage of growth process. We have witnessed the sudden collapse of business empires and houses due to some underlying reasons. Existing theories, though, may be emphasizing upon one factor responsible for entrepreneurship, but collectively they certainly provide a comprehensive understanding of the process of entrepreneurship in general as well as in India. In the light of the points raised here, I have taken four theorists in this chapter for elaborate discussion. All of them established the foundations of theoretical perspective on entrepreneurship. These are: Weber, McClelland, Hagen, and Hoselitz.

Weber: The Protestant Ethic and the Spirit of Capitalism

Max Weber argues that Protestantism had been the catalyst of change in Europe in his monumental work, *The Protestant Ethic and the Spirit of Capitalism* (1976). He begins by pinpointing the fundamental difference between occidental and oriental societies by arguing that rationality was the one axis along which this difference could be identified. However, he narrows his focus of discussion by using the statistics when he compares the Protestants and the Catholics living together in terms of the nature of their work. The Protestants were traders, capitalists, entrepreneurs and skilled workers working on machines. Even in schools and technical institutes, more Protestants were found than the Catholics. A Catholic apprentice working in a guild chooses to become Journeyman and tries to become Master, whereas a Protestant getting the opportunity would become skilled worker in an industry. Weber concludes that the difference lies in the practice of religion and establishes a relationship between religion and emergence of capitalism. In order to explain the Protestant ethics, Weber takes the arguments of Church reformists, particularly Calvin, and Luther from the period of Reformation. The *Bible* was translated and was given a new interpretation. It was Protestantism of Calvin rather than Luther to which Weber gave more importance. Calvinism had great impact on Switzerland, Holland, England and France. The two crucial doctrines were: Predestination and concept of Calling. Luther, while translating the *Bible*, gave the concept of calling. The calling is something which man has to accept as a divine ordinance. It is one's moral duty or responsibility to fulfil worldly duties. While living in this world, he should carry on his duties. Calvin's argument is that people have been predetermined by the God to go to heaven or hell. So some people are chosen and some are damned. Chosen ones are blessed by God and others are cursed. These theologies gave a new meaning to the work, popularly known as Protestant work ethics. This ethics identifies worldly success with spiritual success and provides both a justification and a motivation for the pursuit of earthly endeavours. If one prospers through diligent work, one's prosperity is seen as evidence that one is among those chosen to go to heaven. It also provides a justification for despising those who are less successful, because their lack of success implies that they are among the damned (Weber, ibid.). This created restlessness in the society. This distinction is not because of one's deeds in the past life, rather it depends upon the view that people's role on earth was preordained. Success in one's calling was at least a sign of grace of God. Together these two doctrines produced this worldly asceticism – the one who does not lead a luxurious life, rather lives in austerity. Calvin, on the one hand, emphasizes asceticism and, on the other hand, he emphasizes trade and commerce and enterprizing abilities. To be identified as chosen created a sense of responsibility amongst the Protestants, giving birth to rational action. By giving these concepts, he created religious compulsion so that people work hard, energetically and anxiously, as work was the motive. Thus, asceticism and social responsibility together created economic action which was central to the emergence of capitalism.

What is capitalism in contrast to traditionalism? Sombart (c.f. Weber, 1976) made distinction between satisfaction of needs and acquisition as two leading principles. Satisfaction of needs is attainment of goods necessary to meet personal needs, which is economic traditionalism. For example, when during harvesting, the wages are paid on piece rate and the person has a need of ₹ 100 to fulfil his needs and considering that he stops or slows working as soon as he has done work worth ₹ 100. While acquisition entails struggle for profit, it is free from the limits set by needs. This is capitalistic work. The so-called spirit of capitalism lies in what Benjamin Franklin and Ferdinand provide in certain features of work:

1. Time is money: Time is equated with money. If one wastes time, he wastes money he could generate by working during that period of time.
2. Credit is money: Capital and credit are indispensable. Financer is a useful member of the society. Without credit human affairs cannot be carried on. Whenever one lends credit, one gets interest on it till the other returns the money. Lending at a reasonable interest rate and that to a poor is the bottom line of the credit.
3. Money makes money: Money is of prolific, generating nature. Money can beget money and its offspring can beget more and so on. Profits rise quicker and quicker.
4. Stick to one's words: The good paymaster is the lord of another man's purse. Punctuality, fair means, and justice in one's dealings is the key to make money. Never keep money beyond the time promised lest a disappointment should shut up a friend's purse forever. Stick to one's words to pay back the money. The sound of one's hammer at five in the morning till eight at night heard by the creditor makes him satisfied and may increase the time to pay back, but if he sees one at pub, when one should be working, he sends for his money the next day.
5. Keep an exact account of one's expenses and income. If one plans in a methodical and rational manner and keeps proper record, then one may even save without any inconvenience.
6. Save and invest: Plan economic activity in rational and methodical manner. Do not spend recklessly. It is the spirit of capitalism. In capitalism, one keeps on earning more and more.

Max Weber finds a relationship between the Protestant ethic and the spirit of capitalism. Weber further studied and compared between the prominent religions, such as Judaism, Hinduism, Buddhism and Confucianism, and economic development of the related countries. In his study, *Religion of India* (1958), he found that in India these types of attitudes, outlook, world view and rational scientific attitude had not developed. He did not see any counterpart of Protestant ethic in case of India. In view of Weber, the gradual development and maturation of the most organic stable society, in which everyone is born into a certain caste and limited to a certain trade, is responsible for preventing development of a capitalist economy in India (Aron, 1967). The Hindu social system is based on stable hierarchical *varna* system – Brahmin, Kashtriya, Vashya and Shudra. Each *varna* comprises a number of caste groups which again are hierarchically arranged, and the membership to each caste was based on birth. Thus, there was a segmental division of society along castes. Each caste group is endogamous and had to carry out a prescribed occupation and a large number of restrictions were imposed on social interaction and relationships besides restrictions on religious and social practices. The caste hierarchy was strictly followed and on any violation, one could be ostracized. Due to assigned and fixed work, occupational mobility was restricted. Weber took two principal doctrines: The idea of transmigration of soul (reincarnation) and the idea of *karma*. As per Hindu belief, the soul does not die, it keeps changing the body. The conduct of an individual in any one incarnation, in terms of enactment of one's caste obligations, determines his fate in the next life. If one has faithfully carried out his duties, he has a possibility of moving up in the hierarchy in the course of successive incarnations. The idea of *karma* relates to the sins committed in the previous life. The present life is a result of the past deeds. There is no emphasis of worldly achievements, rather people felt resigned to their fate. There is an important emphasis upon asceticism – renunciation of pleasures in this life in Hinduism, but it is other worldly – moving out of the material world. No emphasis was placed on this life. To quote Zeitlin (1969, p. 147), 'This resulted in an extreme devaluation of the world: none of them enjoined the adherent to prove himself or his grace through action or work. Quite the contrary, the highest good was a contemplative flight from the world. Indian asceticism never translated itself into a methodical, rational way of life that tended in its effects to undermine traditionalism and to change the world'. According to Weber, religious ritualism is the strongest principle of social conservatism. One condition of social change in history has been a break with this ritualism, a break which is the work of the prophetic spirit and the prophetic idea – not to be found in India (Aron, 1967, p. 228).

Weber saw many social and cultural conditions, which should have given rise to modern rational capitalism, but he regards Indian religion as one factor among many which in his view may have prevented capitalistic development. Critical observations of Weber's theory raise a number of issues. For instance, Milton Singer (1972) comments that if a man's present conditions are determined by his past actions and his future will be determined by his present and past actions, then he is master of his fate, why then should he be pessimistic, fatalist and passive and an incompetent failure. Huntington (1968) argues that capitalism also developed in those societies where Protestant ethic was not prevalent, like France, Belgium, and Italy. Hoselitz (1960) argues that Protestants could not develop industries in France because they were not given political security. Robert Kennedy and Yale Brozen are of the view that entrepreneurship developed rapidly in those societies where ethical values provided independent capacity of decision-making. Carroll made an empirical investigation of Filipino manufacturing entrepreneurs showing that ethical values have some effect on entrepreneurial growth but to consider them all in all and final would be unrealistic (c.f. Sharma, 1980). Tripathi (1971) brings out that the initiative of the Parsis was not due to their religion and culture and in his view, the exposure to new ideas and values were the common factors between Parsi and other non-Vaisya Hindu entrepreneurs. Nevertheless, Weber finds Jains in India comparable to Puritans, thus a positive relation between Jain ethics and commercial capitalism on which Tripathi comments that Jain ethics is more rigorous than Hinduism, but the position is quite reverse. Many critics argue that there is no unified system of values in Hinduism. The beliefs and practices of Hinduism vary considerably. The period when Hinduism became systematized, trade and manufacturing reached a peak in India. However, business success was seldom a preferred goal for the Indian mind. Judge (2012, p. 171) states: 'Can we say that lack of rationality did not allow the capitalism to emerge in India? The answer from the perspective of Weber is positive. Did Protestant ethic cause capitalism? The answer is negative. Therefore, the issue is that whether Protestant ethic was a product of capitalism instead of being its cause. Hence, Weber's thesis remains incomplete'.

McClelland: The Need for Achievement

The need for achievement theory given by American psychologist David Clarence McClelland explains entrepreneurial behaviour. McClelland, in the first chapter of his book *The Achieving Society* (1961), raises the question that why certain countries have accumulated wealth at a faster rate and certainly to a much higher average than other countries. He narrows down to understand some of the forces that produce economic development and these forces lie largely in man himself, in his fundamental motives and in the way he organizes his relationships with his fellowmen. McClelland explores what modern psychology can contribute to an understanding of why some men concentrate on economic activities and are conspicuously successful. According to him, it depends upon personality type why some people become entrepreneurs.

He begins by developing two, one verbal and one graphic, instruments to test for psychological variable he calls need for achievement of American college students as well as through parent-child interviews in order to establish which child rearing practices fostered high need for achievement and which practices did not. In the process, he tries to establish a link between high need for achievement and desire to enter business by analysing the achievement motivation in four countries Germany, Japan, India and Brazil. In order to avoid cultural bias, a comparative study was made in United States, Turkey, Italy and Poland. Third, at the same time research was carried out with regard to the motives and other behaviours of actual business entrepreneurs.

Motives have been defined as 'affectively-toned associative mental-networks arranged in a hierarchy of strength' within a given individual. There are three social motives: need for achievement (N/ach), need for affiliation (N/aff), and need for power (N/pow). McClelland described these three basic social motives as socio-psychological needs. Of these three motives, whichever is predominant in strength will tend to shape individual attitude and behaviour the most. Thus people display a hierarchy of social motives arranged in the order of strength in different persons. As such, they are like standard activities with a certain amount of propelling force and it is then that this potential force is aroused and leads to activity we refer to as need for achievement or achievement motivation. Need to achieve has been conceived as a desire for excellence, or urge to improve not so much for the sake of social recognition or prestige, but to attain an inner feeling of personal accomplishment. McClelland, in his study, found that the persons who have high need for achievement, would perform better and they would seek out situations in which they could get achievement satisfaction. He pointed to a possible link between achievement motive and economic development by discovering how parents or particularly mothers produced a strong interest in achievement of their sons and found that the mothers of the sons with high n/ach have set higher standards for their sons. They expect self-reliance and mastery at an earlier age as compared to the mothers of the sons with low n/ach. But how specifically does a high level of n/ach result in more rapid economic development? The link is the entrepreneur and the McClelland's primary interest is in entrepreneurial role behaviour which shows six characteristics.

1. *Risk Taking:* All theorists agree that entrepreneurship involves taking risk of one kind or the other. McClelland suggests a continuum running from a situation of little or no risk in which actions are prescribed by tradition or specialized knowledge to situations where there is no precedent or knowledge for deciding what to do. The entrepreneur falls somewhere in the middle of this continuum. He is called upon to make calculated or moderate risks in which some skill and some luck are involved.
2. *Energetic and/or Novel Activity:* By definition entrepreneurial role involves doing things in a new and better way. His studies showed that people with high n/ach appear to work harder when there is some degree of mental challenge or a new angle of approach for successful solution. He is interested in something which will give him achievement satisfaction and he is constantly seeking new solutions to old problems. The problems and stresses caused by uncertainties of business impel them to work more than others.
3. *Individual Responsibility:* The entrepreneurial role has also generally been assumed to imply individual responsibility that is, an entrepreneur is the one who ultimately is responsible for making decisions. The subjects with high n/ach would probably have done less well, if they had been told exactly what to do rather than whom they were working for, themselves or the

group; they do not respond positively to suggestions telling them what they should do, or think, or believe. A man may get achievement satisfaction from having contributed to the success of a group enterprise so long as it is he who made some of the decisions contributing to a successful outcome and he, therefore, has some way of telling how well he has done.

4. *Knowledge of Results of Actions:* An entrepreneur ordinarily has definite knowledge as to whether he has done a good job or made some correct decisions. People with high n/ach tend to perform significantly better under well controlled experimental conditions when they have positive and definite feedback as to how well they are doing. For a businessman, success is measured in terms of money as a symbol of achievement, but McClelland, in contrast, found through his study that people with high n/ach are not influenced much by money rewards, as they are interested in achievement.
5. *Long Range Planning:* This entrepreneurial role component relates to the planning activities of the entrepreneurs. A successful entrepreneur considers more alternatives and their consequences before they actually happen to him, i.e. he anticipates future possibilities, because the nature of industrial entrepreneurship appears to require more investment in the future, a longer time span, more planning ahead rather than just reacting to emergencies as they arise. The people with high n/ach tend to anticipate a future event before it occurs.
6. *Organizational Abilities:* Yet another kind of planning is organizing human activities in the firm. If an entrepreneur is ever to accomplish more than he can by his own efforts, he must organize the activities of other persons. People with high n/ach prefer experts over friends for problem solving tasks. They would rather work with someone who can help in solving the problem than with someone they know and like. This is an attitude which promotes business success in firms in the sense that choosing personnel in terms of their task oriented skills should contribute more to business efficiency than choosing them in terms of other personal qualities.

This shows that high n/ach leads people to behave in most of the ways they should behave if they are to fulfil the entrepreneurial role successfully. The parallel between the behaviour evoked by high n/ach level in a society can produce more rapid economic development. McClelland primarily being a psychologist argues that high need for achievement is a personality trait and one who shows this trait shall be a successful entrepreneur. At the same time, however, he realized that the personality attribute that is n/ach itself is a product of community structure and he studied some of the social conditions like child rearing practices and socialization process which takes place in the family affecting the personality characteristics of an individual. He further reiterates that it is desirable to stress on meeting certain achievement standard somewhere between the age of 6 and 8 years. It should neither be too early for the boys' abilities nor too late for him to internalize those standards as his own.

Besides the direct impact of family environment, there are some indirect influences as well which may affect n/ach levels. For instance, the younger children of the family and boys with stronger physique have higher n/ach. The parents placing high standards of excellence, the institution of slavery, tropical climate (which is hot, humid and showing little variations), hostellers, besides the joint family, authoritarian father, and broken family are all associated with low n/ach. Now the question is why people with high n/ach tend to become successful entrepreneurs? We have a number of types of behaviour which do characterize high n/ach across cultures. A person with high n/ach tend to travel more and hence is exposed to more and new information and such people are also willing to leave home and are more upwardly mobile, particularly if they are at low socio-economic level. They have special attitude towards time, generally they are in hurry or busy, sharp, active, tense and fast. They will not waste time and talk more in anticipatory tenses. Persons with high n/ach play more competitive and individualistic games. His study of Olympic Games held in Greece found the players having high n/ach.

McClelland was of the view that need for achievement can be developed through training and experience. For this McClelland conducted experiments in number of countries including India. In India experiments were conducted in Kakinada in Andhra Pradesh and Vellore in Tamil Nadu in 1961 for five years to inculcate need for achievement in the minds of young boys to become entrepreneurs. The impact of training programmes on participants was observed and he reached a conclusion that the training programme positively influenced the entrepreneurial behaviour of the participants. In the case of India, he gave recommendations to accelerate economic growth which includes increased communication, population control, and emancipation of women, reorienting school teachers, and improvement in engineering education. People must break from traditional ways if they are to live at a high economic level, and develop values, motives, and social institutions conducive to economic growth. For this he laid emphasis on child rearing practices, children's tales, and different forms of popular culture (McClelland, 1965).

The contribution of McClelland has remained very relevant till date. Much of his findings have led to the reinterpretation of the issues. It is his experiments and understanding of inculcating n/ach through training that led to the initiation of entrepreneurship development programmes (EDPs) in India. Precisely, entrepreneurs can be created or made through training rather than just being born or natural entrepreneurs. Despite being a great contribution, McClelland's theory also got critical evaluation. He relates need for achievement directly with entrepreneurship, but it may be argued that n/ach may be a crucial but not the only factor for entrepreneurship. As we know in a country like India, it is more of economic policies of the government which may affect the development of entrepreneurship. Also looking sociologically, though the child rearing practices and socialization process at family level influences personality traits but the significance of peer group, school, teachers, also make important contribution in the personality formation. Many studies conducted on n/ach clearly depict that person with high n/ach performs better than the others.

Hagen: The Withdrawal of Status Respect

Based on the study of communities of three traditional societies, namely Japan (non-colonial), Columbia and Burma (colonial), in *On the theory of Social Change*, Everett E. Hagen (1962) writes that economic growth always requires creative innovation or change. Innovation is a fundamental prerequisite of technological progress. Changes in traditional behaviour are necessary for economic growth but will be adopted only if either considerable creativity is devoted to the task of making them acceptable or social tensions and pressures are so great that these change men's attitudes. Both conditions may be necessary. Creativity will not be forthcoming except as tensions within society which lead to changes in men.

Innovational Personality

The major qualities that constitute creativity or in other words the qualities/characteristics of an entrepreneur are: (a) openness to experience, tendency to perceive phenomenon as explainable, creative imagination, (b) confidence in one's own judgement, (c) satisfaction in facing and attacking problems, (d) a sense of duty to achieve, (e) intelligence, and energy, (e) an understanding that the world is somewhat threatening and that constant effort is required to deal with it successfully, (f) creative person is alert in observing the world around, (g) has confidence, and (h) creative imagination entailing tendency to leap far ahead where others had not reached. Creative individual is not necessarily a happy man who faces problems with pure pleasure; rather, most creative individuals are driven by creative activity by an incessant anxiety. This is the product of frustrations of one kind or another experienced in early life. Thus, innovative activity is always a reaction to some degree of anxiety.

Authoritarian Personality

Many characteristics of authoritarian personality are simply the opposite characteristics of the creative individual. Uncreative individual's unconscious processes are unproductive. As a child, the authoritarian individual perceived the world as doctorial, subject to sudden changes, not responsive to analysis. The child perceived these sudden changes as not accidental but the play of some wilful powers far greater than his own. These experiences were very painful, have been pressed down out of his conscious mind to the unconscious. As they have created fear and rage and dangerous urges, he seals his unconscious processes. In early life, he dared not express his rage against superior authorities but when he becomes senior, father, and older brother, he can satisfy his aggressiveness by his domination over his inferiors. Each traditional adult individual in traditional society presents strong resistance to the questioning of authoritative decisions. This resistance is an important obstacle to change.

The Anxious Innovator: Much innovation may result from only moderate creativity combined with intense drive; a highly anxious individual may be a more effective innovator than an individual with high creative capacity but fewer motives to use it. Hagen has tried to show that in every traditional society, the members of a group or some groups are somewhat dissatisfied with their roles, and seeds of change exist which would eventually disrupt the traditional structure, personality and culture. Such a group emerges when the members of some social group experience what he calls 'The withdrawal of Status respect'. What is it? Status is one's identity; it includes one's purposes and values in life. Status involves what one does, believe and all his relationships to other persons. Due to some reasons when it is impossible for him to believe that the activity which he was carrying out is no longer useful and worthy element and accorded due respect, the result is inner conflict and tensions in the individual. One feels humiliated and mistreated. The consequence of such a situation is the occurrence of 'Withdrawal of Status Respect' entailing three following conditions:

1. When a traditional elite group is displaced by force from its previous status by another traditional group.
2. When any superior group changes its attitude towards a subordinate group.
3. A group may migrate to a new society that considers its ways alien and refuses to recognize what the group considers its rightful status.

Whatever may be the cause, withdrawal of status respect causes conflict within individuals. The anxiety and rage thus created in adults will alter the home environment in ways that will in turn affect the personalities of the next generation and over several generations. This is important for social change. After one or more generations, a type of personality-retreatist emerges. If social tensions are more severe, a ritualistic type of personality emerges. Out of ritualism-retreatism may develop which may give way to innovational personality, in some cases to a special type of innovational personality to be called reformist. Hagen emphasizes retreatist type of personality, because it may bring social change according to him.

Retreatist: A retreatist is the person who, during the process of personality formation, has met the problem of being unable to satisfy conflicting values by repressing them from his consciousness without being able to replace them by others. He may be withdrawn, indifferent, drunkard or disinterested in the world around.

Ritualistic: The ritualist meets the conflict of values that threatens his identity by a kind of defensive behaviour which acts in the accepted and approved ways of the society. He is neat, methodical, and dependable, but he acts without initiative, imagination or vigour. Thus, he is going through things what others expect him to do.

Innovational: An innovative individual seeks a satisfactory identity by activity contrary to the values of the society. In doing so, he is seeking the acceptance from his society of new goals, new values. In some degrees, he is seeking to change the existing society.

Reformist: The reformist is also an innovator seeking change, but the one who cannot satisfy his needs without imposing his values on his fellows. He acts openly and directly to change the accepted ways of his society. He is rebellious and may attempt to establish a new society.

These are the ways of adaptation by the individual caused by contradictory demands of his culture.

Hagen emphasizes the importance of identifying the psychological dimensions of structural change, but his bias towards psychoanalysis pushes him to ignore other factors which are also responsible for the economic growth or have at least the same importance as psychological factors have. While discussing the effects of withdrawal of status respect, he sees only the positive results, though its effects may also be reverse leading the society to more difficult and complex conditions. One may accept Hagen's thesis that the retreatist develops through anxiety, but it is very difficult to prove that only the withdrawal of status respect creates anxiety leading to development of a creative or innovative personality. There may be n-number of factors leading to anxiety among people, but anxiety does not always leads to creativity. Besides anxiety, there are many other influences on the formation of personality. The rapid economic development of Japan is not the result of non-colonialism and vice-versa, and the lack of development of Burma and Columbia is not the result of colonialism as such. The Samurai community of Japan (Hagen, pp. 103–104) had traditionally enjoyed a high status, which was lowered when they were defeated by the other group led by Tokugawa with superior weapons. After the fall of Tokugawa, Samurais studied, got skills in metal work and armaments, worked very hard to regain their lost status and contributed to entrepreneurial development of the country. Antioquenos in Spain were of equal status with other immigrants, but not looked upon equal by the Columbians. They never considered themselves inferior, but their resentment in 18th and 19th centuries led to change in personality and they emerged as creative and started showing their worth in 19th and 20th centuries and became dominant in Columbian economy leading to a massive rise in industrial production in the 20th century (ibid., pp. 122–123). In Burma, during different colonial rulers, the Burmese became retreatists as colonizers were against their customs, way of life and religion and considered them inferior and traditional which led to intense emotional pressure and a complete absence of status respect. Best way to show or excel is business and Hagen remarked that it takes 30 years between complete independence and economic growth. Hagen writes (p. 59) that in Burma, the adults are authoritarian and shows that in every traditional society the members of some groups are somewhat dissatisfied with their roles and the seeds of change exist there eventually disrupting the traditional structure, personality and culture.

Accepting the thesis of Hagen, these two countries should have been very developed by now, but this has not happened in their case. Therefore, due to inherent weaknesses of the theory of withdrawal of status respect by laying an overemphasis on psychological dimension, he ignored other factors which might also be responsible for economic growth. He sees only one side, whereas the effects of withdrawal of status respect may be the opposite, instead of good results, it may lead the society to more complex conditions. His proposition that retreatism emerges through anxiety as a result of withdrawal of status respect, which further creates innovative personality is difficult to apply at empirical level. It is impractical to wait for generations to emerge creative personalities.

Hoselitz: Social Structure and Economic Growth

Bert F. Hoselitz has extensively worked on sociological aspects of economic growth (1960), and economic development. He has been greatly concerned with the practical difficulties of the peoples of Asia, Africa and Latin America. He is of the view that in creating economic development plans for any change, it must be both economic adjustment and cultural change. He discusses the social structural variables and economic growth of advanced countries vis-à-vis the less developed countries. To begin with, he tries to examine what particular kind of behaviour is typical of the businessman or entrepreneur, as different writers have defined it differently. One definition, for example, divides the functions of the businessman into the following parts: the capitalist, who supplies financial funds and other non-human resources for the enterprise; the manager, who supervises and coordinates productive activities; and the entrepreneur, who is the planner, idea man and maker of final decisions in a productive enterprise. These functions can be separated, although they may be performed by the same single person and, on a level of relatively low economic development, often are performed by one man. In contrast, in modern corporations, the functions of capitalist, businessman and manager are ordinarily performed by different individuals. Hoselitz discusses three major functions of the entrepreneur: supply of capital, leadership/ability to manage, and make/create/produce things.

The Supply of Capital

It is a necessary feature of economic development. New productive enterprises can be started with relatively little capital. There are two sources of local capital in less developed countries:

1. The government which can raise the needed funds by taxation or domestic or foreign borrowing.
2. A second source is the local, native class of merchants, traders, moneylenders, and people with inherited wealth-landowners.

In view of these two major sources of funds, two types of enterprises are possible in less developed countries.

1. There would be publically-owned, often large-scale and complex enterprises where entrepreneurs' functions are performed by officials of the government and where various functions are divided among a number of men.
2. The small private firm, operated by an aggressive, bold individual would be a modern version, in less developed countries, of the capitalist entrepreneur.

Ability to Manage

In less developed countries, the leaders of economic growth will either be of the manager type or the entrepreneur type. The political decisions as well as the sources of capital for investment will determine which of these two forms of business leadership emerges. If economic development is strictly controlled by government, or even if public enterprises are widespread, the managers will be more prominent and will influence the ideas and practices of enterprise in the developing country. By contrast, if public enterprises are limited to a few industries, and if sufficient private capital is available, a climate of genuine enterprise may prevail. If economic development is conducted mainly by private leaders when less developed countries have enacted laws to protect labour and its employees, then economic development with small and medium sized factories owned by private entrepreneurs is preferable for growth. In less developed economies, moneylenders and traders cannot be the future source of industrial entrepreneurs, because a strong desire to make profits is not enough; they must also have an ability to manage. An industrial entrepreneur must hire a group of persons, organize them and direct them.

Production of Commodities

The industrial entrepreneur, who operates a small industry, must participate fully and often constantly in the actual production processes. He is a man who gets his hands dirty, implying that he keeps on trying new techniques of industrial production. He also takes risk of production of commodities, his wealth is invested in his factory, and he depends on market to give him good prices for his products. Hoselitz explains three types of business leadership which are important for economic advancement of less developed countries. At the two extremes are the managers and money-lenders/merchants and between them is industrial entrepreneur. The personality of industrial entrepreneur contains the elements of the two types, but more important is that he is a person who likes to make things, to produce, and to create.

He further suggests that to encourage a spirit of enterprise, social institutions need to be established which make it possible for independent individual enterprises and at the same time allows the development of personalities suited to productivity, working, and creativity. Favourable social institutions can exist as a result of political action. Political acts are important for the development of personalities associated with industrial entrepreneurs. A person's character is determined, to a large extent, by biological needs and the early social contacts during infancy and childhood. But the objective, external conditions, the social structure and political framework of a society also determine the actions/behaviour of a person.

Hoselitz assumes that enterprise can develop only in a society in which the culture permits a variety of choices, and in which the social processes are not so completely rigid that they do not encourage the development of personalities interested in enterprise. Hoselitz argues that planners will be needed to direct the course of economic development for underdeveloped countries. He assumes that entrepreneurship can only come out of a developed cultural base. Thus, entrepreneurs can be developed where the society is well developed. Hoselitz's theory of entrepreneurship raises significant concerns with regard to his assumptions. He assumes that less developed countries have rigid cultural practices which do not let the people become creative/innovative and, therefore, entrepreneurs do not emerge in such societies, rather they have traders and merchants and the public sector enterprises are run by bureaucrats or managers. In contrast, the developed countries have entrepreneurs who also depict the characteristics of capitalists and of managers/leaders. Less developed countries, to develop economically, need more number of entrepreneurs and that is possible with the intervention of government/political decisions, as there would be entrepreneurial growth. For instance, various state governments of India, realizing the fact, launched a number of entrepreneurship development programmes and even in each Five-Year Plan gave much importance to industrial development. A number of incentives were given to nurture entrepreneurship, but still we are far away from attaining the desirable base of entrepreneurship. Too much of political interference, bureaucratization, lengthy procedure, and corruption in all relevant departments have thwarted the growth of small-scale industries in different states of India. Thousands of small-scale units are either sick or have made hardly any progress since their inception. To change the social institutions of any society is a long and slow process.

A Critical Note

We have a large number of theories of entrepreneurship, but taking sociological significance of the above mentioned four theories provide a sufficient base to theorize entrepreneurship in Indian context. Though each of the theory emphasizes one factor but in combining all of them and making it applicable at different stages of the entrepreneurial process, as Sharma and Singh (1980) have given in multivariate model, results may be encouraging. How far these theories of entrepreneurship contribute to the still ongoing debate that entrepreneurs are not born but are made raise a critical question. One may immediately agree that in India certain inherent factors, like caste, community, family and religion, are important but this is not a scientific justification. A cursory look at Indian reality reveals that people who have economic resources and social networks belonging to traditional trading castes dominate the business and industrial entrepreneurship. As McClelland emphasizes that entrepreneurs can be created, therefore, to develop a country, more and more entrepreneurs should be created through human capital, that is education, training and skill formation. Hoselitz adds to it that for the purpose we need to change the cultural values and social practices and here the role of political institutions is most crucial. Nevertheless, to create or make entrepreneurs, the political will is crucial. Various strategies and incentives of the government to encourage taking up to entrepreneurship can be a milestone in this direction.

Suggested Readings

Hagen, E.E. (1962). *On The Theory of Social Change: How Economic Growth Begins*. Homewood, IL: Dorsey Press.

Hoselitz, Bert F. (1960). *Sociological Aspects of Economic Growth*. New York: Feffer and Simons Inc.

McClelland, D.C. (1961). *The Achieving Society*. Princeton, New Jersey: D. Van Nostrand.

McClelland, D.C. (1965). Achievement motivation can be developed. *Harvard Business Review*, 41(6–24), 178.

Weber Max (1958). *The Religion of India* (Tr. and ed. by Hans H. Gerth and Don Martindale). New York: The Free Press.

Weber, Max. (1976). *The Protestant Ethic and the Spirit of Capitalism* (Tr. by Talcott Parsons) London: George Allen and Unwin Ltd.

3

Innovation and Entrepreneurship

Innovation had become the industrial religion or a mantra in the late 20th century. As a matter of fact, entrepreneurship in the present times can predominantly be theorized in terms of innovation. No entrepreneurial activity is possible without being innovative, as it has virtually become an essential instrument of entrepreneurship. Innovation as a word has Latin origin, which appeared in English language in middle of 1500s and it means 'to create something new, novel, to bring in novelty, to bring change, or finding new or different ways of doing things'. Though earlier theories discussed in the previous chapter discretely emphasize the creativity and innovation but there is a need to make sense of its practical meanings in terms of how does one achieves it. It begins from creativity, that is, creativity is the ability to develop new ideas and to discover new ways of looking at the problems and opportunities in contrast to the earlier practice. Innovation is the ability to apply creative solutions to the problems and opportunities to enhance or to enrich people's lives (Zimmerer and Scarborough, 2006). Levitt (c.f. ibid., 2006) says that creativity is *thinking* new things, and innovation is *doing* new things. Entrepreneurs succeed by thinking and doing new things or doing old things in a new way. It is like making new blends, that is mixing up of the material, giving a new look to showroom, evolving new market strategies such as innovative advertisements targeting the psyche of young people. If it touches their mind or emotions, it is a hit product. It is an idea, thought, behaviour or a thing that is new or it is different than the earlier ones. In the modern free competitive markets, consumers have access to multiple goods for the same need, but any one thing which is different and appealing would fetch the demand. Scholars have defined the term innovation by focusing on one or the other feature of it ranging from denoting change, sharp break with the established ways of doing things, to creating new capability.

In a developing country like India, innovation may simply be defined as a 'diffusion', 'remix' or 'fusion' of already existing concepts and values which reproduce something fresh. Ettlie and O'Keefe (1982) empirically investigate the question as to what constitute innovation, innovative values, attitudes and intentions in an organization and they arrive at following characteristics: (a) Experimenting with new ideas, (b) Enjoying change, (c) Facing uncertainty in order to try new ideas, (d) Not giving up or becoming upset when errors are made in doing new work, (e) Valuing unconventional behaviour, (f) Finding problems to solve, (g) Finding new uses of existing methods or existing equipment or existing service, (h) Demonstrating originality, (i) Working on a problem which causes great difficulty for others (j) Providing critical input towards a new idea, and (k) Providing an evaluation of proposed idea.

Innovation is a process through which new idea, new product, new techniques, new solutions to the problems are introduced in the socio-economic system besides the spheres of science and technology. In the process of innovation, braving the failures is fundamental for any individual. Innovation may trigger from a vague or wild idea, but nurturing it may result into repeated failures before it comes out with something new or different. Thus, innovation is a process of becoming new, different and appealing. The economy and society of any country grows and develops due to innovative capabilities of its people. In the context of developing economies, the technology has remained the central issue for the development of capacities for innovation. Sullivan, Munir and Dougherty (1998, p. 272) inform that 'most discussions of innovation have centred on transfer of technology, appropriate state intervention and provision of incentives for innovation'.

Consequently, the innovation in developing countries has primarily become a domain of economists who analyse such issues at either the country or industry level. For economists, change in government policy would automatically lead to innovations and people would rather be forced to innovate new ways of production, management, and marketing of the goods.

Most of the sociocultural theories of entrepreneurship lay emphasis on the family and early socialization of a person for emergence of innovativeness. Just a few years back electric cars, smart televisions, mobile phones, e-commerce and e-transaction were a dream for any Indian. It is as a result of innovations made by some which helped in making it an everyday reality. Drucker (1985, p. 27) defines innovation, 'It is the act that endows resources with a new capacity to create wealth. Innovation creates a resource until man finds a use of something in nature and endows it with economic value. Until then every mineral is just another rock, every plant is a weed'. The things which we take for granted were not there before these had been innovated by some entrepreneurs. The concepts of purchasing power, of hospital, the school, the modern government, management, designing of textbook, and newspaper are innovations of last few centuries which revolutionized our understanding, working, and efficiency (ibid.).

To have a comprehensive understanding of the concept of innovation the arguments of two great contributors, namely, Joseph Schumpeter, the economist turned sociologist, and management legend Peter Drucker have been presented here. The chapter has been divided into three parts. The first part examines the views of Schumpeter on the meaning and concept of innovation, whereas the second part elaborates the opportunities or sources of innovation available in and outside the industry as explained by Drucker. The possibilities of innovations in India have been discussed in the third part.

Entrepreneurship as Innovation

Schumpeter (1883–1950), an economist, a main figure in the literature on entrepreneurship is aptly regarded as the father of theory of innovation and entrepreneurship in terms of their inseparable link. He, during different phases of his life, viewed different aspects of entrepreneurship making his approach truly interdisciplinary covering economics, psychology, and sociology. Schumpeter came from an entrepreneurial family, but he could never become a successful entrepreneur despite his few attempts at making living through investments. However, as it turned out, he became the leading scholar to work out the history of entrepreneurship in economic theory. He emphasizes that while ordinary economic behaviour is more or less automatic in nature, the entrepreneur always has to think very carefully about what action to take since he/she is involved in doing something that is fundamentally new. His writings on entrepreneurship could be divided into two phases. Up to 1940 he was mainly interested in developing his own ideas in order to integrate them into a novel system of economic theory which was centred on economic change or development. In the last decade of his life, he mainly looked into the sociological aspects of entrepreneurship (Swedberg, 2000) which are of present interest for the chapter.

Schumpeter defines entrepreneurship 'as the making of a "new combination" of already existing material and forces: the entrepreneurship consists of making innovation, as opposed to inventions, and that no one is an entrepreneur for ever, only when he or she is actually doing the innovative activity (Schumpeter, 2000 p. 51)'. According to him, the motivational significance of an entrepreneur entail three elements, which are as follows:

1. The dream and the will to find a private kingdom usually also a dynasty;
2. The will to conquer, the impulse to fight, to prove oneself superior to others, to succeed for the sake of success itself;
3. The joy of creating or getting things done, exercising one's energy and ingenuity.

Swedberg (ibid.) interprets in a simple form these three elements as: (a) The desire for power and independence; (b) The will to succeed; and (c) The satisfaction of getting things done. Therefore, it is quite clear that according to Schumpeter, money *per se* does not motivate an entrepreneur.

Later in life, Schumpeter began to take notice of a number of institutional factors responsible for weakening entrepreneurship and contributing to the stagnation of capitalism as a social system. He noticed that people were getting used to change thus posing less opposition to entrepreneurship which made for less strong-headed and original entrepreneurs. The big corporations were also beginning to develop innovative technologies in a routine fashion by putting together teams of specialists. Schumpeter also made it clear that the entrepreneur did not have to be a single person but could equally well be an organization, either a political or an economic one. What mattered was the behaviour, not the actor (Swedberg, 2000, pp. 15–17). Schumpeter (ibid., pp. 51–61) begins his article on 'Entrepreneurship as Innovation' as 'to produce means, to combine material and forces within our reach. To produce other things or the same things by a different method means to combine these materials and forces differently. New combinations appear discontinuously, then the phenomenon characterizing development emerges. Development is then defined by the carrying out of new combinations'. New combination of productive means covers the following five cases:

1. The introduction of a new good, that is, one with which consumers are not yet familiar with or of a new quality of a good.
2. The introduction of a new method of production, one not yet tested by experience in the branch of manufacture concerned, which need by no means be founded upon a discovery scientifically new and can also exist in a new way of handling a commodity commercially.
3. The opening of a new market, that is, a market into which the particular branch of manufacture has not previously entered, whether or not this market has existed before.
4. The conquest of a new source of supply of raw materials or half-manufactured goods, irrespective of whether this source already exists or whether it has first to be created.
5. The carrying out of the new organization of any industry, like the creation of a monopoly position or the breaking up of a monopoly position.

To carry out new combinations and for understanding of the issues involved a few concerns need to be addressed:

1. It should not be essential that the new combinations should be carried out by the same people who control the productive or commercial process which is to be displaced by the new. On the contrary, new combinations are embodied in new firms

which generally do not arise out of the old ones but start producing beside them. For example, it is not the owner of stage-coaches who builds railways.

2. When carrying out new combinations by employing means of production, we must never assume that the carrying out of new combinations takes place by employing means of production which happens to be unused. There are always unemployed workmen, unsold raw material, unused productive capacity and so forth. This certainly is an incentive to the emergence of new combination. As a rule the new combinations must draw the necessary means of production from some old combinations. New combinations mean simply the different employment of the economic systems' existing supplies of productive means.
3. New possibilities are continuously being offered by the surrounding world, new discoveries are added to the existing knowledge and then why should not an individual make use of new possibilities according to the market. He can keep pigs instead of cows, choose a new crop, may grow flowers instead of paddy.
4. Usually, we are in the habit of thinking and work in an accustomed track, as they have become part of subconscious even when new suitable options are available. A new and another kind of effort of will is necessary for a new combination. Mental freedom is needed.
5. In carrying out new combinations, financing is fundamentally necessary. The capitalist credit system has grown out of and thrived on the financing of new combinations in all countries, even though in a different way in each country. Bank is important. Banker himself becomes the capitalist par excellence. He makes possible the carrying out of new combinations. We call the carrying out of new combinations as an enterprise and the individuals whose function is to carry them out are called entrepreneurs.
6. For Schumpeter it is the entrepreneurial functions which make entrepreneurs. It does not include all heads of firms or managers or industrialists who just operate an established business but only those who actually perform that function.

7. One is an entrepreneur only when he actually carries out new combinations, and loses that character as soon as he has built up his business, when he settles down to running it as other people run their businesses. Hence it is rare for anyone to always remain an entrepreneur throughout his active life.
8. Being an entrepreneur is not a profession and as a rule not a lasting condition.
9. Entrepreneurs do not form a social class, such as landowner or capitalist or workmen do. Undoubtedly entrepreneurial function will lead to certain class positions for the successful entrepreneur and his family.
10. The function of entrepreneur itself cannot be inherited. Inheritance of the pecuniary result and of personal qualities may keep up his position for more than one generation and can make enterprise easier for the descendants.
11. Entrepreneurs are not found only amongst certain communities or some groups but are randomly distributed.
12. There may also be reaction of the social environment against the one who wishes to do something new. The opposition may be in the form of legal or political impediments. Different manifestations of condemnations would finally be overcome by winning over the consumers.

In view of Schumpeter, an entrepreneur may indeed be called the most rational and the most egoistical of all. He is more self-centred. His task is breaking up the old tradition and creating the new one. Though it applies mainly to his economic action, but it also extends to the moral, cultural and social consequences of it. An entrepreneur retires from arena only when and because his strength is spent and he feels no longer equal to his task. The theory of Schumpeter introduces the concept of innovation and also tries to resolve the issues concerning innovation and innovative activities.

Sources of Opportunities for Innovation

Peter Drucker (1985) approaches the concept of innovation in a different way from Schumpeter, for he looks into it from the management perspective. Drucker begins by pinpointing the source of the innovative ideas. He suggests that the systematic innovation begins with an eye on opportunities, some located within the business/enterprise, whereas some others are outside the sphere of business/industry. Systematic innovation means monitoring seven sources for innovative opportunity. However, the lines between them are blurred, overlapping. These are like seven windows of the same building and each shows some features, though these features are also visible from other windows. The first four sources lie within the enterprise. They are visible primarily to the people within that enterprise. Actually, these are the symptoms which indicate towards change. The entrepreneur needs to identify these symptoms which in view of Drucker are highly reliable to be worked on.

1. *The Unexpected:* An unexpected thing or situation may occur anytime in anybody's life. Sometime it may be an unexpected success and on another occasion it is unexpected failure or even unexpected outside events. In his view, no other area offers richer opportunities for successful innovation than the expected success. Failure also cannot be rejected and rarely go unnoticed. For instance, the failure of one company gives opportunity to other competitors to innovate and produce better goods at reduced price with more efficiency. Outside events are not recorded in the information and figures but often they are very important, such as change in the export-import policy or tax rebate/subsidy by the government may even be more important. For example, Covid-19 pandemic is an outside unexpected occurrence but it has provided opportunities to innovate in terms of E-entrepreneurship, online shopping stores, manufacturing of sanitizers and masks besides vaccinations. Such unexpected situations/occurrences may influence any enterprise, and provide a new and fresh perspective.
2. *The Incongruity:* Incongruity is a discrepancy or a dissonance between what is and what ought to be or between what is and what everybody assumes it to be. What one perceives that consumers will buy and what actually they buy is a symptom of an opportunity to innovate? So incongruence is a symptom of change. There are several kinds of incongruity:
   (a) Incongruent economic realities.
   (b) Incongruence between reality and the assumptions about it.
   (c) Incongruity between perceived and actual customer values and expectations.

(d) An internal incongruity within the rhythm or the logic of a process.

3. *Innovation Based on Process Needs:* The weak points of an enterprise's workflow, processes and system provide opportunities for innovation. It improves the process that already exists; redesign the old and existing process. It is better to say like necessity is the mother of invention. The growing or changing needs of the system enforces the incumbents to innovate. For instance, in some industries the process has been shortened with the introduction of new technology. Woollen textile mills have computerized the machines and as a result the work burden has reduced tremendously and, at the same time, it can produce high precision and quality goods in a much lesser time. In the middle of the last century, the *lathe* machines were wooden but as demand increased these were replaced with iron and later with steel *lathe* machines. The process of manufacturing machine tools gave opportunities to many to innovate better *lathe* machines.
4. *Changes in Industry or Market Structures:* Both these structures apparently appear to be stable and may last for years, but actually market and industry structures are quite brittle and with a small scratch, may disintegrate very fast. To continue to do business as before is almost a guarantee of disaster and company may reach extinction. Actually both of them are constantly changing and thus providing ample opportunities to innovate to adapt or adjust to changes. Sometimes changes may be very abrupt, such as fashion industry, and other times may be slower like in food industry and market.

   The next second set of sources, which are three in number, involves changes taking place outside the enterprise, but provide ample opportunities to innovate. These are changes in the social, philosophical, political and intellectual environment.
5. *Demographic Changes:* These are defined as changes in population – its size, age structure, composition, employment, educational status, and income. Demographics have major impact on what will be bought by whom, and in what quantities. Drucker argues that changing demographics is both a highly productive and a highly dependable innovative

opportunity. We may cite a few instances in this regard. Great demographic catastrophes of the past, such as Bhopal gas tragedy, earthquake in Bhuj and Tsunami, had immediate effect on society and economy. Recent fear of and lakhs of deaths due to pandemic Covid-19 around the world have had a very powerful impact on the economy and societies of the world. People's needs and requirements have altered significantly, thus providing opportunities to innovate alternative strategies. Historically speaking, migration of the people from one place to another has created an abundance of entrepreneurial opportunities. Catering to all kinds of needs – food, dress, houses, medical of immigrants – a large number of entrepreneurs have emerged in Canada, America, Australia and African countries. As their number and size increased in North America, the distinct needs of Indians were fulfilled by the entrepreneurs. Age composition of any society is another significant variable. In India, we have a large population of young adults whose needs are distinct from the aged population. The Valentine Day (14 February), which is equally popular in India as well, has been expanded into seven-days celebration with each day offering a new concept. The aged people buy for comfort not for fashion which provides a lot of opportunities to entrepreneurs. Infant mortality has decreased and life expectancy has increased in India. Now more number of children is in schools and we have a variety of schools with diverse type of facilities. Providing elderly homes/facilities up to five stars is yet another novel idea. For instance, setting up of 'heavenly homes' for elderly at Doraha, Punjab, was an instant success. The ever expanding travel business/resort business, package tours are result of demographic changes.

6. *Changes in Perception, Mood and Meaning:* Due to the growth of technology, there are significant changes in the way people perceive the world. People change their perception about a certain product, brand or even industry. Drucker gives an interesting illustration of seeing the glass as half full or as half empty. Mathematically, there is no difference, but if perception changes from seeing the glass as half full to seeing it as half empty, then there are major innovative opportunities. Facts do not change, meanings change. The data on the occurrences of diseases like cancer, AIDS, longevity of people in

India points towards the health of the people which has become a new concern over the last three decades. A need for a number of health clubs, gyms, and health foods/diets, yoga, besides the jogging shoes, suits and accessories has emerged. Now there is a market for health care magazines, herbs, shrubs, alternative medicine systems like homeopathy and Ayurveda. Perception of physique and beauty has changed to thin or zero size for girls and muscular bodies of boys. When a change in perception takes place, the facts do not change. The meanings change from glass as full to glass as half empty. Thus, there are ample opportunities to innovate, even in case of food which middle-class people had been taking in India for long has undergone qualitative changes. There are people like Rajiv Kapoor, Ranbir Brar, or Vikas Khanna, who have taken food as a full time occupation and emerged as celebrities just by twisting the traditional recipes.

7. *New Knowledge:* Not just scientific and technical but any new knowledge in any field offers ample entrepreneurial opportunities. Knowledge-based innovation is the super star of entrepreneurship. It gets publicity and thus money. This innovation has the largest lead time of all innovations. Long time span is required from the emergence of new knowledge to its becoming applicable to technology and still more time is taken to use technology to become a product. New ideas are developed constantly and new knowledge is added continuously. More often there is convergence of several different kinds of knowledge and it is never based on one factor, for example, Computer uses five different types of knowledge. Each might have developed independently but when they come together, they might produce something extraordinary. New knowledge can be applied to anything like customer service, market strategies, sustainability, and business ethics in entrepreneurship (Drucker, 1985).

Dana (1998, pp. 75–76), on the basis of studies of a variety of models that helped number of countries to promote entrepreneurship, concludes that entrepreneurial response to opportunity is culture-bound. 'Entrepreneurship should not be defined on the basis of opportunity, but rather cultural perception of opportunity should be considered; individuals from various cultures are culturally influenced in the perception of opportunity, and in turn react differently to that which may or may not (according to cultural values) be considered to be an opportunity for entrepreneurial behaviour'. Nevertheless, the sources of opportunities for innovations as elaborated by Drucker are exhaustive and may be relevant for any budding/nascent entrepreneur in general.

The Indian Context

India in a neo-liberal phase is striving to move towards self-sufficiency, indigenous manufacturing, and promoting local entrepreneurs for the speedy development of the country. At the same time, there is a cut throat competition in the market between MNCs and the Indian corporate houses and big entrepreneurs. In such a scenario, it is only on the basis of consistent innovation of any kind, nature or extent that Indian entrepreneurs would sustain their enterprises. The liberalization of Indian economy in 1990s has led to a greater awareness about innovation in Indian business and industry. Therefore, innovation has become a buzzword in the modern entrepreneurial ecosystem. Many social scientists have worked on the theme in India and provide concepts, models, and theories for entrepreneurship development. Empirical cases based on Indian society compiled in *Entrepreneurship and Innovation* by Kanungo (1998) provides conceptual models for development by putting contentious issue of innovation in the backdrop. It is very difficult to take one or the other model for developing any economy; rather there is always a need to integrate the environmental factors and behavioural dispositions that facilitate creation, continuity and growth of enterprise.

The reports of Global Innovation Index provide valuable insights into any country's innovation models. The Government of India has launched several significant initiatives for propelling innovation, such as the start-up India initiative, Accelerating Growth of New India's innovations, Atal Tinkering Labs, new Intellectual Property Rights policy, Smart City Mission, Uchchatar Avishkaar Yojana, etc. The comments of Chandrajit Banerjee, Director General, Confederation of Indian Industry (2020, p. ix) are quite relevant in this regard, 'All these initiatives, coupled with phenomenal research and innovation from the institutions, industry and society are cementing India's position as an innovation and knowledge hub. However, the financial dimension plays a critical role in fructifying these innovation efforts'. Every other day we come across innovative practices of the people from across the different strata, but unfortunately they disappear on the way to turn the innovation into a real product. Still the country suffers from lack of innovation infrastructure.

Other than the science and technological innovations to generate profits, innovations can be of many other types, such as social innovation, sustainable innovation, green/urban forest innovation, and responsible innovation are the new non-economic terms in use. The emergence of social media in its various forms has depicted that common people of any society may show innovative abilities, or may at least be *jugaad* innovations. Their representation of everyday reality in the form of postings, meme' is no less innovative. But the point is that whether they would ever be able to translate their innovative skills towards entrepreneurship. In the Global Innovation Index, 2020, India is ranked 48th out of 131 countries with a score of 35.59 (Switzerland is ranked at the top with a score of 66.08). Thus, India being among the top 50 countries clearly depicts its innovation ecosystem for entrepreneurship, but the deciding factor is that who will finance them to turn their innovative abilities into production? This is a big challenge and also an opportunity. During the times of Covid-19 pandemic, a number of communities, individuals and start-ups have been found to rise to the occasion to create solutions to specific issues. Even the five-star hotels in the city started providing home delivery of food items to keep their business going. Now the government should actively come forward and provide finances to start and sustain the ventures. As we know, under corporate social responsibility (CSR) policy of the government under the Indian Companies Act 2013, the big profitable companies have to contribute 2 per cent of their annual profits to social activities which was amended in 2019 to include contributions to incubators and research projects in publically funded universities, Indian Institutes of Technology (IITs), and national laboratories.

Innovation is a continuous process and an entrepreneur can never be complacent. The moment he behaves complacently, he would be displaced by some other innovative entrepreneur. Innovation, nevertheless, is central to an enterprise development and India needs to develop its ecosystem to support entrepreneurship. Innovation and entrepreneurship go hand in hand and India has the potential to become a global hub of innovation. Existing literature on Indian Innovation system clearly reveals that innovations need to address the entrepreneurship development. Vyas (2005) argues that productivity, profit and growth of an enterprise are closely linked to its ability to innovate successfully. Imitation is believed to be an inferior and non-entrepreneurial act, but accelerating technological change has made the innovation increasingly difficult for small and nascent business. To counter it, he proposes a strategy of imitation to facilitate entry and subsequent consolidation through incremental innovation.

After having a comprehensive understanding of innovation in entrepreneurship, it is much relevant to examine entrepreneurial development in India at the empirical level. In forthcoming chapters, the focus will be on the contribution and role of various stakeholders in the development of entrepreneurial eco system in India.

Suggested Readings

Drucker, P.F. (1985). *Innovation and Entrepreneurship: Practice and Principles.* New York: Harper & Row.

Kanungo, Rabindra N. (ed.) (1998). *Entrepreneurship and Innovation: Models for Development.* New Delhi: Sage Publications.

Schumpeter, J.A. (1934). *The Theory of Economic Development* (pp. 62–94). Cambridge: Harvard University Press.

Schumpeter, J.A. (2000). Entrepreneurship as innovation. In R. Swedberg (ed.), *Entrepreneurship: The Social Science View* (pp. 51–75). New Delhi: Oxford University Press.

4

Development of Indian Entrepreneurship

After having a fairly exhaustive understanding of the concepts, theories and schools of thought on entrepreneurship, it is appropriate to examine its various dimensions in Indian context. Before we focus on entrepreneurship at empirical level in India, it is significant to explore the process of development of entrepreneurship where we find a few facilitating but more of hindering factors in its growth. It is pertinent to divide the vast and complex development of Indian entrepreneurship into historically relevant time zones. For the purpose it is put under three phases. Phase I and II represent the colonial India, whereas the phase III shows the nature and character of Independent India's entrepreneurial development as a result of its own plans and policies. The categorization does not mean that nothing is important before and after these phases. Actually, the time between 1600 and 1850 – the period which has not been taken into account here, is like foundation of modern Indian entrepreneurship. And after the liberalization of Indian economy in 1991, the nature of entrepreneurship altered significantly in post-liberal era which will be briefly touched upon in this chapter. The time duration of these phases is as follows:

- Phase I: 1850–1900

- Phase II: 1900–1947
- Phase III: 1947–1991 (June)

To trace the history of Indian entrepreneurship, it is much relevant to examine the roots of Indian capitalist development and it lies in the establishment of English East India Company (EEIC) set up by ex-army officers, a corporate on 31 December 1600, and continued to dominate the market for the next 275 years. In 2000, it celebrated 400 years. In 1618, it negotiated its first trade agreement with Mughal Empire and in 1657, it became the permanent Joint Stock Company and thereon the story of personal and corporate gains began and laid the foundation of modern multinational culture, financial management, and business administration. In 1690, the East India Company established its base in Calcutta at a time when Bengal was regarded as paradise on earth due its riches, wealth and property. The artisans of Bengal had been producing high quality muslin, cotton, and calico, and had a better standard of living than their counterparts in England (Robins, 2006). Nafziger (1971) informs that in 1750, India was as urbanized as England, France and Italy. However, over a period of time, the company became an illustration of its executive malpractices, stock market excesses and human exploitation. The stalwarts of the time like Adam Smith, Edmund Burke and Karl Marx made critical evaluation of company's existence and practices. Then how could it survive and could get legitimacy for its actions is to be located in the colonization of India.

In view of Meeta and Rajivlochan (2020, pp. 13–58), one of the important reasons for their presence for such a long period was their ability to systematize information to manage their money better; they commissioned surveys about possible products for which there could be a market. The English East India Company displayed a keen sense of the importance of information. On the other hand, in 17th and 18th centuries, the Indian merchants though showed a plenty of entrepreneurship, yet it was lack of regulation, lack of legal systems, and a certain inability to systematize information to improve efficiencies in Indian business, besides the inability to recover debts, that led to their marginalization. Good management of money and resources were responsible for the success of the company and rise of colonialism in the country. Trust and honour is no substitute for laws of contract which were written. The English East India Company spent much time and effort on taking care of its soldiers. It was able to pay the Indian soldiers regularly, consistently and organize their supply lines. Invalid soldiers were given land to settle, cash gratuity, and pension besides many other provisions. Therefore, as Meeta and Rajivlochan (2020, p. 25) write, 'The company was able to offer greater security to the average Indian businessmen. And for the rich businessmen who were their business rivals: the company made it difficult for them to operate independently of the company'. They brought out the fault lines at the level of policy of Mughal rulers in comparison to the East India companies (English, European, Dutch and Portuguese) who enjoyed a lot of ease of doing business in India. They were even allowed by their local rulers to raise their own armies. While in the absence of state support to business, the Indian merchants did not get protection against looting and piracy on high seas or even at home. Piracy hit the merchants powerfully from the 17th century onwards. The system of passes (first introduced by the Portuguese) for the safe passage became common practice amongst other European companies. Indian traders had to spend money on getting the passes and had to pay custom duty on the cargo. The Indian rulers failed to provide protection of property which was the key to doing business when it was fiercely competitive in India. In 1858, the Parliament replaced company with direct British rule in India.

At the turn of the 18th century, India was a predominantly agricultural country and manufacturing was confined to textile goods and handicrafts, which contributed a very small share in the total economy. Entrepreneurship was found amongst artisans, both rural and urban. Artisanal products like cotton, and metal products of bronze and steel of Bengal, Kashmir, Mirzapur, Varanasi, Gaya, Puri were famous. From the ledgers of the English East India Company, Meeta and Rajivlochan (2020) find 91 different types of textile products, 41 types of other products, including spices and fragrant wood exported to Europe. The weavers of Bengal wove *malmal*/cotton[1] so fine that it could pass through the finger rings. Facilities for transporting the goods, such as roads were not developed. Same was the case with waterways trade with distant places was only in small parts that is, Ganga and Indus rivers in north and rocky rivers in south. As there was no safety on the roads, the traders were going in caravans to escape theft and violence. On the way there were different provincial rulers, local chieftains and zamindars that had put custom barriers and were charging heavy duty resulting into the rise in prices of goods. Tripathi and Jumani (2007, p. 2) quote the visit of Thevenot in the first quarter of the 18th century who counted sixteen customs points within a distance of less than 60 miles. Very often they were looted on the way by thugs. The basic character of the Indian business in the 18th century was commercial rather than industrial. The merchants, even those with vast financial resources, showed no interest in promoting industrial undertakings or attempting technological innovations (Tripathi and Jumani, 2007).

Tripathi (1971) informs that the existence of innumerable systems of currency was yet another adverse factor, at the turn of the 19th century, as there were about 1,000 currencies in circulation in India. Some of them even depreciated in value every two-three years. Even in the absence of any effective and clear-cut system of exchange, bankers and moneylenders fixed their own arbitrary exchange rates. In the absence of any unified money market governed by single bank rate, there were different bank rates for Western-style banks, traders borrowed from banks upon *hundis* and much higher rates were charged by moneylenders on peasants and artisans. Moneylenders even charged up to 12 to 18 per cent interest rate to agriculturists. These political and economic factors led to the regional markets-each limited to 200–300 miles-and the so-called village self-sufficient economy.

Ray (1994) writes that the development of regional markets, self-sufficient villages proved detrimental to large-scale undertakings. Tripathi (1971, p. 103) identifies two more factors of relatively less significance. First, the religious system of education which prevailed through the 1800s emphasized the importance of a man's calling. Second, business was held in low esteem in India throughout the period. Kautilya's belief that a businessman was a thief but was not called so, seemed to have become a commonly held view in later years. The dual nature of economy in colonial India had organized and unorganized sectors, which had their own institutions and forms of organization. During this time trade and business was flourishing in the *bazaars* only. In the *bazaar* economy, the world of commerce and credit, the capital was there through indigenous bankers, moneylenders, traders, the Jagat

Seths, Nagar Seths, Marwaris, Parsi, Bohras, Khojas, Memons, Khatris and Banias. It was from the *bazaar* that the Indian industrial capitalism emerged in the second half of the 19th century when India was a dependent country. The first factory, a cotton textile, was set up by an entrepreneur from Parsi community in 1851 at Navsari in Surat (Ray, ibid.). There were parallel foreign enterprises to Indian enterprises, as Levkovsky (1972) writes that capitalist mode of production was not homogenous. They developed with different speeds, forms and in different branches of economy. On the flip side, feudal relations had also started disintegrating by the end of the 19th century and that was a pre-requisite for the development of capitalism. The peasants were deprived of their means of production and were ready to sell their labour in the factories at a cheap rate. Shirokov (1980) explains the exploitation of factory workers.

As we take up the next phase of entrepreneurial development of India in the 20th century, we find that though the Indian Industrial production was restricted to a few goods, like cotton mills developed in Bombay and Ahmedabad largely under the Parsi and Gujarati enterprises, but the 'real boom conditions' favoured the Indian industry to increase during this phase. Industry grew fast especially from First World War to 1947. In the early 20th century, heavy industry like steel, engineering, electric power and shipping started making a beginning. Later, at this time around 1919, the Marwaris also entered into industrial production. The famous Birlas made good fortune during this time. Tripathi and Jumani summarize (2007, p. 90), 'New enterprises sprang up in the wake of rising opportunities created by the war: apart from the Marwaris, new social collectivities or caste groups were drawn to the modern sector and industries, to which they had so far remained indifferent, began to attract them. The commercial sector too began to draw individuals and groups hitherto uninvolved in business'. Nevertheless, there were a number of government restrictions; even the basic machine that is, *lathe* was not allowed to be manufactured by Indian entrepreneurs. The connections of *bazaar* bankers and merchants helped them to enter the industry from World War I to the Independence of the country and as a result, the factory system grew fast. The great depression was not so severe in India as in other developed economies, but still it had its impact. Tripathi (2004, p. 226) writes that World War II came as Godsend for

Indian business. British set up a large-scale industry, largely to meet the needs of the war, such as guns, ammunition, tents, leather shoes, military uniform, etc. which did not have much significance for the industrial development of the country and its people. There was no connection between small and large-scale industries. As a result, the artisan production was ruined by the emergence of large-scale industry. We have illustration of Japan where artisanal commodity production was integrated with medium and large industry. Their skills did not get ruined, whereas in India they got ruined with the emergence of industrial development. With the mechanization of yarn production introduced in 1821, artisans of Bengal, who were producing high quality cotton, had their thumb and index finger cut to curtail competition from them. We also know that the cotton fields were turned into opium cultivation. Due to the lack of incorporation of artisans into industrial production, our process of industrial development remained slow; as a matter of fact, we are experiencing now what Britain had experienced some 250 years back. Japan took only 50 years to reach that stage. Indian capitalism has not emerged from within, rather it has been imposed from above.

The scholars have assigned a number of reasons for the slow entrepreneurial development in India. Weber (1958) stressed sociological factors, that is, religion, ritualism, *karma*, belief and caste system to explain the backwardness of India. Buchanan (1934) says that religious philosophy that is *karma* besides caste, *purdah*, joint family system have remained major hindrance against industrial development. Gadgil (1971) is of the opinion that economic factors are responsible, which he identifies as small capital resources, late development of organized banking, high profits from moneylending, inability of banks to afford long term industrial loans, existence and prevalence of more profitable activities in *bazaar*. Quite often colonial exploitation is blamed for the lack of entrepreneurial development of India, but Meeta and Rajivlochan (ibid.) discard the arguments of colonialism by emphasizing the fact that many countries were devastated with two World Wars, yet they could manage to recover pretty well. Japan was never colonized, but devastated due to World War II; similarly, China began at a lower base than India in 1950, but today its economy rivals that of the USA.

India got Independence in 1947 and Ray (1994) raises a question why at that time economy was backward, and predominantly agricultural with massive poverty, Though India possessed a large and fairly sophisticated modern industrial complex, the roots can be traced to traditional merchant communities and, as Tripathi mentions, India at Independence was a proto-industrial society. The industrial policy resolution of 1948 stresses the greater participation of the state in economic activities, and thus a new phase begins in which Indian welfare state played the guiding role with economic planning through Five-Years Plans, and other economic measures, such as import and tariff policies and control of prices and distribution of goods, which were launched for balanced economic development of all regions. The leaders' vision of a socialist state encouraged political interference and a system of industrial licensing was devised where the existing and new industrial undertakings could not be established without the prior procurement of license from the Central Government. To procure the needed goods and equipment, they were required to get permits which discouraged the private enterprises. As a matter of fact, the Government of India was deciding what to produce, how much to produce and where to produce and what will be the selling price. Large-scale industry remained largely in the public sector dealing with scarce resources, vital sectors requiring huge investments. Small and medium industry which largely were engaged in consumer goods opened in the private sector but with lot of restrictions.

Along with Independence, the country was also partitioned into two – India and Pakistan. India faced a setback as it's large finest, fertile cotton and jute growing areas, skilled workers, and successful businessmen like Cutchi Memons had moved to Pakistan. Thus, the common type of industries emerged which then started competing with each other. In the initial one-and-half decade, the annual growth rate in industrial output rose to 150 per cent from 0.6 per cent growth during 1937–47 due to centralized planning and other protective measures. Due to obvious drawbacks in the planned economy of India, it resulted into concentration of industries at a few places like Bombay, Ahmedabad, Calcutta, Kanpur, etc. Also there emerged a concentration of small and medium industries which contributed to inefficiency, because most of these were bogus units. Further there was concentration of certain types of industries. As a result, we had lopsided, skewed entrepreneurship in few sectors producing certain goods at certain places. Who were these entrepreneurs? Their roots can be traced to traditional business communities, like Parsi, Marwari, Gujarati. Most of these businesses were family enterprises like Tata, Birla, Kirloskar, Mafatlal, Singhania, Modi, Godrej, Larsen and Toubro, Khataus, Amins. The family owned and managed businesses have remained a prominent form of doing business in postcolonial India. Most of the successful entrepreneurial communities, business families and business houses were/are found to be concentrated in the 'entrepreneurial belt' stretched from Rajkot in Gujarat to parts of Maharashtra – Mumbai/Pune/Kolhapur. Though family is always considered the most valuable resource of generating capital, know-how, and trustworthiness, but the same resource have had become a hindrance when it came to expansion and diversification of business. There were clashes of interests, ideologies and vision between brothers, fathers and sons, uncles, nephews and among cousins. The sons, being educated and highly professionalized, wanted to modernize and diversify to which business patriarchs objected strongly. The succession crises, division of property and inheritance, and competition have remained serious challenges. Though we cannot ignore the contribution of some individual entrepreneurs like hotelier M.S. Oberoi, Bhai Mohan Singh of Ranbaxy-a pharmaceutical company and many others who diversified the entrepreneurial base of India.

Monopoly capitalism showing itself through public sector and nationalization of various institutions led to strict bureaucratization, red-tape, corruption, deficit budgets in the public sector industrial units. Moreover, there was no competition from foreign goods, which restricted private entrepreneurship. Due to restrictions on trade and tariff, a lengthy, extensive and expensive system of trade emerged. Restriction on movement of goods, export and import of the goods also discouraged the private entrepreneurs. Faulty industrial policy led to the making of informal sector so powerful and that too sans the work ethics giving livelihood to bulk of the Indians remained stagnant. In view of Nafziger (1971) state planning agencies largely have been performing entrepreneurial functions, for they assist in the creation of new institutions, in other words, the Government of India has largely been playing the role of an entrepreneur through its public sector predominance.

Within the three decades of Independence, the country developed a closed economy where the pace of growth was slow, profit rates and saving rates were low, the rate of industrial development remained low. All this indicate a lack of entrepreneurial skills in the public sector. The persistent low growth rates of GDP and per capita income, rising level of unemployment were the significant indicators of need for overhauling the economic policy. The fiscal deficit and imbalance of payments were determining the character of Indian capitalistic development. The economic crisis did not come as a jolt from the blue, rather it accumulated over a decade or so. Pre-liberalization phase, precisely 1980s, has a special significance because by this time savings and affluence of upper middle class had created favourable conditions for industrial investments on the one hand and a consumerist boom for domestic industrial production on the other. Thus, under the pressure of consumer demand, new industrial entrants and the changing global trade regime, the then young Prime Minister, Rajiv Gandhi, in mid-1980s undertook a gradual liberalization of the industrial policy. The success story of Maruti Suzuki points towards it. But due to misplaced priorities of the government, the gap between the income and expenditure of the government resulted into sharpened fiscal deficit as well as deficit in the balance of payments, and huge foreign debt. It led the government to take a policy decision in July 1991 on liberalization of Indian economy. The economic liberalization policy or new economic policy or the structural adjustment programme intended to bring reforms in market structure, encouraging private enterprises and opening the trade borders, covering a wide spectrum of policies including fiscal, industrial, trade, public and labour. Thus, a new era of entrepreneurship began. It is relevant to briefly touch upon the liberalization policy and its expectations, while the socio-economic consequences of the post-liberalization phase will be examined in Chapter 13: Globalization and Entrepreneurship.

The first of the three major entitlements of economic liberalization policy is marketization, which means making the Indian economy a market economy where there is free competition, where efficiency and quality would prevail and thus integrating with the world economy. The second is privatization which was of two kinds, namely denationalization and deregulation. Denationalization means changing the ownership of public sector assets to private sector and deregulation meant the opening up of the reserved areas or sectors for private players. Under this policy some of the big public sector enterprises, which were largely experiencing huge losses, were deregulated, meaning that now private individuals could enter into such enterprises, thus initially reducing the number of reserved industries to eight from seventeen. The policy makers believed that the deregulation of these industries would increase competition and hence improve the production, its quality and would be more efficient on the one hand and, on the other, would relieve the burden of the government. The third, globalization was an attempt to bring more foreign direct investment (FDI) into the industrial sector. The existing strict restrictions with regard to import and export were removed with the hope that now there would be free flow of goods and services amongst the countries which would benefit both producers and consumers. There is no doubt that the policies do not have uniform impact, but all these measures affected different sections of the society differently.

It is significant to mention that the economic liberalization policy of the Government of India made every section of the society to have a kind of experience where people across state boundaries simultaneously experienced certain forms of information, entertainment and market. There was increased international flow of capital, goods, services, people and information. Manuel Castells (1996), a Spanish sociologist, has argued that ITC (Information, technology, communication) is leading to the formation of a 'global network society' in which organizational and national borders dissolve. Many new entrepreneurs from within and outside the country entered into the Indian business. Repealing of MRTP (monopoly restrictions on trade practices) Act, which was supposed to prevent concentration of economic power through foreign collaboration and privatization, simplified these various regulations.

Following various measures of the Indian government there began the growth of transnational corporations which could base certain operations in countries where labour is the cheapest and take profits where taxes are the lowest. Multinational corporations entered Indian economy through various formats, namely:

1. Franchise – that is giving the brand name of the MNC to the entrepreneur in host country against loyalty, such as subway, McDonald, Starbucks, etc.

2. Maruti Suzuki represents the partnership/joint venture where Japanese company has collaborated with the company of host country for some share which is less than 50 per cent.
3. MNCs set up the whole business and then hand it over to the host business. Many of the highway projects fall under this type.
4. MNCs are also acting as distributors or agencies.
5. A few MNCs directly with 100 per cent FDI own and operate business ventures in India. IKEA, a Swedish furniture manufacturer, opened its own stores.

The traditional retail sector underwent significant transformation. The modern retail formats started competing in the market, though the consumers started getting a variety of goods and brands. The consumerist boom in India by the turn of the 20th century encouraged Wal-Mart of USA, Metro from Germany and many others to set up their big stores even in medium-sized cities. The traditional traders and businessmen, who were comfortably placed in commercial centres of the cities, started feeling the heat of the new competitors with a variety of formats, such as discount stores, supermarkets, hyper-marts, and speciality chains (Sharma, 2015). The neo-liberal era in the development of entrepreneurship in India poses variety of new challenges to address.

Note

1. Nafziger (1971) quotes that Indian muslin was used in wrapping Egyptian mummies.

Suggested Readings

Gadgil, D.R. (1971). *The Industrial Evolution of India in Recent Times, 1860–1939*. Delhi: Oxford University Press.

Levkovsky, A.I. (1972). *Capitalism in India: Basic Trends in its Development*. New Delhi: People's Publishing House.

Meeta and Rajivlochan (2020). *Making India Great Again: Learning from our History*. New Delhi: Manohar Publishers.

Ray, R.K. (1994). 'Introduction'. In R.K. Ray (ed.), *Entrepreneurship and Industry in India 1800–1947* (pp. 1–69). New Delhi: Oxford University Press.

Robins, Nick. (2006). *The Corporation that Changed the World: How the East India Company Shaped the Modern Multinational*. New Delhi: Orient Longman.

Shirokov, G.K. (1980). *Industrialization of India*. New Delhi: People's Publishing House.

Tripathi, Dwijendra (2004). *The Oxford History of Indian Business*. New Delhi: Oxford University Press.

Section II

Role of Social Capital in Entrepreneurship Development

5

The Role of Social Capital in Entrepreneurship Development – I

After having an overall theoretical understanding of entrepreneurship in general in the preceding chapters, we now move to the entrepreneurial development in India at empirical level. The existing literature on entrepreneurship clearly states that in India we have community and caste entrepreneurship, for the major share of entrepreneurship is the contribution of a few enterprising traditional business communities. It is their family networks and connections, caste bonding, personal relations and family network of relations to which Granovetter calls 'embeddedness' (1992) in generating trust, in establishing expectations, and in creating and enforcing norms that have remained significant in the emergence and growth of Indian entrepreneurship since the middle of the 19th century. It is precisely their social capital which made them to survive through odds over generations and hence leading the economic development of the country. Coleman (1988) argues that family relations are important in the market and so is the stability of proprietorship. One can see the market as consisting of a set of individual merchants, each having an extensive body of social capital on which they depend through the relationships of the market.

To understand the meaning and context of social capital, contributions of three major theorists, Bourdieu, Coleman, and Putnam, will be examined to provide the perspective for the purpose of analysing the prevalence of traditional business communities in entrepreneurship development. How did they emerge as businessmen? How could they sustain and regenerate themselves through generations? What are the factors of their success? To explore all these questions, let us first learn what is social capital? For the purpose, this chapter is divided into two parts, first would provide an exhaustive understanding of the concept of social capital encompassing the writings of Bourdieu, Coleman and Putnam in this context. The second part would present the cases of a few prominent business communities, namely the Marwari, the Gujarati, the Parsi, and the Sindhi communities, who by the virtue of their stock of social capital have emerged as successful entrepreneurs. The second part is further divided into two parts. Part (a) will explore the role of social capital in the context of two traditional business communities, that is the Marwari and the Gujarati, whereas part (b) will examine two more business communities, namely the Parsi and the Sindhi in the next chapter.

Origin of the Term Social Capital

By all records social capital may first have appeared in a book authored by Lyda Judson Hanifan published in 1916 in United States to highlight the social context of education. After his retirement he went back to his village in Virginia, which at that time was a much less developed state, to work with people to develop school system. He concluded that grave social, economic, and political problems of the communities in which he worked could be solved only by strengthening the networks of solidarity among their citizens. He observed that older customs of rural neighbourliness and civic engagement, such as debating societies, barn raisings and apple cuttings had fallen into disuse. Gradually, these customs had been almost wholly abandoned owing to which people had become less neighbourly. Community social life gave way to family isolation and community stagnation. Writing in 1916 to urge the importance of renewed community involvement to sustain democracy and development, Hanifan coined the term 'social capital'. He referred to social capital as 'those tangible assets that count most in daily lives of people: namely goodwill, fellowship, sympathy and social intercourse among the individuals and families who make up a social unit (c.f. Coleman, 1988).

What does Social Capital Mean?

Before we actually take up the role of social capital with regard to the traditional business communities, it is relevant to understand what the social capital means and how its relevance has been resurged over the last few decades in the Western world. Sociologist Pierre Bourdieu first introduced the term in 1972 while distinguishing among various forms of capital and he specifically elaborated the concept of social capital. Till then we were aware of the capital which had only economic connotation. It was the money-capital which was basic to start any enterprise. Anyone believed that these traditional businessmen have capital so they are able to start, diversify and sustain themselves for generations. As a matter of fact, it was their sense of solidarity, relationships, trustworthiness and connectedness which worked more than economic capital. Bourdieu (1986, p. 16) argues that capital is accumulated labour, which when appropriated on a private basis by agents, enables them to appropriate social energy in the form of reified or living labour. He elaborates thus, 'capital can present itself in three fundamental guises: as economic capital, which is immediately and directly convertible into money and may be institutionalized in the form of property rights. As cultural capital, which is convertible, in certain conditions, into economic capital and may be institutionalized in the form of educational qualifications; and as social capital, made up of social obligations (connections), which is convertible, in certain conditions, into economic capital and may be institutionalized in the form of a title of nobility'? For him, the title of nobility represents 'symbolic capital, presupposes the intervention of the habitus, as a socially constituted cognitive capacity. It is membership in a group which provides each of its members with a collectively owned capital, a credential, which entitles them to credit which may be instituted by a common name (name of a community, family, a class, a school, a party) maintained and reinforced through exchanges. The profits accruing from membership in a group are the basis of the solidarity which makes them possible. The volume of the social capital possessed by a given agent thus depends on the size of the network of connections he can effectively mobilize' (Bourdieu, 1986, p. 21). In other words, he explains, 'the network of relationships is the product of investment strategies, individual or collective, consciously or unconsciously aimed at establishing or reproducing social relationships that are directly usable in the short or long term, i.e. at transforming contingent relations, such as those of neighbourhood, the workplace, or even kinship, into relationships that are at once necessary and elective, implying durable obligations subjectively felt (feelings of gratitude, respect, friendship, etc.) or institutionally guaranteed (rights)' (ibid., p. 22). It reaffirms the limits of the group, the limits beyond which constitutional exchange-trade, commensality or marriage cannot take place. It explains why in traditional societies the whole group is involved in arranging a marriage than the agents directly concerned. Even in modern societies, families continue to control these exchanges through institutions by producing occasions, places or practices which bring together individuals as homogenous as possible in terms of existence and persistence of the group (ibid., p. 22).

Coleman put the term social capital firmly and finally on the intellectual agenda in the late 1980s. He (1988) defined social capital by its function. It is not a single entity but a variety of different entities, with two elements in common: they all consist of some aspect of social structures, and they facilitate certain actions of actors, whether persons or corporate actors, within the structure. Coleman also discusses the forms of social capital: physical, human and social. Social capital is productive, making possible the achievement of certain ends. Social capital is embedded in the structure of relations between and among actors. Certain properties of social capital can be employed in the creation of human capital. With the development of idea that the concept of physical capital, as embodied in tools, machines, and other productive equipment, can be extended to include human capital as well. Just as physical capital is created by changes in materials to form tools that facilitate production, human capital is created by changes in persons that bring about skills and capabilities that make them able to act in new ways. Social capital, however, comes about through changes in the relations among persons that facilitate action. He further adds (ibid., pp. S100–S101), 'If physical capital is wholly tangible, being embodied in observable material form, and human capital is less tangible, being embodied in the skills and knowledge acquired by an individual, social capital is less tangible yet, for it exists in the relations among persons'. Just as physical capital and human capital facilitate productive activity, social capital does as well. For example, a group within which there is an extensive trustworthiness and trust, it is able to accomplish much more than a comparable group without that trustworthiness and trust.

The value of the concept of social capital lies first in the fact that it identifies certain aspects of social structure by their functions. The function is the value of these aspects of social structure to actors as resources that they can use to achieve their interests. It is important to identify those aspects of social relations that can constitute useful capital resources for individuals. For Coleman these are obligations and expectations, trustworthiness of the social environment, information channels, norms and effective sanctions. People always do things for each other. If an individual does something for B and trusts B to reciprocate in the future, this establishes an expectation in A and an obligation on the part of B. This form of social capital depends upon trustworthiness of the social structure, which implies the actual extent of obligations held and the obligations to be repaid. An important form of social capital is the potential for information that inheres in social relations. Information is important in providing the basis for action. One of the means by which information can be acquired is through the use of social relations. For instance, a person who is not greatly interested in current events but who is interested in being informed about important developments can save the time of reading a newspaper by depending on spouse or friends who pay attention to such matters.

Effective norms can constitute a powerful form of social capital. A prescriptive norm within a collectivity is that one should forgo self-interest and act in the common interests. A norm of this sort, reinforced by social support, status, honour, and other rewards, is the social capital that builds young nations, strengthens families by leading family members to act selflessly in 'the family's' interest, and in general leads persons to work for the public good. Some of these norms are internalized, whereas others are largely supported through external rewards for selfless actions and disapproval for selfish actions.

All social relations and social structures facilitate some forms of social capital and actors establish relations purposefully and continue them when they continue to have benefits. For instance, the closure of social networks is a set of effective sanctions that can monitor and guide behaviour. The intergenerational closure of a joint family provides a quantity of social capital available to each parent in raising their children with regard to their school matters as well. Closure of the social structure is important not only for the existence of effective norms but also for the trustworthiness of social structures that allows the proliferation of obligations and expectations. Thus, we may say that closure creates trustworthiness in a social structure.

For instance, when I joined voluntary organizations functioning in the city, I found my social capital has been enriched substantially. We all are members of one club, have solidarity among members and in time of need, try to help each other. And collectively we put pressure on administration to provide us space to hold meetings. Both social capital in the family and social capital in the community play roles in the creation of human capital in the rising generation. The parents help the children to do homework and teach them the chapter they did in the school so as to do well in the class. Here is a case in which the human capital of the parents, at least as measured traditionally by years of schooling, is low, but the social capital in the family available for the child's education is extremely high. These examples illustrate the importance of social capital within the family for a child's intellectual development. It is true that children are strongly affected by the human capital possessed by their parents. The social capital of the family is the relations between children and parents (and, when families include other members, relationships with them as well). In other words, if the human capital possessed by parents is not complemented by social capital embodied in family relations, it is irrelevant to the child's educational growth that the parent has a great deal, or a small amount, of human capital (ibid., p. S110).

Social capital within the family that gives the child access to the adult's human capital depends on both the physical presence of adults in the family and the attention given by the adults to the child. Even if adults are physically present, there may be a lack of social capital in the family if there is absence of strong relations between children and parents. The social capital that has value for a young person's development does not reside solely within the family. It can be found outside as well in the community consisting of the social relationships that exist among parents, in the closure exhibited by this structure of relations, and in the parents' relations with the institutions of the community. Coleman (ibid.) even proposes that if an individual comes into contact with his neighbour, and they with other neighbours, there will be an accumulation of social capital. It may immediately satisfy his social needs and it may bear a social potentiality sufficient to the substantial improvement of living conditions in the whole community.

Robert D. Putnam (2002) describes social networks and the associated norms of reciprocity as social capital, because like physical and human capital (tools and training), social networks create value, both individual and collective, and because we can 'invest' in networking. Social networks are, however, not merely investment goods, for they often provide direct consumption value. In fact, the very large international literature on the correlates of happiness suggests that social capital may actually be more important to human well-being than material goods. Studies have shown that human happiness is much more closely predicted by the access to social capital than by access to financial capital. The single most common finding from a half century's research on the correlates of life satisfaction in countries around the globe is that happiness is best predicted by the breadth and depth of one's social connections. Your extended family represents a form of social capital, as do your Sunday school class, the people you meet regularly on your commuter train, your college classmates, the neighbourhood association to which you belong, the civic organizations of which you are a member, the Internet chat group in which you participate, and the network of professional acquaintances recorded in your address book.

Putnam, on the basis of existing debates, brings out a classification of different types and dimensions of social capital:

1. *Formal versus Informal Social Capital:* Formal social capital is available when one is a member of a club or a labour union, whereas informal social capital is to be found in the game of basketball in the school, or people who have gathered at the auditorium to watch a drama.
2. *Thick versus Thin Social Capital:* Some forms of social capital are closely interwoven and multi-stranded, such as a group of workers working together at the factory, or visiting the

families on weekends. There are also very thin, almost invisible filaments of social capital, such as the nodding acquaintance you have with the person you occasionally see waiting for bus at the bus stop, or even a chance encounter with another person in an elevator.

3. *Inward-Looking versus Outward-Looking Social Capital:* Some forms of social capital are, by choice or necessity, inward-looking and tend to promote the material, social, or political interests of their own members organized along class, gender, or ethnic lines and exist to preserve or strengthen the bonds of birth and circumstance, whereas others are outward-looking and concern themselves with public goods.
4. *Bridging versus Bonding Social Capital:* Bonding social capital brings together people who are like one another in important respects (ethnicity, age, gender, social class, and so on), whereas bridging social capital refers to social networks that bring together people who are unlike one another.

The second half of the 20th century saw the rapid spread of inventions and innovations scarcely imagined when the century began. There are new technologies for entertainment (notably television), for communication (cheap and nearly universal long-distance phone service, fax machines, electronic mail), and for information (the Internet). These new technologies have had myriad effects on social capital. On the one hand, they have undoubtedly enhanced our ability to maintain our social networks even across vast spaces, but, on the other hand, they have also facilitated a withdrawal of some people from civic and social life. It is hardly surprising that technology's effects on social capital building are mixed (Putnam and Kristin, 2002).

Communities

There have been a few communities throughout the world, who have been the trendsetters in trade and business and many of them later took to manufacturing as well. For instance, Filipino and Chinese in Philippines, Samurai in Japan, and Chettiars in South, Marwaris in East, Gujarati Jains and Banias, Parsi, Khojas, Memons, Bohras in West, and Khatri, Arora and Bania in North in India, besides many other communities at regional levels. In India, the business communities are groups of castes with a common regional origin and a traditional involvement in trade. Their names typically indicate geographical or in some cases linguistic origin, for instance, Gujarati, Marwari, Sindhi, Punjabi (Timberg, 2014). Max Weber was the first one to recognize the significance of social structure of a community in determining entrepreneurial attributes and economic development of its members. Communities manifest social solidarity, pride in their values, family relationships, trust-worthiness, and other kinship and neighbourhood networks and cooperation which are supporting their people in economic endeavours. An empirical examination of business communities of India reveal the significant contribution of social capital in its various forms helping them to develop, diversify, and sustain over the time. The major emphasis would remain on the role of their stock of social capital besides providing a general background of the community. To begin with, let us focus on one of the most successful and wealthiest business community, that is, Marwari community, who virtually control half of the Indian assets, followed by other business tycoons.

The Marwari

In common parlance they are known to be hailing from Rajasthan state of India. To be more specific, they belong to erstwhile Marwar region; it is technically the old state of Jodhpur in Rajasthan. Significant group of traders and industrialists come from Shekhawati region spread from Jaipur to Bikaner. The regional culture assigns lot of importance to commerce and trade. Their traditional occupation has been trading and moneylending and thus they were exporters, financers and bankers. Marwaris as a community includes several castes. Tod (c.f. Timberg, 1978) has mentioned 128 merchant subcastes, that is Baniya caste of *vaishya varna* members in Rajasthan. Prominent amongst them are Aggarwal, Maheshwari, Oswals, Khandelwals, Porwals, who follow the Jainism, and the Vaishnav religion. Just to take note of a few Marwari business houses, we are immediately reminded of Bajaj, Khaitan, Dalmia, Birlas, Goenkas, Oswals, Poddars, Modi and Gwalior Mills. Thomas A. Timberg has extensively worked on the Marwaris, and his first book was published in 1978 and again in 2014, that is the post-liberal era of India, he traces their history from Jagat Seth to the Birlas. Much of the analysis of Marwari businessmen in the chapter is based on his work (Timberg, 1978, 2014).

The process of migration of the Marwaris began in the 16th century around 1564 when they came to Bengal to supply ration to Raja Man Singh's troops. By the last decade of the 16th century, waves of Marwaris had moved to the central India and to Bengal as well in search of trade opportunities. The next impetus of their migration came in the 19th century with the opening of the Delhi-Calcutta rail route, as this place had a flourishing trade centre of the British at that time. Timberg gives a detailed explanation of their long and arduous journeys that how these traders used to reach Delhi on camelbacks and then they would take train to Calcutta. G.D. Birla, a pioneer Marwari industrialist wrote, 'the nearest railway station to Delhi was either Ahmedabad or Indore. To travel by camel was sheer torture and migration was done in groups called *sangh*' (De, 1995, p. 26).

Why did they migrate so far? One of the major reasons for it was that in their homeland economic opportunities were limited. The land largely being barren provided little scope for agriculture and trading activities within. This region had a number of princely estates and frequent battles were going on between them as a result of which there was a fall of many princely regimes. The traditional prosperous land trading route from India to Middle East, Central Asia and Europe passed through Jaiselmer, Rajasthan had lost its significance. The Jat and Maratha insurrections devastated the Shekhawati region. Besides a long list of battles over the time, the region also faced a number of epidemics, particularly plague which created a havoc in the area. Finding limited opportunities locally they started looking towards other places. The fall of Mughal Empire and with the rise of the British, the local traders and merchants started migrating to the emerging cities along the coast, like Bombay. At that time the East India Company had spread its wings in and around Calcutta. Attraction to these centres of business activities due to the simultaneous expansion of railways, even up to Shekhawati region later in 1920, further facilitated the migrations. The popular saying is that a Marwari went to *Pradesh* (foreign land) with an empty pot and came back with pot full of coins. The myth was and still is that wherever there are no means of transportation, the Marwari would successfully venture out and reach there.

Most of the Marwaris in Calcutta started as commission agents of the British traders, while others were engaged in speculation in opium, gold and silver. Opium produced in Bihar and eastern UP was exported to China through Calcutta. It is hard to find a Marwari who is not religious. Religion and rituals form a central place in the daily life of the Marwaris. The food habits of the Marwaris reflect a strong *vaishnav* influence. They are pure vegetarians particularly, the Marwari Jains. However, the younger generation is gradually shifting to non-vegetarian food.

Role of Social Capital

1. Marwaris show a strong sense of community belongingness and solidarity. Some well-established big firms, two cloth merchants – Nathuram Saraf of Mandawa and Jhunjhuwala of Chirawa ran *basas* (*sarai* (inn) with community kitchen) which provided free boarding and lodging to the persons coming from Marwar in Calcutta and as a matter of fact, any Marwari newcomer was welcome to stay and take food in the *basas*. G.D. Birlas's father, Shiv Narain, also, to begin with, stayed in a *basas* in 1860. Such *basas* were run by big firms on cooperative basis in other major towns too where free boarding and food was served to the newcomers. This kind of social bonding, help and cooperation towards one's own community helped them to progress.
2. Through the social connections, the newcomer would soon get to work as apprentice with the established businessmen. After learning the techniques of business and profit sharing and accumulating some capital, he would start his own business through the social networks. Marwari traders and merchants became very successful and started controlling cotton, sugar, tea, and opium export trade, besides moneylending. They emerged as exporters, importers, stockbrokers and speculators. They got pre-eminence in Calcutta next to the British.
3. Back home, in Rajasthan, they built big *havelis* for the families. Marwaris have had evolved a very pragmatic system of reproducing the social capital through a customary practice. After working for many years, when they would get older, they return home to the family. Only the young men migrated out to do the business, whereas women and children stayed back

and were subsequently joined by the returned elderly men. As a part of the family tradition, it was the obligation and expectation from the elderly to train the young ones to replenish the human capital that is, to teach the young ones the tricks of trade, ethics and nuances of business to prepare them to migrate. This provides a clear illustration of social capital creating human capital by imparting training and skills to take up the hereditary occupation of the family, though they never cared much about formal education.

4. A number of traits inculcated in personality, primarily through family and kinship networks, may be identified in the case of Marwaris contributing to their unparalleled success. Timberg (2014) traces their ability to adapt to situations and flexibility of mind as important traits in their extraordinary success. Das (2014) adds that the virtue of being risk-takers and trustworthiness have central place in their business life. De (1995) writes that Marwaris have uncanny knack for business. In the words of Deepak Khaitan, the former President of the Chamber of Commerce, it is the ability of Marwaris to take risks, strong financial acumen, excellent man management, and flexibility in approach that have made the Marwaris to go up (De, 1995).
5. One of the most important factors is the community solidarity among Marwaris. The newcomer, to begin with, as was the prevalent practice, would work usually as a clerk, accountant or an agent to British firm or in some enterprise where he would learn the tricks of trade as well as save money and then he would be helped in setting up his small business, which gradually he, with his hard work, skills, book keeping, and business acumen, would expand.
6. Being very calculative and farsighted, they are relatively late entrants into the industry as compared to the Parsis, though they had enough capital. They finally joined industry during the interwar period. When the Tatas had set up a steel plant, the Marwaris were largely in trading. When they entered into industry, they surpassed all other business communities within the next two decades. The Marwaris had set up 52 industrial houses and established control over 30.5 per cent of the industrial assets till Independence (De, 1995).

7. From Bengal, they moved to Ahmedabad, Bombay and other parts of eastern India. The Marwaris are virtually found all over India, except in the southern part, and have entered into all kinds of businesses. For instance, about two centuries ago, known for their keen business sense and enterprising spirit, the Sikh ruler, Maharaja Ranjit Singh, invited them to Amritsar city of Punjab to promote business in the holy city. Beginning from 32 business families, the number of Marwari families has risen to 2,000 with the passage of time. The Marwari community is the richest and the most successful community of the city due to their hard work, diligence, honesty, work ethics and above all a strong sense of community belongingness. They are cloth commission agents and traders and manufacturers of woollen garments and shawls, in addition to trading in tea leaves. The community has its own temples, schools, libraries, hospitals and hotels in the city.
8. The Marwaris have strong family relations. They could migrate and live at a place for a long time only because of their strong adherence to living in joint families and families back home have continued to be a great source of human capital. The norm of the community is to marry within the community and even within the caste. Thus, they have a great way of preserving the social capital to which Coleman (1988) characterizes as the intergenerational closure. The existence of intergenerational closure provides a quantity of social capital available to each parent in raising their children. Closure creates trustworthiness in the family, which allows for the existence of effective norms and the proliferation of obligations and expectations. Though they are extremely simple, thrifty and conservative in day-to-day life, but when it comes to the occasion of marriage, they flaunt their money like anything. The weddings are greatly extravagant and exaggerated functions. Lavish marriage ceremonies are source of accumulating as well as show of the possession of their social capital. They know how to use physical capital to create social capital.
9. The community has also remained a great source of financial support to its members when a newcomer wanted to start his

own business. Usually the well-off Marwaris would pool in some money to help the community member to set up business. Later they also started their own banks, The Bank of Rajasthan, Bikaner, are illustrations. Badridas Goenka became the first Indian to be appointed as the Chairman of the Imperial Bank of India in 1933 which later was named State Bank of India.

Collectively they developed various institutions like temples, schools, hospitals besides forming business associations which helped them to trade more easily.

The Marwari, community has undergone transformation, precisely after the liberalization of the Indian economy, from the provincial to cosmopolitan. Their traditional outfit – *dhoti kurta* and *galabandh* jacket and *pagdi/topi* – are on their way out. The Marwari women's lifestyle has also changed. The younger Marwaris have realized the significance of education to learn the new techniques of business. Aditya Birla studied in Michigan Institute of Technology and Deepak Khaitan did MBA from Geneva. The formal training of the younger generation also changed their style of functioning and doing business. Though we are mainly focusing on the Marwaris as a business community, but it is relevant to mention that quite a large number of them are now professionals, intellectuals, and art lovers. Recently published business literature-autobiographies and biographies of great Marwaris, like one by Medha Kudaisya (2003), give important insights about how their social capital reproduces itself in the post-liberal era.

The Gujarati

The Gujarati business community belonging to Gujarat state of India includes a number of religious and caste groups. Gujarat has a history of a large number of powerful merchants, such as Virji Vora of Surat, Shantidas Zaveri and many Nagarsheths from Ahmedabad with business prowess. The Patidars, the Bohras, the Parsis hail from Gujarat. Tripathi (2004) explains, 'This is understandable because the region had long been witness to the most thriving commercial life in India, and its long coastline had always been home to major ports'. They are found in 164 towns of Gujarat and are largely engaged in petty business/shopkeeping as they lacked enough capital and religious leadership discouraged Western education as well. They could not compete with the industrial giants like Parsis. Bohras (Daudi) got converted from Hindu trading caste to Islam. They had to suffer a lot at the hands of Sunni rulers of Gujarat during 1411 and 1554 for not embracing the Sunni sect. Again their persecution was repeated during the reign of Aurangzeb in 1566–67. At present the prominent entrepreneur among them is Azim Premji of Wipro. The proportion of Muslim Bohras in the total economic activity of the state got reduced due to India's Partition as most of them migrated to Pakistan.

Among the Gujaratis, the most dominant and successful business community are the Patidars. They are also described as the Jews of India. The Patidars originally belong to Kanbi caste, which is the most widely spread agriculturalist caste in Gujarat. It comprises three surnames – Patel, Desai and Amin. Patels were cultivators and Desai and Amin were *jagirdars.* Patidar means a landholder, a term which was originally used for Kanbis. In 1931 census, they returned themselves as Patidar rather than Kanbi. Now they have stopped using the term Kanbi and they do not marry their daughters to non-Patidars. The Patidars in Gujarat are divided into four sub-castes – Kadavas, Levas, Anjanas and Matis.

Patidars are concentrated in the Kheda district where the land is fertile, with sufficient rainfall and thus good for agriculture and villages are large. The Patidars are rich and form the dominant caste of the local villages. They constitute 42 per cent of the landholders, holding 71 per cent of the land and contribute 70 per cent of the village income (Pocock, 1972). The Patidars depict a very interesting case of upward social mobility through changes in occupations. They had become tax collectors during the Mughal rule as a result of which they claimed equality with Rajputs who previously dominated the area. The Rajputs lost their landownership to the Patidars and had become their tenants. They started growing cash crop Indigo in the 19th century which led them to have close contacts with the merchants of the region. Knowing the prestige of the merchants, they started claiming the *vaishya* status, a step down from Kashtriya in the *varna* hierarchy. Now they became traders and merchants and started small enterprises, as they moved to other places. Under the British and Gaikwad of Baroda, they became quite prosperous (Tambs-Lyche, 1980). The Patidars present an interesting movement from agriculture to trade and trade to industry. There is, in fact, an overlapping of the three. A farmer growing cash crop was travelling to far off places and even crossing the borders to sell his produce, so he himself was trading his produce and whatever he would earn from selling the produce was invested in land back home.

In 1920s, a violent political agitation took place against the land revenue administration in Kheda district which was ruthlessly repressed by the British and many peasants lost their homes. Later, during the Civil Disobedience movement led by Mahtama Gandhi, a large number of Gujarati Patels moved to other parts of India and even to foreign countries. In fact, all those who supported the British could not stay back due to insurgency and those who fought against the British could also not stay in Gujarat due to perpetual harassment (Panigrahi and Panda, 2000). This was the major push factor which led to the international migration of Gujaratis for trade and hence beginning of their progress across the borders. The Patidars, though occupy lower status in the caste hierarchy, yet through business and trade they became economically, socially and politically powerful. Therefore, they are now the dominant caste of Gujarat and are entrepreneurs par excellence. Some household names of Gujarati entrepreneurship are Reliance, Adani group, Kotak Mohindra, Sun Pharma, Zydus Cadila, Torrent, Intas, Syntel, Wipro, Amul, Parle, Asian paints, Pidilite, Waghbakri, etc.

Role of Social Capital in the Success of Gujaratis

1. Gujarat occupies the most developed region or terrain, right from Rajkot to Gandhinagar-Ahmedabad-Anand-Baroda-Baruch-Surat-Navsari up to Mumbai. The building of roads, railways and also sea route opened up the expansion of the markets. In India this belt may be considered to be economically the most advanced region of India surely due to geographical and historical reasons. It has major ports, trade routes connecting the major business centres of the time.
2. As is true for other cultures, amongst Gujaratis also there is a proverb that the best vocation is self-reliant agriculture, trading is next and service is the lowest. Culturally. it has been inculcated that doing business or trade is far more superior and over the time they have developed a merchant model

which predominates in Gujarat, that is, '*naukri chhoro, vyapar karo*' (leave job, do business). The merchant ideology evaluates the business as of high prestige. For a person from Punjab this may sound ridiculous, but the big hoardings around the cities remind the one that business carries more prestige for them than any other vocation.

3. Gujarat could develop entrepreneurial environment or culture. They have developed a business ethics where most of the business dealings were completed by the word of mouth. The trust and honour were the essence of business dealings. Tripathi and Mehta (1990) inform that the founder of Ahmedabad textile mills was a Brahmin and the next was a Kanbi Patidar. Their argument is that it is not religion or caste but it is the kind of exposure one has to new ideas and values that really matters. Interestingly, the Gujaratis could develop an entrepreneurial culture wherever they settled entailing the role of primordial ties, social and kinship networks and use of informal and family resources. And a person born and groomed in a business family is likely to be naturally inculcated with business values, and ethics without any conscious effort (Bal, 1998). Even when multinational companies started venturing in India after the liberalization of the economy, they also chose Gujarat as entrepreneurial base. The Gujaratis could develop complete entrepreneurial ecosystem.
4. The most important factor is their community belongingness. Rutten (2001) writes that the Patidar caste group is seen to be more prone to partnership with family and kinship than others. The role of primordial ties is significant in their success story. Their usual practice is to have joint ownership or to run family businesses.
5. The Gujaratis have a community tradition to help or support a new entrant. The community members may help with finance to start own business or the newcomer may be asked to join the business as an apprentice to learn the skills and develop capabilities. The Gujaratis' past reveals the entrepreneurial spirit of its people when they have been travelling across seas to sell their produce and there are many instances of the merchants of Gujarat, such as Mulla Abdul Ghafur and Virji Vora whose ships worth lakhs of rupees in those days were

looted many times by the prevailing sea pirates. Yet they rose to emerge as the richest merchants within a few decades in Surat. Such was the spirit for earning money. When even Shivaji looted Surat, they resurged with much vigour.

6. Gujarat as a trading capital had its extensions up to Fiji, Mauritius and many African countries in the 18th century. During the 19th century, the famines in Gujarat forced some of the Gujaratis to sail across the Arabian Sea and settle in East and South Africa. In fact, the Patidars became one of the biggest communities of Indians in East Africa where they realized the merchant ideal of Gujarati culture to a great extent. Most of them with more money migrated to England during 1960s. A study of the London Patidars (Tambs-Lyche, 1980) reveals that about two-third of the respondents came from East Africa. Later, the exodus of Asians from African countries also pushed many to England. The pattern of migration of the Patidars to England may be described as a chain migration where people chose to migrate on the information supplied by kin and village mates. Even in alien lands they tended to form a community and thus concentrated in a few areas; London and Leicester have emerged as the Patidar centres. Besides shopkeepers, they were house owners keeping paying guests, moneylenders, wholesalers, agents, and brokers.
7. The chain migration pattern reveals the role of social capital, when the families and wider kinship group was helped to migrate to foreign shores, now to America, on the basis of marriage or otherwise. When the American immigration policy was liberalized in 1965, many Gujaratis opted for American citizenship with the consideration to sponsor their close relatives. There are cases of the Patidar families who have extended their families and kinship a hundred times through chain migration. In the 1980s, the Gujaratis started motels and stores for which they needed family members and they soon became prominent in hospitality business. Most of the retail shops, gas stations, and once even newspaper stands were owned and run by them. Fisher informs (1980) that many Gujaratis were professionally employed while simultaneously running a business with the help of wives, children, kinsmen

and friends. The power of social and human capital is such that many areas in America are in the making of 'Little Gujarat'.

8. A substantial portion of the Gujaratis (80%) being Patidars were doing businesses of varied kinds in Canada, particularly in Ontario. Israel (1994) mentions that the Patel community life is organized in a range of sub-castes in which marriages are arranged in the context of Unions of Villages, each with its own governing body. There are six such Unions and members of all of them have migrated to the UK, United States and Canada. There is hardly any corner of the globe where they have not reached today and they are best known for their entrepreneurship.
9. Tripathi (2004) writes that by the turn of the 18th century, India was amongst the most industrialized countries of Asia, but actually it was confined to textile goods and handicrafts. Ahmedabad was known for its textile manufacturing – cotton, silk and wool. Nagarsheth Shantidas Zaveri was dealing with precious stones. While Virji Vora was travelling far and wide to trade his variety of goods. Besides trading in opium for some time, they took to moneylending and became prominent bankers, but most of the Gujaratis mainly remained engaged in cotton cultivation and producing textile and since then Gujarat has remained the major centre of textile production. The first cotton textile industry was started by a Nagar Brahmin Ranchhodlal Chhotalal in Ahmedabad which became operational in 1861.
10. Bal (2006), in a comparative study of two most diasporic communities from India, the Patidars and the Jats of Punjab, explores why despite having number of common features – both are landowners, middle class status and the position of dominant caste between the two – have they performed differently in foreign lands. The Patidars are the most prosperous community and the Jats are also the wealthy people in Punjab. The Jat immigrants in the US, Canada and England are largely confined to blue-collar jobs in the unorganized sector, whereas the Patidars have shown great business acumen. They are best known for their entrepreneurship. Rutten (2001), in a comparative study, informs that the Patidars have a strong sense of jointness and family feelings. In his view, they, being

agriculturists and landowners, had always played an emotional role in tying the family members together, as a result, family-centric behaviour and attitude had become an important characteristic of the Patidars.

11. The nature and type of work taken up by the earlier emigrants also played a significant role. When a new emigrant comes, he/she largely depends on his/her friends and members of the community to search for a job. As a result, the new migrants tend to get concentrated in the one kind/type of jobs (Bal, 2006). New Gujarati immigrants often get absorbed into the businesses of their relatives, community men and friends as business activity always needs extra people to work. In the process, the newcomer also learns the ropes to climb in business besides establishing networks. Rutten's (2001, p. 175) study also informs that 'Patidar caste are seen to be more prone to partnership within family and kinship than others. Their sense of status and preference to operate without the assistance from outside the family makes them form partnerships within families. This emphasis on jointness is often carried to the extent of an ambition where the business is owned solely by members of his or her own joint or extended family'. Studies have shown that family members are the most trustworthy and least costly collaborators in business. Ethnic resources – families, rotating credit associations, enforceable trust, multiplex social networks and ideologies besides religion encourage and support the founding of new business firms (Light and Rosenstein, 1995).

The Gujaratis continue to dominate the entrepreneurial scenario of the country. The Ambanis and Adani are often rated among the richest persons of the world. They have spread their wings to all kinds of businesses within the country and beyond it. The new, young entrepreneurs have ventured into ICT sector as firmly as ever.

Suggested Readings

Bal, Gurpreet (1998). Communities and culture in entrepreneurship development in India. *The Journal of Entrepreneurship*, 7(2), 171–182.

Bal, Gurpreet (2006). Entrepreneurship among diasporic communities: A comparative examination of Patidars of Gujarat and Jats of Punjab. *The Journal of Entrepreneurship*, 15(2), 181–203.

Bourdieu, Pierre (1986). 'The Forms of Capital'. In J.G. Richardson (ed.), *Handbook of Theory and Research for the Sociology of Education* (pp. 241–258). New York: Greenwood Press.

Coleman, James S. (1988). 'Social capital in the creation of Human capital'. *American Journal of Sociology*, Vol. 94, pp. S 95–S 120. Supplement: Organizations and Institutions: Sociological and Economic Approaches to the Analysis of Social Structure.

Pocock, D. (1972). *Kunbi and Patidars: A Study of the Patidar Community of Gujarat*. Oxford: Oxford University Press.

Putnam, Robert D. (ed.) (2002). *Democracies in Flux: The Evolution of Social Capital in Contemporary Society*. New York: Oxford University Press.

Tambs-Lyche, H. (1980). *London Patidars: A Case Study in Urban Ethnicity*. London: Routledge & Kegan Paul.

Timberg, T.A. (1978). *The Marwaris: From Traders to Industrialists*. New Delhi: Vikas.

Timberg, T.A. (2014). *The Marwaris: From Jagatseth to the Birlas*. New Delhi: Penguin Books.

6

Role of Social Capital in Entrepreneurship Development – II

This chapter is in continuation to Chapter 5 in which two business communities, namely Marwari and Gujarati, have been discussed by tracing their origin or roots from two states of India, Rajasthan and Gujarat. In this chapter, two other communities, Parsis and Sindhis will be discussed. Also, from the perspective of social capital, the family businesses are also going to be described and examined. Parsi and Sindhi though grew, developed and flourished in India, but owing to certain historical reasons, they have been displaced from their native places and they chose to adopt India as their homeland. At their native places before the displacement both these communities were progressive, hard-working, and engaged in business and trade. It is important to examine the trajectories of their performance at the places they migrated. One may say that it was their indomitable spirit and inherent entrepreneurial qualities which helped them to rebuild their lives and businesses. However, it would be a post facto reasoning. The important thing is to locate the fundamental element in these two communities which shaped them. It is in this context that the role of social capital becomes important in facilitating us to have an in-depth understanding of these successful business communities. Social capital (Coleman, 1988) in the family is analytically separable into at least three different components: financial capital, human capital, and social capital. Financial capital is approximately measured by the family's wealth or income. It provides the physical resources that can facilitate achievement, for instance acquiring knowledge and skills, and the financial resources that help in overcoming family problems. Human capital is approximately measured by parents' education, capabilities imbibed, skills learnt and their business experience provide the potential for a cognitive environment for the younger generation that aids its learning the skills and building the capacity. Social capital within the family is different from either of these. It is the family and kinship connections, networks, primordial ties, which help to build business linkages, as Nadel (1957) identifies two types of relationships, namely network and pattern. It is network that is interlocking of relationships and operates in case of business families. However, network does not simply indicate the links between persons, but it is an additional linkage of the links. It is this interrelatedness or interlocking of the relationships amongst the displaced business communities, which greatly helped them to re-establish in an alien scenario. In contrast to a person from the non-business family, a man born in business family has better advantage to do business, for he develops the entrepreneurial acumen/behaviour in the course of everyday experiences and it becomes a part of his personality. The main difference, as Coleman (ibid.) expresses, is of the time and effort spent by the father with the child on teaching him various practices of doing business.

The following part II(b) focuses on two prominent business communities of India that is, the Parsi and the Sindhi with an emphasis on the role of social capital in their success. In part III of this chapter, the role of social capital has briefly been examined in the context of family businesses in India.

The Parsis

The Parsi, pioneer of industrial entrepreneurship in India, played an outstanding role in the growth of industry in second half of the 19th century. The first mill of India, that is the cotton textile mill, was established in 1854 by a Parsi, Cowasjee Nanabhoy Davar in Bombay (Tripathi and Mehta, 1990). Tripathi further comments, 'Cowasji Nanabhai Davar, a Parsi merchant of Bombay, has the distinction of being the first Indian to float a cotton mill, and his Bombay Spinning and Weaving Company was the first truly successful industrial venture in the country' (2004, p. 96). Another prominent Parsi, Dinshaw M. Petit's father Maneckji was among the early pioneers of the industry in Bombay and the founder of the first composite mill in the Presidency (ibid., p. 118). Though Parsis were late entrants to trade and business as compared to Marwari, Gujarati and other communities, but they became the first to enter into industry. Their journey reveals a number of issues, but it was primarily their human and social capital which turned everything in the right direction for them.

Most of the information available on Parsi entrepreneurs has been provided by Amalendu Guha, a historian, through three of his articles published in *Economic & Political Weekly* in 1970 and in 1984. He informs that to escape persecution by the Muslims who forced them to convert to Islam, the Parsis fled in the boats from their homeland Persia (modern day Iran) in 697 AD and reached the Gujarat coast, near Navsari. Nineteen years later they moved to Sanjan – a port in the Gulf of Cambay. For the next 700 years, nothing was heard about them and the possibility is that they might have assimilated with local population and took to native occupation of farming. Sanjan was overrun by Muslims in 1315 and Parsis were once again uprooted. Next they settled in Surat-Navsari area in the 15th century. The Parsis, at this time, were primarily an agricultural community. Some Parsis were awarded *jagirs* by Mughal kings for their skills. By 17th and 18th centuries there were famous shipbuilders among the Parsis of Surat. A Parsi shipbuilder of Surat built warships in 1672. Besides shipbuilding, they also were engaged in foreign trade, export and import, and in textile manufacturing. Major export from Surat was cotton and silk textile and the Parsis were actively engaged in it. They were primarily engaged in trade with the Persian and Arabian gulfs.

Since Bombay was emerging as a hub of commerce in the early 19th century, many Parsis migrated there and established themselves as guarantee brokers, contractors, and suppliers for troops, importers and exporters, shipbuilders, general traders and moneylenders and hence emerged as a dominant business community. The less fortunate amongst them worked as weavers, carpenters, artisans, liquor brewers and retailers of imported alcoholic drinks (Tripathi and Jumani, 2007, p. 40). Under the system of regulated trade from Bombay, Parsi also exported opium to China. According to 1864 census of the Bombay Island, the

Parsis, though only 6 per cent of its population, accounted for 17 per cent as wholesale traders, engaged in broking, banking and money-changing. Also of all the alcohol dealers in Bombay, 21 per cent were Parsi liquor dealers. Thus, they were in a favourable position for capital accumulation. Towards the middle of the 19th century, the Parsi traders, shipbuilders and financers of Bombay came into textile industry. Desai (1994) mentions the outstanding contribution of three families to textile industry, namely Wadia, Tata and Petit, who later diversified to paper and silk industry, steam navigation, Indian railway builders, iron and steel industry. They also worked as secretaries, managing agents and managers of the mills. Guha (1984) writes that in fact what brought a sharp turn to the fortunes of the Parsis was the quick expansion of trade with China in the wake of the industrial revolution of England. Trade in opium and raw cotton was then the mainstay of the Parsi Seths. Money earned through these businesses was used to acquire landed property, and in the process, the Parsis also emerged as the largest landholders in Bombay. By the middle of the 19th century, they owned almost half of the island of Bombay, with one quarter of it being the property of a single family, that of Wadias. These properties brought huge income in rentals to them, as they were renting these to Europeans and others (Tripathi, 2004).

A number of Gujarat towns, such as Surat, Broach, Navsari and Cambay had a large concentration of Parsis, and in these cities, the Europeans, particularly the English, had depended on the services of Parsi middlemen, agents and brokers. It reveals that Parsi community did not stick to one place, as it kept on frequently moving, exploring and venturing into new vistas. The Parsis are the most mobile, diasporic community found almost in all countries of world, though in small numbers. It is also the most urbanized community. Interestingly, towards the end of last century, 90 per cent of them were residing in metropolitan cities, 9 per cent in cities and only 1 per cent were residing in rural areas (Guha, 1984). The famous and successful Parsi entrepreneurs, to mention a few, are Tatas, Godrej, Wadias, Mistry, Mehta, though they are successful actors, scientists, academicians, professionals as well. At present their population in India according to the 2011 Census is 57,264. India's Parsi-Zoroastrian population has been falling every decade since 1941. In 1961 their number was nearly one lakh in India. Between the 2001 and 2011 censuses, their numbers fell from

69,000 to 57,000. A study by Parsi demographer Ava Khullar (c.f. Nair, 2017) listed low fertility, migration, late marriages, and exclusion of kids born to women married to non-Parsi as the prominent reasons for their decline.

Role of Social Capital in their Success

1. The Parsis are the most closed-knit community. They are strictly endogamous in terms of marriage. The pressure of the community is so strong that they either tend to marry within their own community or do not marry at all. Invariably, one may find a large number of persons who never married. Despite the fact that this community fears the danger of being extinct, they wish to preserve their own community identity, traditions and practices under all conditions.
2. Zoroastrianism is their religion where they worship the fire. Fire is most pious to them. They do not observe caste system like Hindus do, but within themselves they form a closed group with a Panchayat at its head, which is the custodian of the strict Parsi life. Therefore, their community solidarity and belongingness is very strong.
3. The strong sense of community solidarity helped them to make the best use of economic opportunities. As a community, they developed close contact with the British East India Company, though the Dutch and the French were also trading with their help in India. Local traders depended on the British and the Dutch for protection on seas. During 1750–1850, the Parsis prospered most as the closest allies of powerful European agency houses at the top.
4. The pattern of their occupational mobility depicts a movement from agriculture-artisan to trade and from trade to industry. Being a small community in India, the trust, cooperation, mutual help and networks, besides their basic Gujarati linguistic identity, have all the more remained strong to keep them united. Most of the Parsi enterprises follow the business ethics strongly and that is the reason for their long term sustenance and their spirit of enterprise in post-liberal era. Even in present times, the Tatas, and Wadias of Bombay Dyeing and Go-first airlines and many other Parsi enterprises appear to be the most honourable, trustworthy, genuine, and reliable.

5. Their methods of business organization depict the role of family ties. Their businesses are family enterprises and family members are their working partners. From 1830s they started joint stock companies when they worked as apprentice for European firms. Normally, a young Parsi would not start his career in his own firm but as an employee in a European firm where he would get training in their business methods, which he could subsequently use in his own business. They built ships for the English East India Company from 1730 onwards.
6. Besides the social capital, their human capital also reveals distinct features. For instance, most of them have had formal, modern, Western education including technical skills and managerial know-how. They picked up English despite being a Gujarati linguistic community.
7. Their comprador role from 1750–1850 (Guha, 1970) to British patrons as stable collaborators and most reliable allies brought them close to political power. They showed a strong affinity with British in terms of dress, food, mannerism, language and way of life. It is generally argued that the Parsis were the beneficiaries of British rule, but Guha (1984) writes that they also were victims of their policies, since British monopoly capitalism would not tolerate rivals in the same market. Later, in the nationalist struggle Tatas, Wadia, Petit, and Godrej even provided financial help. Godrej is known for his association with Gandhi and his Sawdeshi movement.
8. There are enough illustrations of the Parsis helping their community members financially to do business. The Bank of Bombay, Oriental Bank Corporation, and Commercial Bank of India were established by Parsis from 1840–1845. It depicts their capital accumulation as well as financial acumen.
9. Their pattern of spatial and occupational mobility as a community is worth mentioning. They migrated from rural to urban areas during the early 17th century and by 18th century, they were migrating from urban to urban areas in favour of Bombay. And by the middle of the 19th century, half of their population and in 1881, 70 per cent of their population was urbanized. Accordingly, they moved from manual to non-manual occupations, primary to secondary and to tertiary occupations, that is from agriculture and artisan crafts to trade

and then trade to industry. Guha (1984) refers this to intra-community structural change, an embourgeoisement of more or less the entire Parsi community.

10. As we trace the reasons for the success of Parsis, the theory of Hagen (1962) that withdrawal of status respect and the minority group morale are reasons for the emergence of innovative personalities among samurai community of Japan, Burmese, and Antioquenos in Columbia, may be true for Parsis. Guha (1984) writes that even now the community has a sense of rootlessness, despite having Gujarati linguistic identity, have failed to integrate well with the nation. Weber (c.f. Judge, 2012) makes a similar comment on Jews. He points out that minority communities that are directly or indirectly excluded from political influence, work very hard in the economic action, e.g. Poles living in Russia and Eastern Prussia, Huguenots and Jews in France, and some religious sects in England.
11. Guha (1984: p. 129) traces the causes of the success of the Parsi community. He identifies four major causes: (a) Advantage of belonging to the economically the most advanced region of India, (b) Numerically less imposing presence of Europeans in the Bombay presidency was a boon for them, (c) The Parsi social outlook is important for entrepreneurial success, (d) What was striking in the Parsi society was its density and coexistence in constant social interaction therein of numerous artisans and traders. The Parsis are the most fascinating community, not only in terms of doing business but also in terms of business ethics and lifestyle.

The Sindhis

This is the business community which has its roots in the Sindh province of Pakistan. During the Partition, the Hindu and Sikh Sindhis were forced to migrate to the Indian side. Historically, Sindh, being a prosperous region, was invaded by foreigners – Persians, Greeks, Scythians, Kushons, Afghans, Moguls. Thus there has been an assimilation of various cultures in the region, which has had an influence on its people, culture, religion and outlook. After Mohammed Bin Qasim's invasion of Sindh in 711 AD, it has been under the Muslim rulers for the next almost 1,100 years. In the 16th century, the Mughals had made inroads into

India and, in 1592, Emperor Akbar annexed Sindh after which it remained under Moghul rule till the British conquered Sindh in 1843 and, in 1847, the British made it a part of the Bombay province for easier administration. During most of this time, the Sindhi Hindus were not allowed to own land owing to which they took up trading, money changing and administration. Within Sindh, it was the beautiful city of Thatto that had been the major marketplace, as far back as in the 12th century. Markovits writes (2008), 'The first mention of Banias of Sindh occurred in Arab and Portuguese documents concerning Muscat at the end of the 15th century. Thatto is mentioned as Muscat's most important Indian trading partner, and its Hindu merchants, the Bhatias, appear to have been the main participants in the trade between Sindh and Arabia'. Thatto, one of the richest cities of the Orient, had its own textile manufacturing producing high quality calicos and baftas, chintzes and muslins, as well as fine silken goods. Shikarpur, previously under direct Afghan administration, was taken over by the Talpurs, a Baloch clan, in 1824 and subsequently also began to emerge as a centre of business.

The Hindu Sindhi business community identify themselves as Hyderabadi, Shikarpuris, Sahitis and so on identifying with their place of origin. As a caste group, they form the majority of the community in India. In terms of sects or sub-caste, the two primary divisions in the group are Amils, and Bhaibands. The Amils were a class of government servants, an educated class, and worked as teachers, lawyers, doctors and bureaucrats. The Bhaibands were traders, shopkeepers and businessmen. A special term, Sindhiworki are Bhaibands who are referred as Sindhis who go abroad for trading in material manufactured in Sindh.

Though Sindh never had a rigid caste system, the traditional caste hierarchy among Sindhis classified Brahmins at the top, amongst them were *daryapanthi* and *nanakpanthi*, trading castes, namely the Lohanas, Bhatia and Khatri. The Lohana sub-castes are namely *amils*, *thakur*, *udasi*, *masand*, and *bhai*; religious castes were the *saraswat*, *pushkarna*, *jajak* and *bhat*: occupational (artisanal) castes, *sonara* and *wanhan* are placed at the bottom. Later, the hierarchy changed due to modern values and now the Lohanas, who were predominant economically and numerically, considered themselves superior to all, as the Brahmins were socially and educationally not progressive.

In 1941, before the Partition of India, Sind had a population of 45,35,008 of which 12,29,926 were Hindus. They made up about one-fourth of the total population. Most of the peasant population in this area was Muslim, while the Hindus occupied positions as merchants, shopkeepers, moneylenders, landowners, teachers and administrators. The mercantile specialization of Hindus in Sindh was related to the Islamic proscription against taking money at interest. The Sindhi Hindus filled this vacuum and met the needs for credit and trade (Barnouw, 1978). As per Census of India, 2011, the population of Sindhis in India is 27.72 lakhs. Though Sindhis are found to be living in almost all the states and UTs of India in small or large numbers, but 95 per cent of them live in central and western states of India, Gujarat state has 42.70 per cent, Maharashtra accounts for 26.10 per cent, Rajasthan has 13.9 per cent, Madhya Pradesh has 8.80 per cent, Chhattisgarh has 3.40 per cent, while Delhi, Uttar Pradesh, Assam, Karnataka and Andhra Pradesh have just 1 or less than 1 per cent of the Sindhi population. Punjab has only 462 Sindhis living according to 2001 Census.

The Role of Social Capital in the Resurgence of Sindhi Business Community

1. Sazz Aggarwal (2012, p. 219) writes about a woman living in Mumbai with her non-Bhatia husband, 'Ours is a very small and tightly-knit community, and we believe in preserving our culture and history'. She further informs, 'We have always been valued for our strict professionalism and ability to keep secrets. We were trusted by the kings; never spoke to outsiders, and mingled only within the community. Our business hub was always the middle East' (ibid., p. 220). After Partition, some families moved back to Jaisalmer, Rajasthan, where they believed they had originally come from, and men moved to Gulf for trade. In Bombay, there is a big settlement in Kandivali where they continue to be a very tightly-knit, close community. Bhatias are strict vegetarians and worship Srinathji. The best thing about the community is the bonding, as they are well knit and connected.
2. Sindhi Banias followed traditional caste occupations of moneylending and commodity trading. Their surplus cash made them to find new areas of trade. Markovits (ibid.) identifies two extraordinary and separate networks and one of

the biggest networks was centred in Shikarpur and was spread through Muscat, Afghanistan, Persia, India, and important towns, such as Bukhara, Samarkand and Kokand of Central Asia. In the early 1840s, Shikarpur had a Hindu majority and as it grew into an important base for trade, Banias from other areas migrated and settled there. From moneylending they moved to money changing, taking deposits and overseas remittances. One of the most important aspects of this was elements of trust and security. It was well-known that no Shikarpuri banker would ever default on a *hundi*, a bill of exchange. Shikarpuris settled and made homes all over the regions in which they did business. Russian revolution pushed them out of many of the Central Asian bases and India's Partition drove them out of Shikarpur.

3. The other network identified by Markovits (ibid.) was Hyderabadi Bhaibands, built up in the mid-1800s. The Bhaibands made use of new technology in communication and maritime transport and travel, and became a global one. These merchants were known as 'Sindhworkis', a term dating from the period when they first discovered that the handicrafts of Sindh were to the taste of their new British rulers. They began hawking lacquer work on wooden articles, painted flower vases, jugs and jars, embroidered linen, brass work, furniture for which Sindh was famous. They further extended their sales across India and as Markovits (ibid.) informs, around 1860 some Hyderabadi merchants extended their peddling operations outside India. Their first destination was Egypt, as it was the first tourist destination. Over the next 50 years, the Sindhiworkis developed a full-fledged international trading network, while continuing to be financed and controlled from Hyderabad. They had set up small shops and started selling goods, handicrafts and curios from other parts of the world. And profits fed a consumer boom in Hyderabad where the merchants and their families lived lives of ease and opulence. It is generally accepted that Sindhi women used to be the most fashionable and they were the trendsetters of fashion. By running their businesses entirely within the community, they were able to strengthen the economy of their hometown and build tighter community bonds like the Thattai Bhati as and other like-minded communities.

4. Aggarwal's (2012) stories of Sindhi reveal that Sindhi families were also engaged in retailing high quality fabric in different cities of China before the Second World War. Sindhi are smart, courageous and emancipated people. One Khemch and Mahtani, a Bhaiband trader, went abroad for business. He started 50 small shops in Western Europe, South America, and Northern Africa. He traded spices from India, silks from China and perfumes from Paris, taking them all over the world. It was not just the merchants who travelled to work, all young Sindhiworkis men worked in different positions around the world along with these merchants and they were living together collectively in their shops. Sindhi merchants are found at international ports like Singapore, Hong Kong, Indonesia, Ghana, Mombasa, Gibraltar and many other places (Barnow, 1978). There is hardly any place in the world where Sindhi are not found. It was a common practice for men in the family to travel and live abroad, coming home to Sindh only every three or four years. The children and women were living behind in all women families.
5. Most of the Sindhi Hindus migrated to India after the Partition in 1947 via Karachi and primarily settled in and around Bombay, a large number, 20,000, in Ulhasnagar (Bombay) and in Pimpri (Pune), where they struggled hard, stayed in camps but they continuously looked for business opportunities and some of them could soon start trading in cloth and grains, as they did in Sindh long time back. The bulk of the Sindhi refugees were traders. Only about 2 per cent of the approximately half million Sindhi, who fled to Bombay state in 1947–48, were farmers. Barnouw (1978, p. 449) informs, 'The rioting which broke out in West Pakistan after partition thus can be seen as due not only to religious conflict but also as due to the politically channelled protests of peasants against moneylenders. Like the Jews of the middle ages, the Sindhi moneylenders were a convenient scapegoat'. Barnouw writes that Sindhi in Poona (now Pune) still form a community apart, largely endogamous, have a more eclectic and liberal religious outlook, influenced by Sufism and Sikhism and other religious traditions. He illustrates that several of the trading groups, such as Jews, have a rather liberal cosmopolitan outlook.

6. Lawrence H. Fuchs (c.f. Barnouw, 1978) identifies such factors as the levelling effects of trade, the experience of persecution, the vulnerable marginal position, as well as travel abroad and familiarity with different cultures and such patterns have been exemplified by Sindhis. The Sindhi business community does not include only the trading castes. Occupation has ceased to be a feature of the caste system. Caste among Sindhis is, thus, highly flexible. They, being not caste conscious, are hospitable and inclusive which has facilitated their assimilation with the local population and as a matter of fact the existing literature does not reveal any anti-Sindhi protests anywhere. Most of them are bilingual which gives them chance of greater communication. The main traits in their own words are: 'confidence, endurance, hard work, smart, intelligent, be your own boss, never-say-die, money-minded, have a great pride of the community'.
7. The Hindus of Sindh had a system of Panchayat or village community which was governed by its headman (Mukhi) responsible to the general body of the community. At some places the office was hereditary, whereas in some cases it was periodically elected. The Panchayats were based mainly on caste. The Lohanas formed most of the village panchayats while the remaining castes, except Brahmin and Amils, formed joint committees with the Lohanas wherever their number was not sufficient. The functions of Panchayat were mainly social and religious. Even after the displacement from Sindh, the community spread a network of Sindhi educational and cultural institutions throughout the country and tried to reproduce their social structure by reformation of Panchayats to maintain the basic tenets of cultural life. Now panchayats were based on region, instead of caste.
8. The Sindhis are of a very determined character for preserving their lost prestige, economic or social. By patience, perseverance and skill they have survived through their darkest periods of history and have by quick assimilation strived for rapid social progress without destroying their cultural purity and status. After Partition, while re-establishing themselves, they mostly dispersed in the urban areas throughout the country and distinguished themselves as suppliers of consumer goods at the cheapest rates. They have a distinct trait of quick adaptability in their character (Aggarwal, 2012).

9. Just like Marwaris, Gujaratis, and Parsis, the Sindhis have also entered into manufacturing/industry through trade, as they had requisite technical experience and the accumulation of the capital and rational use of the profits earned from trade. The friends and family members helped them more than the government in arranging the entrepreneurial prerequisites (Bal, 1998). In the beginning of the settlement, the community had a strong sense of unity and community members helped each other to set up businesses. They also have practices of regenerating their social capital by training the young ones in the trading acumen during their leisure time. Children are asked to serve in shops and industries run by their fathers, kins, and community members. Thus, the children gain the experience which also develops their aptitude/keen interest towards their hereditary/family occupation.
10. The feeling of loss of status and minority group morale, due to forced migration played a significant role in the development and rise of Sindhi community, as Trivedi (1983) affirms on the basis of her empirical study carried out in Rajasthan. Their credibility to mould themselves according to the situation, the distinct trait of quick adaptability, and the cosmopolitan outlook helped them to get success as businessmen and entrepreneurs.
11. Hinduja is the most prominent Sindhi firm. They come from a town – Shikarpur in Sindh. The Sindhis have a strong sense of community and culture. They view themselves as highly westernized, and it is known that the fashion in pre-Partition era used to surge from Sindh. Numbering over two million in India and one million abroad, the Sindhis are largely a business community (Dorin, 2003), though we find a few in Bollywood as well.

The Punjabis

Dorin (2003) has mentioned the Punjabi business community as the prominent entrepreneurs along with the Marwari, the Gujarati and the Parsi in terms of owning assets and global turnover. The major trading castes of the Punjab are the Khatri, Arora and Bania comprising both Hindus and Sikhs. Census of 1911 shows that Khatris of Kapoor, Khanna, Mehra sub-castes were dominant in

Lahore and the Aroras in Multan and Banias in Delhi. By 1921, the Khatris were already controlling some 300 and the Aroras around 50 industrial establishments. Thus, the Punjabi business community actually refers to a few traditional trading castes. The records reveal that they travelled across Afghanistan, Central Asia, Iran, and Russia during the period from 16th to 19th centuries in caravans to sell their produce. Their kinship network was spread across Delhi, Multan, Lahore, and Amritsar (Bal, 2017). Prominent business groups among them are Thapars, Narangs, Mahindra, Hero group, Escorts, Ranbaxy, Usha Shriram, Apollo tyres, etc. They primarily remained traders of the goods and entered into industry only during the middle of the 20th century, particularly the Punjabi refugees due to India's Partition, as they were given a few incentives/concessions by the Government of India. The bicycle industry of Ludhiana is an example of the refugee entrepreneurs (Singh, 1994). Harish Damodaran, in his book the *India's New Capitalists* (2008), does inform us about many successful Jat businessmen/industrialists right from the middle of the 20th century, who ventured into sugar, brewery, transport and hotel industry, to the present times. Another successful entrepreneurs of Punjab are the Ramgarhias. Ramgarhias are the traditional artisanal group, whose hereditary occupation is smithy and carpentry are predominantly found engaged in machine tool industry, steel re-rolling mills, agriculture implements, in addition to iron-based industry. The industrial development of Punjab owes a lot to the contribution of Ramgarhias (Bal, 1995). Thus, in case of Punjabi entrepreneurship we may say that it is found across various caste groups and dispersed in various regions of India.

Family Businesses

Besides the traditional business communities, the family owned and managed businesses are a noticeable form of doing business in India. Though family businesses are passing through difficult phase all over the world, yet in India, as Dutta (1997) informs, almost 99.9 per cent of all firms are family-owned or family-controlled. The family business is constantly evolving and is very diverse. In Indian society, the family support for the businessman is critical to his survival. Akhilesh Mittal (2019), in his article in *Business India*, narrates the legend of the Agroha *biradari* to which prosperous Aggarwal merchants like Bajajs and Mittals belong. There were one lakh merchants in Agroha town (present day located near Hisar in Haryana). The market worked on inter-business lending rates of 2 per cent. If one of the businesses failed, each of the 99,999 other businessmen would donate one rupee and a brick so that the insolvent businessman could restart his business and rebuild his home. He further adds that this phenomenon can still be seen in India's stock markets where insolvent brokers are saved from ruin by community loans and advances (c.f. Dutta, 1997). Almost every small enterprise is family run in India, as it provides the initial resources, capital and networks. India ranks 3rd globally in terms of number of family owned businesses which contributes some 70 to 80 per cent of national GDP annually.

In this part of the chapter, the focus would be on the successful business families that how the social capital of the family has helped generation after generation to evolve and sustain their businesses. There are a very few studies on family businesses in India, though almost all the enterprises had been functioning on family basis. Patvardhan (1990, 1995) examined the evolution and performance of five western India's family businesses, that is, Dahanukar, Apte, Dandekar, Sathe and Parkhe, in addition to the house of Garwares who contributed to economic development of the country in the first half of the last century. None of them had a previous business background but mainly started their businesses under the inspiration provided by Gandhi's call for Swadeshi in the early 1930s and largely engaged in consumer products with a medium level of technology. Most of them had a single product line and were relatively less capital intensive and were mainly oriented towards domestic market. They relied heavily on their own funds and scrupulously avoided bank borrowing. They were largely generous and egalitarian in management and in their approach to industrial relations. They achieved notable success in business, but the relatively free economy in 1940s was transformed to one of regulation and control after the Independence of the country. All the five businessmen had limited success in expansion and diversification, for they did not have the techniques of market forecasting, project preparation and industrial inputs.

The history of the growth of B.D. Garware family enterprises from Garware motors to plastic, paints and shipping reveals the growth, expansion and diversification of business. In family enterprises it is always the idea, motivation, hard work, decision-making and the propensity to adapt and change lies with an individual, the pioneer of the enterprise. Later for his sons, the second generation joining the business is not that challenging, and similarly, for the third generation it is rather a smooth sailing to enter the business. The initial organization forms a nucleus of an expanding business empire. Thus the entrepreneurial initiative may prepare the ground for the foundation of what Tripathi and Mehta (1990) called as 'entrepreneurial continuum'. They presented detailed studies of nine successful business families/houses/groups, Tatas, Mafatlals, Kirloskars, Larsen and Toubro, Khatans, Amins, Lalbhais, Walchands, besides Ranchhodlal Chhotalal of Gujarat and Maharashtra. Though Ranchhodlal Chhotalal was pioneer of cotton textile mill in Ahmedabad, but his sons and grandsons could not create new edifices over the foundations laid by the predecessor and thus failed to have entrepreneurial continuum largely due to the demands of social reference group. In contrast, the Tatas have had a strong human and social capital in the form of modern education, Western technology, close relatives and trusted employees and hence the entrepreneurial continuum conformed to the values and ethics of Tata House. The social linkages of the houses with trading background made their work much easier, conclude Tripathi and Mehta (ibid.).

It is not surprising to note that most of the studies have been conducted in the 'entrepreneurial belt' in western India, for most of the successful business families and business houses are found to be concentrated here. Gopalakrishnan (2014) quoted Raghavan, who enlists five aspects which made family firms distinctive. These are:

1. Tradition: Deep understanding of origins and acceptance of founding principles.
2. Risk Management: Take a conservative approach to risk.
3. Hands-on role: Keep closely in touch with details of business.
4. Long-term view: Not as driven by quarterly earning pressures.
5. Thrift: Treat money spent as their own.

A number of studies have informed that joint family system has remained the most conducive to doing business. In joint family, three or more generations are living together under the same roof, eating food cooked in the common kitchen and share common property. The most important aspect of family business is that they all are family members having primary relations which bind them together. In a traditional patriarchal household, the roles and relations are hierarchically structured. The patriarch is head of the household as well as owns and manages the family business. The sons always remain lower in the hierarchy and, thus, follow the orders of the father. The sons are generally not expected to take independent decisions to expand and diversify the business. Family businesses also developed the Indian fabric of values, traditions and practices, as Dutta (1997, 65–67) writes:

> There are three kinds of patriarch in the Indian family business. The first is the entrepreneur-patriarch, who is accepted within the family as being the founder of the business and its prime mover... he has both power and authority vested in him irrespective of his standing in the family hierarchy. In Weberian terms, he is a charismatic leader and plays a greater role in business and family... . The second category of patriarch is the eldest son of a successful businessman, who inherits the patriarchy when his father dies or is unable to continue, in Weberian terms, his authority is more traditional than charismatic. He is constrained to work with consensus of the rest of the family. The third type of patriarch is rarest. He is not the senior sibling but rises to head the business by sheer dint of capability. This shifts the balance of power within the business and the family.

The Indian family business patriarch starts off with the advantage of being the undisputed leader. Traditionally he is only the steward of the family wealth even though he may have built it up all by himself. To circumvent the tax and inheritance laws, assets are seldom held individually. This forms the basis of the continued existence of the family business across industries and generations. The patriarch gains authority by being the mature and trustworthy relative who plays an active role in the nurturing and development of the family by sacrificing individual agendas for collective benefits. The leadership requires the ability to attract loyal, able family members and professional managers through a complex matrix of obligations and exchanges (Dutta, 1997). The patriarch feels satisfied after he has handed over the growing business to his son. The son realizes his obligations and responsibilities towards his family and tries to fulfil all these toward parents, sisters and brothers. The son starts getting apprenticeship lessons early in life. There are many cases of top business family's sons present on the shop-floor during vacation from schools. The family business has been innovative in its financial management and survived antagonistic government policies (ibid., 1997). Family members only run the business. A very few specialized services may be taken from outside. These can be managers, directors, consultants, auditors, etc. otherwise they depend more on friends and peer group for advice in times of challenges.

As is true for internal family relations, the business families have inter and intra family competition, conflict, rivalry and cooperation. After the liberalization, these business houses face the bigger challenges of producing cheap and best goods for the international market. Though family is the most valuable resource of social capital, but the same resource may become a hindrance when it comes to expansion and diversification of business. After the liberalization the conflicts in Indian business families have grown, as they face new set of challenges. Due to differences of attitudes and aspirations of family members the management challenges have remained serious. A report of Confederation of Indian Industry on family business informs that 13 per cent family businesses survive till third generation, only 4 per cent go beyond third generation and in fact one-third of businesses disintegrate because of generational conflict. Majumdar (2014) presents ten big family feuds by taking up the cases of Ambani, Apollo, Bajaj, BPL, Chhabria, Kirloskar, Mafatlal, Modi, Ranbaxy and Shri Ram, which ultimately weakened or even ruined the businesses. There were clashes of interests, ideologies and vision between brothers, fathers and sons, uncles, nephews and among cousins. The sons being foreign educated and highly professional wanted to modernize and diversify to which patriarchs like Bhai Mohan Singh of Ranbaxy, Raunaq Singh of Apollo objected strongly. The succession crises, division of property and inheritance, and competition have remained serious challenges.

R.V. Raghvan (c.f. Majumdar, 2014) having experience of working with professional and family companies quotes American evidence for four findings on family versus non-family businesses. One, that family businesses were 25 per cent more profitable; second, that listed family business shares performed better; third, that mutual funds showed better return from family businesses; and lastly, family businesses have less mortality compared to non-family businesses. There is no doubt that the highs and lows of family businesses indicate the strength of social capital which kept them running the enterprises successfully. The brothers of Ambani group can always reconcile and be together, though assured profits and success can even be intoxicating. Family businesses have survived through the British rule that encouraged manufacturing only in restricted sectors of limited goods. The regulated and controlled economy of post-Independence India when there was less competition, produced for the local market, enjoyed government subsidies and were protected under MRTP, accelerated the growth of family business. Family businesses have further flourished in post-liberalization phase despite the emerging competition from MNCs. The family values, close-knit structures of family, family/kinship relations, mutuality and trustworthiness will continue to give an edge to family business which forms the 'backbone' of the Indian economy.

Suggested Readings

Aggarwal, Saaz (2012). *Sindhi: Stories from a Vanished Homeland*. Pune: Black-and-White Fountain.

Barnouw, Victor (1978). The Sindhis, Mercantile Refugees in India: Problems of their assimilation. In Sylvia Vatuk (ed.), *American Studies in the Anthropology of India* (pp. 447–459). New Delhi: Manohar.

Desai, Ashok V. (1994). The Origins of Parsi Enterprise. In Rajat Kanta Ray (ed.), *Entrepreneurship and Industry in India 1800–1947* (pp. 99–108). New Delhi: Oxford University Press.

Dutta, Sudipt (1997). *Family Business in India*. New Delhi: Response Books.

Guha, Amalendu (1970). Parsi Seth as Entrepreneurs 1750–1850. *Economic & Political Weekly*, 5(35), 107–115.

Guha, Amalendu (1970). The Comprador Role of Parsi Seths 1750–1850. *Economic & Political Weekly*, 5(48), 28 November.

Guha, Amalendu (1984). More about Parsi Seths: Their Roots, Entrepreneurship and Comprador Role, 1650–1918, 21 January. *Economic & Political Weekly*, 19(3), 117–119+122–132.

Markovits, Claude (2008). *The Global World of Indian Merchants 1750–1947: Traders of Sindh from Bukhara to Panama*. New Delhi: Cambridge University Press (paperback).

Section III

Entrepreneurship across Gender, Caste and Class

7

Women Entrepreneurs

Empowerment and Development

Let us be very clear at the outset that the meaning of entrepreneur is gender neutral. For both men and women it is taking initiative to start some business or commercial activity, risking their money, providing leadership, making decisions with farsightedness, innovating and producing something new or different. It is only the prefix, women, which makes entrepreneurship distinct as well as problematic. The existing literature has never depicted anything specifically like male/men entrepreneurs, and entrepreneur by default means male entrepreneur, whereas the research and studies on women entrepreneurs and their entrepreneurship are widespread across the spaces. Why so? To be precise, the problematic is gender, that is, the way genders are constructed in the society results into the assignment of gender roles to men and women. No doubt, the entrepreneurship has remained gendered for pretty long time and it is only recently for the last three to four decades that women entrepreneurs have created a distinct space for themselves in the world of business. Thus, entrepreneurship is not gender-neutral rather carries its specificities.

Situating Women/Gender in the Context of Entrepreneurship

The gender aspect of entrepreneurship has recently begun to be addressed. Due to the existential conditions of women in Indian society, they are subordinate, deprived, unequal and have low status. The space of women is considered to be in the four walls of the house. Women, though now are getting education and some are going for higher education even, yet they are not taking to work the way it should have happened. Why is it so? One is non-availability of jobs, unemployment level is very high due to the size of the population with low economic development and the other which is the most important is the prevailing sociocultural practices. The marriage of the daughter weighs heavily on the minds of the parents. Their mindset is so prepared that girls themselves also tend to believe that it is their obligation to get married first and free the parents from the burden. With such an ingrained mindset, to be economically independent takes a back seat.

After marriage the everyday reality pushes them to look for an additional source of income to support themselves and their families. Nearly 90 per cent of the working women are engaged in the unorganized sector where they tend to work for long hours. They get low wages as compared to men and their quality of work life is bad and they also face various kinds of discrimination. Women from low caste and class are the most exploited in the job market. In most of the cases their work conditions are not at all conducive to their reproductive roles. The process of globalization brought a number of work opportunities for women by making the goods of the world accessible to them through the new and diverse formats. In the case of the middle classes, the modern gadgets have entered average households thus releasing women from the drudgery of the household chores. The family size has come down, by making one or two children a norm in the urban settings. As a result, women have free time as well as the enforced needs push them to look for alternative work opportunities. However, for a large mass of lower class women socio-economic reality has marginally changed.

Many studies have emphatically substantiated that once women begin to earn, they save more and also try to invest in the health and education of their families (Aga, 2012). Agarwal (1994) has shown that if women have more income, then they tend to spend major portion of it on the studies and well-being of their children, whereas men tend to spend major share on themselves, and invariably on liquor/narcotics. Thus, it is desirable to let the women generate more income. How can it be possible? Job market is already saturated. It is difficult for women to break the glass ceiling[1] or the barriers to make their forceful entry into the job market which is already unfavourable due to stereotypes towards women and the prevailing macho corporate culture. Over the time, we all have understood that the way to women's emancipation is through economic independence. It is argued on the basis of empirical studies that the best way to empower women is through entrepreneurship. The experiences of women of other countries also suggest that more and more women are taking to entrepreneurship. In the United States of America and Canada, more than 30 per cent of all businesses are with women (Mattis, 2000; Richardsen and Burke, 2000). The latest trend reveals that even women who hold managerial positions find entrepreneurship more conducive to their dual roles. Many of them are leaving jobs in the formal sector to opt for self-employment/entrepreneurship.

Entrepreneurship is not only creating jobs for themselves, but also for at least other five persons. There are many entrepreneurs who are excelling in what they do and are paving the path for other women as well. Entrepreneurship has also been found to be the most conducive to the traditional gender roles. In other words, as entrepreneurs, women would be able to carry out their family roles effectively. More and more women are breaking free from the traditional, gender-specific roles and occupations and venturing into the business world. Entrepreneurship is also being pursued by the state as an alternative to providing jobs. Women entrepreneurs in India are a precious resource and as a matter of fact, women entrepreneurship has become a cliché in the modern Indian society.

A considerable research has been conducted on women entrepreneurs and entrepreneurship in India. The pioneer studies of 1980s, though a few, have focused on the socio-economic profile of the women entrepreneurs, whereas the literature of the 1990s reveals that the research began to focus on the heterogeneity among women entrepreneurs in terms of caste, class, education, age and region. In addition to their adopting new roles, their motivation, orientation, strategies and problems have also been examined. The research on the topic, however, has achieved a higher level in this century when the role of skill development through training, opportunities and performance acquired prominence. Women themselves started negotiating their capacity, articulating own agency to bring transformation in their lives. It is relevant to mention that the research on women entrepreneurship has remained multidisciplinary, but whenever we examine the entrepreneurship in the context of women it is very important to treat the woman as a gendered category – the way gendering takes place in the society. The moment we begin to take into consideration the social construction of gender by using concepts and terms accompanying it, it obviously points towards the fact that work is also gendered. However, the domains of business, trade or commercial activities do not fall in the gendered domain of women's work. Since entrepreneurial ecosystem is predominantly male dominant, women tend to face more and more challenges because of structural barriers. Women with their own grit, resilience and hard work have overcome such socially created disparity and have created a niche for themselves. Dix (1991) even calls women as 'natural entrepreneurs', gifted with an individualism. In the absence of any distinct theory of women entrepreneurship, the attempt in this chapter is to provide a comprehensive view of various dimensions of women entrepreneurship from gender perspective. As we know, women do not constitute a homogenous group, therefore, their entrepreneurial activities also vary across caste, class and regions.

Why do Women Become Entrepreneurs? Motivation and Orientation

A set of existing studies on motivation of women to become self-employed or to start business has discretely taken the cognizance of the so-called pull and push factors. Some other researchers on the basis of empirical studies, have found that most of the women are self-motivated and their orientation to start business is mainly due to financial reasons. It may be in order to earn livelihood, to supplement the family income or to earn more money. Also there are some women who have taken over or inherited a business (push factors). Whereas for some women doing business may be the result of pull factors, that is, to be one's own boss, desire for independence, passion to pursue innovative ideas, a hobby, or a quest for distinct identity/space. It has also been argued that in the case of women entrepreneurs, it is neither an instance of push nor pull, rather both these pressures work simultaneously. For women of upper-middle class, it is more a pull or attraction, but for lower caste, class, and disabled women it is largely a push to do some business as a means of livelihood or to add-on the family income. The intrinsic rewards of having self-satisfaction, self-realization and self-fulfilment at work further motivate them to be entrepreneurs.

We may also understand the motivation of women in terms of practical needs and strategic interests to become entrepreneurs. It is precisely the needs of a woman and her family which is the central feature, alongside her strategic interest to be satisfied and self-reliant along with a sense of achievement and empowerment. Whatever may be the dominant motivating factor, it is quite evident that presently more and more women in the society have developed awareness, built capacities, taken initiative, and made choices in this direction of becoming entrepreneurs.

How do Women become Entrepreneurs?

As discussed above, there may be push or pull factors for a woman to decide to take up business activity, but the most important for her taking the steps towards achieving this goal are self-motivation, hard work, skill formation, and commitment in a competitive market. Here, we may discuss by taking the arguments of Burt (2000), who argues that any woman entrepreneur would bring three kinds of capital to enter into the market. The first is financial capital – cash in hand, savings in the bank, any investments coming due, and lines of credit. The second is human capital, natural abilities – charm, health, intelligence and looks – combined with skills acquired in formal education and job experience give the abilities to excel at certain tasks. Third, her relationships with others as social capital. She has friends, colleagues, and contacts generally through which she gets opportunities to use her financial and human capital. The existing empirical studies point towards the use of combination of these kinds of capital. Venturing into the entrepreneurship process, the first entry stage entails the use of her financial capital, that is, whatever assets she has from gold jewellery to cash in personal savings. The second stage of building-up depends on her human capital, whereas for growth and sustenance, the social capital occupies the crucial significance. Most of the women develop their businesses through networks and alliances with their friends, colleagues and contacts, as they become the most potential customers and through these links their business flourishes. Women entrepreneurs are more a product of social network. Caputo and Dolinsky (1998) investigate the role of financial and human capital of household members available to women entrepreneurs in the USA. The husbands' business knowledge and experience greatly contributed to women being self-employed. The sharing of childcare by husbands also facilitated the self-employment of women. Even in India, studies (Singh, 1992; Bal, 1997; Kaur, 2007) have revealed that more number of women belonging to traditionally business families, such as Bania, Khatri, Arora display entrepreneurial orientation. It may be family members' inspiration and support to start business, which, at later stages, contribute to their success.

When do Women become Entrepreneurs?

Most of the women take up to entrepreneurship in their 30s. The women across religion, castes and class are found to be doing business. It is significant to find that in India most of these women start their enterprise after getting married and after a few years of married life. The reason for it may be traced from the common cultural practices of the society. Most of the girls' parents do not want their daughters to set up their business before marriage, because the marriage of the daughter after a particular age is the prime responsibility of the parents and the daughter has no reason to disobey them. However, it has pragmatic explanations emerging out of women's mundane existence. First of all, parents in general still do not want her to be independent and economically self-sufficient. It is believed that a woman belongs to her husband and his family and it is their choice whether they want her to pursue some kind of entrepreneurial activity. Second, as per the sociocultural practices, the parents have to give substantial dowry to the daughter at the time of marriage, owing to which the parents do not want to go extra mile to invest money in her business/enterprise. Third, after marriage, her business would legally be shared by her husband and usually, the parents are not sure of the person or family, as still predominant form of marriage in India is arranged. As a result, they hesitate to invest money in her business, rather they would prefer to give her gold jewellery. Various studies on gender have made it very clear that the economic independence of a woman is the straight route to her empowerment, but making the girl economically independent is not the priority, despite the fact that the regular job of the girl is now an acceptable norm. Thus, in general, the young girls do not have freedom to make choices on their own and they tend to struggle between one set of control to another set of control.

Types of Entrepreneurs

Unlike the developed countries where highly professional women in corporate sector may leave and sometimes lose job to relocate in their own business usually on the same lines in which they have gained experience. In India, we have a few such instances where women entrepreneurs are product of 'Corporate Incubator'. A few women tend to see themselves as 'born to be' entrepreneurs and most of them have evolved into entrepreneurs (Mattis, 2000). Another interesting fact about India is that before becoming entrepreneurs a large majority of women were homemakers. It implies that while deciding on the kind of enterprise or business that one should start, women generally have interest in extending their home skills into the marketplace in which they find themselves the best suited.

Women entrepreneurs, both in rural and urban areas, can be classified on the basis of the commitment to their traditional gender roles. One type of entrepreneurs are traditional, who could be identified as those who are more committed to family roles, domestic orientation, and have limited capital. They engage in home-based production-such as pickle, *papad*, *dari* weaving, embroidery, knitting, piggery, and dairy are found more in rural areas. On the other hand, in urban areas, women entrepreneurs are engaged more in service businesses, such as beauty parlours, boutiques, running shops and retail business. The other type of entrepreneurs is modern or innovative in which are included those who are educated, have technical skills and they try to create things in a new and different way to make money, such as designing, fashion, beauty, jewellery, and food production. They would, alongside, be carrying out the household chores with domestic help. Yet another type, which may be regarded as new generation entrepreneurs have ventured into industrial entrepreneurship-small or medium level of manufacturing – have become their own boss. They largely free themselves from the ascribed family roles. Shehnaz Hussain, pioneer woman entrepreneur and a popular name in beauty treatments and herbal cosmetics industry, is one such instance. Following in her footsteps, there emerged a long time home maker, Vandana Luthra as a wellness and beauty giant who founded VLCC (Vandana Luthra Curls and Curves), and then a world famous fashion designer, Ritu Kumar. Women like Kiran Mazumdar-Shaw, Swati Piramal, Anu Aga and many other young women broke away from the prevalent beauty and boutique options and ventured into clinical, pharmaceutical and biotechnology sectors and who have become the role models for Indian women.

Process of Entrepreneurship

The process of starting any business is no less challenging for the women in our society. It actually involves a lot of decisions to be taken, such as capital, place, size, and product to create a viable business, in addition to the issues involving family and children. Women generally start with a small business. It is evident from the fact that in India more than 90 per cent of the companies run by women are microenterprises and of all the MSMEs, 20 per cent are owned by women. They learn to climb the rope to success with trial and error. Most women (about 79%) finance their businesses through their own savings, borrow from family members, and to a limited extent they seek bank loans. As per the Government of India's order, 10 per cent of all lending of the banks must be for women entrepreneurs. Thus, micro-credit schemes have reduced the anxiety of women to get money, particularly in rural areas, though usually the initial seed money is in thousands only, which may later expand up to millions of rupees. It is because of these reasons that terms like nanopreneurs and solopreneurs have come into use for women entrepreneurs. Women business ownership is concentrated primarily in retail and service sectors and only a small proportion among them has entered the manufacturing sector.

Where to start the business is the next decision one has to make. It has been observed that the place to begin with is invariably located in the proximity to the house, or it may start from the front rooms of the house itself. It provides them security and also helps them in creating work-family balance. Alongside the work they can look after the demands of the children and elderly in the home. As they grow in business and the demand increases, they move to posh locality or in the market hub.

The sources of raw material/products procurement vary according to the nature of the enterprise. Usually, they procure it from the local market. In certain cases they depend upon sources outside the state, but surely within the country. For the purpose they seek the help of their husbands or family members. Women entrepreneurs also seek the advice of the people with commercial and organizational experience whenever needed. It is worth mentioning that most of the women-owned enterprises are being run on informal basis and they do not put any boards, banners to attract customers. In the process, many of them escape the tax and other liabilities to the government in the initial stages. However, such a situation is the reason that accurate data are not available with regard to their number. Women constitute around 14 per cent of total entrepreneurs in India and they contribute roughly around 17 per cent to the total GDP of the country (Ashlin, 2019). As women entrepreneurs are largely running the micro or small enterprises, the extent of their employment is also small.

Nature of Enterprises

Most of the women take up to those enterprises where they have inherent skills or life experiences and have some association with the needs of women. Women enterprises mainly cater to the requirements of women. The nature of entrepreneurship varies from rural to urban areas, within urban area whether in a big city or a small town. A woman's personal liking and aptitude and belief in achievement also affect the nature of her business. Certain kinds of entrepreneurship is confined to rural areas, such as weaving, embroidery, knitting, handicraft, seri-culture (rearing of cocoons), vermi-composting (rearing of earthworms), piggery, bee-keeping, poultry, etc. This type of entrepreneurship is found functional in simultaneity with their traditional gender roles. Women entrepreneurs of urban slums (Indira, 1990) are engaged in petty business like *beedi* making, tailoring, vegetable selling, whereas women entrepreneurs of Delhi (Singh, 1993) are engaged in diverse activities like manufacturing high tech engineering goods, electronic goods, and cane and leather goods. Kamla Singh (1992) found tailoring to be the most common service type enterprise in three districts of Haryana. In Amritsar, Bal (1997) has found that enough money has gone beyond the beaten track and women are running restaurants and computer centres, also the beauty and wellness centres, and boutiques. Women entrepreneurship reveals an association between caste and type of enterprises. The upper castes and class women are running big businesses which require more capital investment and are based on specialized skills and a certain level of education, whereas the scheduled castes and lower class women are engaged in petty businesses or in micro-enterprises. A relatively recent study (Unni et al., 2021) explains the nature of entrepreneurship within the Indian middle class women from interdisciplinary perspective.

As women are engaged in those entrepreneurial activities which largely cater to the needs of women, and they have some inherent skills, most of their customers are also the women. The sale is local and volume is small. Most of the women sell their products through the informal channels, such as through family and friends. Agents and dealers also act as intermediaries in the market who provide the raw material and help to sell the products. Studies on rural entrepreneurs also show that women entrepreneurs are forming themselves into self-help groups with the help of NGOs, who in turn also provide them raw material and help them to sell the produce. Here members pool-in their resources and expertise in the task.

Challenges Faced

A number of empirical studies (Indira, 1991; Singh, 1992; Singh, 1993) inform that women entrepreneurs face quite a number of challenges with regard to getting finance from banks and other agencies as well as to get allocation of adequate and appropriate place for their units to be located largely due to the lack of centralized source of information. Iyer (1991) informs that though there are clear-cut guidelines from the apex agencies to provide easy and timely resources and subsidies to the small-scale entrepreneurs, the lower level support system is not responsive to the extent it should be. Women entrepreneurs also tend to face challenges from customers, agents, and colleagues to run the businesses. At times they feel discriminated when they have to deal with males as agents, dealers, and government officials. Most of them are of the view that men tend to take them non-seriously due to the prevalent stereotypes and mind-set. In the beginning, even the family members are not sure of her capabilities and hesitate to invest in their business. Thus mobilization of finances remained a big challenge to become an entrepreneur.

Though each kind of business presents a distinct challenge to sustain in the market, yet some common challenges are of employees/workers, competition, maintaining quality control and prices. Sometimes they also have to face the rude behaviour and harsh language from the customers (Bal, 1997). But women are taking such incidences as a part of the business they have chosen and they do not get distracted from their objective. In contrast, some women running boutiques and selling readymade garments as well are also of the view that since men can be handled with tact so that they as customers become cooperative and docile.

Watson (2003) in a study of Australian small and medium industries of female-owned businesses demolishes the prevailing notion that women-owned businesses have higher failure rate than the male-owned enterprises. Women are actually over represented in the retail and service industries where business is relatively smaller in terms of employment and revenue as opposed to high technology, construction and manufacturing. After controlling the effects of industry, the study concludes that there was no significant difference in the failure rates for male-run and female-run businesses. In other words, the discontinuation of a business depends upon its nature rather than whether it is run by men or women.

Another study (Peter, Carter and Hamilton, 1996) of small business performance and gender in English and Scottish firms depicts that female businesses under-perform in terms of the number of employees, tax registration, sales turnover, capital assets and range of markets. They are also less likely to own multiple businesses, less eager to plan expansion, and where expansion is planned, their strategies for growth are different from their male counterparts.

Interventions to Promote Entrepreneurship Amongst Women in India

In 1975, celebrating Women's Day, for the first time, the then Prime Minister, Indira Gandhi, appealed to women to become entrepreneurs to improve their own lot as well as for the development of the country. Later, a decade (1975–1985) was dedicated to women when a large number of schemes and programmes were launched for women's economic participation in development. Later on, the earlier emphasis on welfare approach was shifted to women entrepreneurship development. The Government of India launched Entrepreneurship Development Programmes (EDPs) in 1980s for women to train them in entrepreneurial skills. However, the impact of EDPs remained restricted as only a few women could benefit from it. Still another scheme, the Development of Women and Children in Rural Areas (DWCRA) was also initiated in 1982 to provide women with opportunities of self-employment. Women's Development Corporations (WDCs) also privileged the entrepreneurial activities of women. Similarly, the National Policy for the Empowerment of Women, 2001, also reiterated on the economic empowerment of women. Number of institutions, voluntary organizations, NGOs are running training and skill development programmes for women to generate income and earn livelihood, for instance, SEWA (Self-Employed Women Association), the Lijjat Cooperative and many other initiatives suggest the efforts at the empowerment of the poor working class women.

Dumas (2001), in her study, shows that an entrepreneurship training and education programme designed to help low income women to start their own businesses actually accomplished its goal to help women to launch their own businesses, to empower them to achieve self-sufficiency and to advance the economic health of city neighbourhoods through micro enterprise and job creation. A much needed study was carried out by Wadhera and Koreth (2012) measuring achievement motivation in rural women micro-entrepreneurs who started micro-enterprises under the project of ACORD, a non-profit society in 18 villages of Rajasthan. The findings reveal the presence of the need for achievement in women's motivation profile which has a strong relationship with her drive, success, stamina and sustaining of her micro-enterprise. The study also establishes that the absence of the achievement motivation from her profile is strongly related to her failure to sustain or achieve success in her micro-business. The findings bring out a clear relationship between women's successful entrepreneurship and social effects, like positive female empowerment along with their growing social confidence and respect by family, husband and the community.

Some other cooperatives are organizing women in self-help groups and collectively producing food, handicrafts, and other household items. Self-Help Groups (SHGs), consisting 10–15 women from grassroots, particularly from the tribal, poor and rural areas, who could collectively engage in an activity, get together. One woman amongst them functions as a group organizer who helps in the choice of entrepreneurial activity, maintain credit linkage with the bank, and is responsible for the procurement of raw material as well as marketing of the product. A revolving fund of a few thousand rupees is made available through some government agencies. They may collectively pool in resources. Each one may contribute one rupee each day to the pool. They put the money in the local cooperative bank. The bank would provide loan in multiples of the accumulated savings of SHG. The NGOs also help them to procure the loans from banks for self-employment. They have been found successful in terms of regularity of meetings, maintenance of record books, building capital, setting of an enterprise, and effective group savings. They have been found credit worthy and repayment of loan is quite satisfactory. These self-help groups may be producing the goods for bigger cooperatives, such as Fab India, promoting handicrafts of each state. For the promotion of micro-enterprises by facilitating micro-credit, the Government of India took many initiatives, such as Rashtriya Mahila Kosh, Small Industries Development Bank of India, Mahila Vikas Nidhi, MUDRA scheme to support MSEs. One may argue that group interaction, that is, by organizing themselves, can enable them to achieve success.

Empowerment Through Entrepreneurship

Entrepreneurship as a strategy for empowerment of women is one of the successful way. The terms *autonomy, empowerment, control* and *agency* have acquired significance as a result of women entrepreneurship. Women entrepreneurs in general and specifically who are in micro-credit programmes are negotiating for changes in economic hierarchies that they confront. They have access to money, thus, their economic independence leads them to participate in the decision-making process in the families. They are taking their personal decisions, participating in the purchase of major household items, marriage decision of the children, and visit to the relatives. Participation strengthens the abilities and potential of poor women (Weinberger, 2001). Despite being busier after starting the business, they are satisfied and happy doing some creative work. They can fulfil their family needs more easily and conveniently and their status in the family has undergone a change. A gain in self-confidence has been experienced by all women. The women have claimed to have been empowered and are more equipped to negotiate the hierarchical structures of religion, caste, and patriarchy in the society. Their status in the family and community undergoes a change. They are effectively challenging the existing norms and values to improve their well-being. Wadhera and Koreth (2012: pp. 154–155) inform that 'several women, especially those who are successful have experienced an enhanced status in the village. Some have even assumed informal leadership roles in the community – other women consult them on various personal matters and see them as role models'. Though keeping work-life balance has remained a major issue for women entrepreneurs, yet they are able to adjust their timings of work according to the needs of the family. After taking to entrepreneurship women tend to experience social and economic empowerment, besides their contribution to the Indian economic ecosystem. Further, women entrepreneurs in the country have become a driving force in the emerging corporate world by expanding their activities to manufacturing and to information technology sector. However, still there is a long way to go to achieve gender parity in entrepreneurship.

Note

1. Glass ceiling is a transparent ceiling yet so strong to break. The term glass-ceiling was coined in 1986 by two Wall Street Journal reporters to describe the invisible barrier that blocks women from the most senior positions in corporate America.

Suggested Readings

Bal, Gurpreet (1997). Women entrepreneurs: Emerging trends and issues. In Paramjit S. Judge and Satish K. Sharma (eds), *Dimensions of Social Change: Essays in Honour of Professor P.N. Pimpley* (pp. 169–188). Jaipur: Rawat Publications.

Beaumont, S., Singh, K. and Ramachandran, K. (eds) (1992). *Development of Microenterprises by Women*. Ahmedabad: British Council and Indian Institute of Management.

Caputo, Richard K. and Dolinsky, Arthur (1998). Women's choice to pursue self-employment: The role of financial and human capital of household members. *The Journal of Small Business Management*, 36(3), 8–17.

Dix, Carol (1991). *Enterprising Women: The Lives of Successful Business Women*. London: Bantam Press.

Kaur, Kiranpreet (2007). Role of social structural variables in entrepreneurial orientation: A study of women entrepreneurs in Punjab. *Social Change*, 37(1), 77–97.

Wadhera, Kiron and Koreth, George (2012). *Empowering Rural Women: Micro-enterprise Through Achievement Motivation*. New Delhi: Sage Publications.

8

Entrepreneurship Development Among Marginalized Communities

This chapter aims at providing an overall view of the entrepreneurial activities of the marginalized communities of India, namely, the scheduled castes and the scheduled tribes, who through their own capabilities and abilities have proved to be successful entrepreneurs in diverse fields. The scheduled castes and the scheduled tribes are the downtrodden and the poorest of the poor people of India. However, different reasons could be attributed to their position in the socio-economic hierarchy. Due to various historical reasons including the Hindu ideas of ritual purity and pollution and *karma* principle have kept the Dalits away from the equal participation and opportunities in the society. On the other hand, the tribals, due to their geographical isolation, could not have access to the world around for centuries. They remained confined to their limited space. They developed self-sufficient economy, self-governed, and well contained social rules and regulations. As a result, for long they remained insulated from the development process. Both Dalits and tribals do not lack in inherent skills, potential and wisdom, rather the social and economic conditions and constraints have kept them historically deprived. A number of strategies have been used to uplift their conditions. The social reformers and missionaries have been working amongst them since early 19th century. The Government of India has been taking a number of initiatives, and introducing the policies of protective discrimination and programmes to improve their conditions. The education, change of occupation, training and refurbishing of their traditional skills have remained significant. Their own efforts towards mainstreaming through social mobilization, struggles, and social movements have also contributed to their status enhancement. In the present times, the voluntary and citizen sectors have remained quite effective in improving the conditions, particularly of tribals in addition to the government initiatives. The role of NGOs, corporate sector, Self-Help Groups, and social entrepreneurs has been noteworthy in this regard, though far from satisfactory.

The main attempt in the chapter is to bring out how through entrepreneurship by overcoming caste and geographical challenges, the Dalits and tribals have been able to improve their socio-economic and political status in the society. A very limited number of empirical studies have been carried out to present the entrepreneurship amongst them. However, an attempt would be made to identify and discuss the nature, type and extent of Dalit and tribal entrepreneurship in India. The chapter has two parts, one each for Dalit and tribal entrepreneurship. The first part examines the entrepreneurship amongst scheduled castes, whereas the second part takes stock of the emerging entrepreneurship amongst the tribals of India.

Dalit Entrepreneurship

The scheduled castes population in India as per Census 2011 is 16.6 per cent of the total population which is relatively high and in Punjab they constitute 32.8 per cent, which is the highest for Dalits in India. The scheduled castes are dispersed across the states of India in varied numbers and within each state there are a number of caste groups within the scheduled castes category, who usually follow a hierarchical order. An association called Dalit Indian Chamber of Commerce and Industry (DICCI) was founded by Milind Kamble in 2005 to promote entrepreneurship among Dalits with its headquarters in Pune. Businesses owned by Dalits in India exist, but they get very limited opportunities for the development of business enterprises due to sociocultural economic disparities.

However, a section of them, by overcoming the significant inequalities, has become entrepreneurs. Khandekar (2013), informs that only a few thousand have become significant business persons and in his view those 'who do take risk, often reap high rewards'. Similarly, Khade of Mumbai was convinced that he would make more money by starting his own business and consequently, gave up his government job to start his own enterprise despite the major challenge of caste status in the society. We come across innumerable examples where Dalit entrepreneurs had to face twin challenge of caste status and proving their worth.

There are a few detailed studies carried out on the entrepreneurship development amongst the scheduled castes. In this part, three major studies carried out in western, northern and southern India will be elaborated to show how some of the scheduled castes by venturing into entrepreneurship have attained a higher social status in the society. Their mobility on the hierarchical ladder of the Indian society is primarily a result of their own initiative, motivation and hard work. Dahiwale (1989) did the pioneering work in this area. He carried out an empirical research in Kolhapur city of Maharashtra. The study is on five scheduled castes, namely Mahar, Mang, Dhor, Chambhar and Bhangi, who by taking to modern occupations at lower, moderate and also at higher levels have experienced social mobility. Their caste ascribed occupations are menial jobs, such as rope making, drumming skin objects, snaring of the skin, scavenging and removing night soil. These menial jobs are objects of social contempt and the people involved in doing such jobs were considered untouchables, segregated in terms of residential localities, and were discriminated in day-to-day life activities. Out of the total 230 respondents, 30 were treated as control group who were engaged in traditional caste occupations and 200 had adopted caste-free, modern occupations. These were shops of eatables (27.5%), industrial owners and machinery stockists (14%), doctors/advocate/tax consultant/charted accounted (13%), cycle shops (10%), tailoring (8.5%), building and road construction (6.5%), transportation, and painting (6% each), radio/watch sellers and repairers (4%), besides the publishers, distributors and shops selling miscellaneous items. The data clearly reveal that they have been able to take up new occupations, though majority remained engaged in lower modern occupations.

Their process of uplift begins in early 20th century as a result of progressive policies of the then ruler, Shahu Chhatrapati of Kolhapur, who encouraged them to learn new skills and also helped them financially to start businesses. He himself became a role model by hiring services of the scheduled caste people for household and state services. They were appointed in the palace, including his cook, his chariot driver, the gate keeper and even his body guards. Later the role of Jyotiba Phule, B.R. Ambedkar and the welfare activities of Christian missionaries to enlighten the scheduled castes men, women and children through education and information significantly contributed to their mobility. The special programmes and policies of Government of India in enabling ex-untouchables to take to modern occupations have further been attributed to their success.

In adopting higher number of modern occupations, Mangs (35.5%) were leading, followed by Mahars (27.5%), whereas Chambhars were less prone to adopting modern occupations than other castes owing to which they remained engaged in leather activities which still has good scope and wide utility in the changing times. The respondents with modern education and professional or vocational skills found easier access to modern jobs and those who remained deprived of education or were less educated continued to pursue their hereditary occupations. A large number of respondents of modern jobs could single out the factor of their own performance responsible for their occupational mobility and success.

Dahiwale (ibid.) categorically concludes that nearly one quarter of the respondents took to modern jobs and moved away from traditional way of living due to the push of the poverty, unemployment, caste occupation and family background. The reformers' ideologies also found to be effective in deviating from the traditional way of life. The most important has been the constitutional measures, and protective discrimination policies and programmes for the mobility of ex-untouchables into modern occupations and henceforth to their social mobility.

Flamant (2003) conducted a study on the international shoe-makers of Tamil Nadu. The north of Tamil Nadu is one of the important industrial centres of finished leather and shoes for international market. Arab traders operating on the Kerala and Tamil Nadu coasts initiated process of Islamization in the eighth century.

The origin of present day Labbai is uncertain. The British colonizers named the Tamil-speaking Muslims as Labbai in order to differentiate them from the Urdu-speaking Deccanis. 'It appears that the Labbais were generally low castes or those termed untouchables who had converted to Islam, even though some now affirm that they came from all the castes, including Brahmins' (Flamant, 2003, p. 102). Labbais reject caste stratification. With the sudden development and expansion of the leather industry, the Labbai Muslims acquired the reputation of being dynamic businessmen. In the middle of the 19th century, Muttu Meera rather was one of the first Muslims to take up leather trade and tanning. Proprietor of two factories in 1870, he was one of the richest merchants of Madras (present day Chennai). His descendants dominated the leather market in Madras until the end of the 1960s. The tanning in its traditional form was always carried out by the scheduled castes, when Labbai Muslims were responsible for its progressive industrialization during 19th and 20th centuries. Now they are engaged in leather shoemaking and are actually international entrepreneurs as they are exporting their leather goods to Europe, Australia and the United States. These are family businesses where network of kinship operates in management, partnership, capital alliance and transfer. They changed the traditional methods of tanning and have set up factories to produce upper part of the shoes and the full shoes.

With the advent of new generation of managers, greater flexibility is observed with regard to the family and the community and more importance is given to recruiting competent professionals. Owing to the increase in the number of shoe factories, there was a massive recruitment of women which increased two to three times higher than that of men. Women are employed as labour. Nearly 80 per cent men are Muslim who fill all the managerial and administrative posts. Now due to the profits involved in this enterprise, many upper caste Hindus, like Chettiars and Brahmins, have also taken to production of shoes. The degrading tasks such as snaring, desalting, skinning and shearing of hides are left to the scheduled castes. Labbai Muslims perform the more qualified tasks. This study reveals that a low prestige occupation by becoming profitable attracts the high castes to engage into it and sometimes recruited for qualified tasks.

Yet another study by Judge and Bal (2009), and Bal and Judge (2010) on the scheduled castes of Punjab explicates entrepreneurship as a means to empower the scheduled castes. The study maps the nature, extent and level of their entrepreneurship. Punjab has the highest proportion of the scheduled castes to the total population of the state, out of which two districts, Jalandhar and Nawanshehar, have the major share. There are 39 different scheduled castes placed in hierarchy in Punjab. The empirical study has been carried out in Jalandhar and Amritsar districts. Out of the total sample of 1,600 respondents from the villages and cities of Jalandhar and Amritsar, only 133 that is, 95 in Jalandhar city and only 38 in Amritsar, entrepreneurs could be found while only 14 entrepreneurs were found in petty businesses out of the 10 sampled villages. Thus, this study primarily focuses on Dalit entrepreneurs in urban areas. It is significant to inform that two caste groups, namely Chamars/Ad-dhrami and Meghs, alongside a nominal number of Balmiki, Mazabi and Dumna castes, have excelled in the entrepreneurial activities. They have taken to 26 different entrepreneurial activities of small, medium and large-scale. It is found that most of their entrepreneurial activities have some association with their hereditary occupation. It is particularly noticeable in the case of Chamars/Ad-dharmis whose hereditary occupation is snaring and processing of raw hides, tanning of leather, and producing leather goods. They have modified and diversified their skills and have become industrialists, raw hide merchants and commission agents of leather. They are manufacturing a variety of leather goods, namely leather jackets/coats, purses, belts, tool belts, shoes, etc. The second largest group, Megh/Kabir Panthis have utilized their hereditary skills of weaving in sports goods industry, like shuttle cocks, bats and pads of all types, and gloves. In the case of these two communities, earlier the World Wars I and II and then globalization accelerated their entrepreneurial potential. The needs of the war, like leather shoes, gave impetus to caste groups dealing with leather. A variety of their leather goods have a market worldwide. The caste occupation of Balmiki, Mazabi and Doms (known by different names in different parts of the state) was scavenging and they were doing all kinds of menial jobs.

These people by abandoning their traditional occupation have ventured into small business activities, such as readymade garment shops, grocery, tailoring, electrical and mechanical works, meat shop and property dealer. Most of the respondents reasoned out that their traditional occupations were stigmatized. In addition to factors like non-availability of work, economic survival, and education compelled them to modify their skills. Through training and on-the-job practice, and through hit and trial they diversified into different lines of businesses which they find satisfying and profitable. Nearly 60 per cent of the total ventured into business with their personal savings. They started carrying out business activities from residential area, and gradually some of them like Ad-dharmis separated residence and business area, as they moved to better/posh residential areas, while others shifted their business to main market area and kept the same residence.

Through their hard work, perseverance and innovativeness they have been able to earn profits, and moreover, some of them have become multi-millionaires. They have raised their standard of living, become rich, famous and honourable. Their inter-generational occupational mobility has rendered the caste irrelevant to an extent and they have moved up in the social hierarchy. It is well-known that Jalandhar is the stronghold of the Bahujan Samaj Party and many entrepreneurs have contested for political posts. At the time of the study, the mayor of Jalandhar city was a successful Ad-dharmi entrepreneur who could be elected despite the strong opposition from upper castes. The success stories of these entrepreneurs suggest that the way to their uplift is through education, self-realization, and abandoning of the traditional occupations, though they were also apprehensive of the existing caste hierarchy amongst them. The study also points towards the emergence of classes within the schedules castes.

Alongside the detailed empirical studies, a few case studies have also been carried on Dalit entrepreneurs informing that through entrepreneurship they have become millionaires. Khandekar (2013) collected 15 inspiring profiles of both men and women Dalit entrepreneurs, who had to overcome the major challenge of caste stigma in their journey to success. These entrepreneurs are from every sector of the economy. Khandekar (p. xii) writes, 'As per the Dalit Indian Chamber of Commerce and Industry (DICCI), Dalit businessmen pay nearly 1,700 crore as tax to government, their total turnover is ₹ 20,000 crore and they provide employment to 5 lakh people'. The president of DICCI,

Milind Kamble, was awarded Padma Shri in 2013. Incidentally, these 15 Dalit millionaires have mainly started their businesses after 1991, that is, after the liberalization of the economy which proved a boon for them. Most of them are convinced that the new market environment has put them at par with other businessmen while earlier the government issued licences for manufacturing and also decided the quantum of production and the sale price. While climbing the ladder of success, they worked extremely hard, because they were to not only overcome economic challenges, but also to cross the deep ditch of social disabilities. The path to their success is education, often professional, opening of opportunities, and on-the-job training.

Ashok Khade set up his company DAS (name suggests the first letter of the brothers' names as he could not call the company as Khade, which would reveal his caste to the world turning it into a hurdle. He even writes his name as K. Ashok) Offshore Engineering Private Limited in Mumbai makes huge platforms used for extracting crude oil from the sea. J.R.D. Tata is his inspiration and from him he imbibed two things: to do business honestly and to do business not merely for profit, but also for the good of the society. In an answer to one of the questions that what the government should do for Dalits entrepreneurs, his reply was 'Dalits don't need concessions – they need connections. They need to be empowered enough to be able to interact with major companies'. It is significant to note that Dalits have been benefitted from the liberalization of the economy as 'the new market gives equal opportunities to all'. 'Foreign companies are not interested in who you are, therefore caste becomes irrelevant'. Remarkable stories of successful Dalit entrepreneurs from across the country reveal the hardships and caste hurdles faced by Ratilal, Devjibhai Makwana, Malkit Chand, Bhagwan Gawai, Harsh Bhaskar, Hari Kishan, Atul Paswan, Devkinandan, J.S. Phulia, Sarath Babu, Sanjay Kshirsagar and Swapnil Bhingard. Changing with times, education, hard work, honesty, guts to do business, mannerism, punctuality and ethical business practices are the secrets of their success.

It is not only the men among the Dalits who succeeded, but we have a number of instances where Dalit women have overcome the barriers of caste, class and gender to make a place for themselves. Kalpana Saroj started her career at a hosiery factory in Bombay which paid her ₹ 2 a day is now chairperson of her own company – Kamani Tubes. After a torturous child marriage, she tried to commit suicide twice, but destiny had some other plans for her. She went on to buying land from a needy person and constructing a shopping plaza on it and then buying a sick company, Kamani, and turning it around to a profit-making company. She now runs a business empire worth ₹ 1,000 crore in Mumbai, Kuwait and Congo. She ably overcomes the intersection of being uneducated, Dalit and woman with her business acumen. The Government of India awarded her with Padma Shri in 2013. Undoubtedly, these entrepreneurs began with an idea just to earn a livelihood which led them to a remarkable success. The coal changed the life of Savitaben Parmar, who excelled in making tiles, was an inspiration to herself and her view is that 'one may face problems in one's own city, as everyone knows you – go and work in another area. No one would know your caste there'. 'Do not beg – even from government, set up your own work'. She now plans to diversify her business into buying and selling of gold. Her mobility from handling the impure coal to pure metal speaks volumes of her struggle to prove her worth to the world by emerging as a successful entrepreneur. These stories of multimillionaires reveal that Dalits through entrepreneurship have been able to achieve economic equality and it is very clear from the studies that economic mobility leads to social and political empowerment. Therefore, entrepreneurship can be a successful strategy to empower the Dalits of the country.

Tribal Entrepreneurship

Though the tribal art and craft is well known, but due to financial constraints, illiteracy, utter poverty and lack of awareness, the tribals could never commercialize their age-old skills. The Government of India, through the Ministry of Skill Development and Entrepreneurship, has taken initiatives for implementing entrepreneurship development schemes and programmes for the youth and women through entrepreneurship education, handholding and mentorship along with essential linkages with financial and market institutions. Tribals have been motivated to introduce changes by overcoming the structural constraints through government tribal programmes, tribal youth programmes, and tribal entrepreneurship development programmes. The tribals or the Adivasis constitute 8.6 per cent of the total population in India. According to Census 2011, the number of scheduled tribes in India is nearly 10.42 crores. They are found nearly in 30 states and union territories of India and are mainly dependent upon agriculture or on forests. But they have a vast reservoir of art and crafts, traditional skills, wisdom and knowledge. There are nearly 705 ethnic groups amongst them who specialize in varied skills, thus a huge potential for entrepreneurship. After liberalization of the economy, a number of NGOs through Self-Help Groups and with the provision of micro finance (informal financing agencies) have encouraged and empowered them, particularly rural women to connect their agricultural and forest produce with the markets by using some kind of technology. By turning their problems into opportunities there is a rise in the entrepreneurial activities across the tribal groups of the country. Their self-sustaining enterprises range from organic farming based on traditional knowledge and wisdom to varied variety of produce of forests. Trivedi (1991) classifies the major segments of tribal economy, such as forest hunting, hill cultivation, and plain agriculture. He argues that tribals in India are passing through a phase of economic change due to the intervention of modern forces.

One of the pioneering studies on Bhils of Rajasthan by Trivedi (1991) reveals that they accepted new enterprises involving their personal financial risk. Some took to agriculture entrepreneurship, sericulture, spinning and weaving, hotel and restaurants, shop keeping, and manufacturing of the small articles consumed by the region. He (pp. 180–181) argues that 'Entrepreneurial activities have come to the tribals more or less as a movement and it has introduced some basic structural changes in the tribal society. All the tribal entrepreneurs accept that they have gained prestige by taking to enterprise among their people'. The significant aspect of the tribal entrepreneurship is that their natural resources, combined with traditional skills largely handmade goods production, have the potential for local, urban and even global market. That is why they are referred as ecopreneurs, to which Shah (2018) calls as sustainopreneurs of change. As there is a lot of diversity amongst the tribals, so is of their natural resources, skills and goods produced. Their three major resources or sectors are: agriculture, including livestock, farming, horticulture and sericulture, forestry, and handicrafts.

Therefore, their entrepreneurship varies from artefacts, bamboo products to traditional handloom, handicrafts, silk weaving, and metal jewellery, in addition to natural collection of beads, flowers and fruits of the area. Though the process of their mainstreaming had already begun, yet the liberalization and globalization of the Indian economy accelerated the process at a faster rate. The emergence of the concepts of self-help groups, micro-finance, social enterprises and corporate social responsibility have contributed to express their inherent strengths, potential and skills.

Pal (1999) brings out the fact that the production and marketing of tribal handicrafts in Bihar as well in India are carried out under conditions of uncertainty. The interlocking of product and credit markets adversely affects the viability and sustainability of economic activities of poor artisans. Such interlocking has hindered the development of the collective bargaining capacity of the producers, which in turn has undermined their capability to lookout for markets and get better prices. His study brings out an innovative experiment carried out by an NGO with tribal weavers. The same NGO organized marginal artisan producers, became a partner in marketing of products made by tribals with a view to get them access to wider market. The Tribal Handicraft Marketing Cell was started which established links with other prominent agencies of Delhi and Calcutta which specialized in marketing village handicrafts in India and abroad on a non-commercial basis. Later on, a number of activities like rope making, jute work, leaf plate making, oil crushing, bee-keeping, basket making, soap making and brass work were also taken up.

To provide an overview of their emerging entrepreneurship, various cases of a number of tribal entrepreneurs of the country who got to express themselves in the first Global Tribal Entrepreneurship Summit organized in Dantewada, Chhattisgarh by NITI Aayog in 2017 have been presented by Rai (2017). An agripreneur, Tenzing Bodosa from Assam has his customers across the world. His organic farming generates revenue of ₹ 60–70 lakh annually. He has been able to motivate and train a large number of entrepreneurs in the area. A village in Maharashtra, Mendha Lekha is known as India's first bamboo economy village which has a population of 450 persons of Gond tribe. They all work together in cultivating bamboo as raw material for paper industry through which they are generating profits worth crores. The forest produce includes bamboo, honey, *lac*, herbs, leaves, berries, fruits, etc. Another is the success story of a women's Self-Help Group comprising 3,500 women from 127 tribal hamlets of Orrisa's Kandhamal, Sambalpur, Angul and Deogarh areas, who traditionally were selling the Siali leaf locally have entered into a formal agreement with a German company to supply one lakh Siali leaf plates every month which have become very popular in European countries as it acts as a biodegradable alternative to plastic and styroform.

In 2016, the District Collector of Sukma in the southernmost district of Chhattisgarh came up with Aranya – a social enterprise that is now changing the lives of tribals living there. The organization produces Imli Chaska, a sauce made from tamarind, which grows in abundance in the region. Grown organically, the sauce contains 85 per cent fruit pulp as compared to the industry standards of 27 per cent. Nilratan Shende set up a social enterprise EAGL, which is empowering farmers and tribals belonging mainly to the Korku community in Maharashtra's Melghat region by using livestock, mainly goats, and has helped over 200 families break the shackles of poverty. A Hyderabad-based organization, ACL India has incubated 54 social enterprises across five states of India, providing livelihood to over 65,000 women. These women entrepreneurs belong to tribal groups, small and marginal farming communities, livestock holders, weavers, internally displaced, and other vulnerable communities. Through training, skill development, market connections, and other support mechanism, it helps social enterprises to become self-sustainable and profitable. Another social enterprise, Last Forest, started as a marketing platform and it provides livelihoods and training in sustainable harvesting and organic agriculture to tribal groups living in the Kotagiri region of Tamil Nadu. Last Forest runs stores in Ooty, Coonor and Kotagiri, and supplies in wholesale to over a hundred stores across India. The brand sells beeswax products like lip balms, balms and handmade soaps along with non-timber forest products like gooseberry, pepper, soap nuts, black *jamun* and nutmeg. While some other social enterprises are focusing on the education of the tribal children.

The study of Chakraborty and Kumar (2020) presents some empowerment stories of tribals of Jharkhand, who, by using the locally available resources and rich bio-diversity, have started small and medium enterprises. To mention a few, the women running lac business through SHGs, Didi Café, C.M. Kunkal-popularly known as the lorry woman is the owner of Kunkal Enterprise, running transport business, owns 50 large trucks and has employed 300 persons. Nirja's apparel industry is an illustration of an educated woman taken to self-employment, and Tech Solutions are being run by highly educated professional tribals. Doman Tuduan alumnus of NIFT, Bengaluru, created a popular brand Rusica Trends, which is widely appreciated. He is also the mentor for more than 100 entrepreneurs under the start-up India mission. Such is the zeal, hard work and motivation of the tribals to explore their natural resources to generate employment and income.

In addition to government efforts, major initiatives have come from voluntary sector. Iyengar (1998) traces the movements of voluntary initiatives for tribal development in the state of Gujarat, which, according to him, began much before government interventions were planned after Independence. The tribal areas of the state in general and tribals in particular report higher incidence of poverty. He classifies the major voluntary initiatives in tribal areas into four categories:

1. On Gandhian principles of rural reconstruction and development.
2. Initiatives based on professional approach and technical and technological solutions.
3. Initiatives based on the mobilization and organization of local people for struggle and development.
4. Initiatives aimed at an efficient delivery of inputs, i.e. implementation of government and other sponsored development programmes.

He suggests that although every initiative has had some significant impact on the lives of tribal people, the ones based on the mobilization and organization of local populations promises results that are most sustainable in the long run.

Khakhalary (2017) suggests that government should modify and upgrade its policy and programmes which would be helpful for tribal entrepreneurs in venturing into the '2E' market, being e-preneurs that is, electronic platform, engaging in e-commerce and eco-preneurs, implying environment friendly products and services. Iyenger (1998) suggests a professional approach in the implementation of policies and programmes should be a must to ensure efficient and equitable delivery. National Knowledge Commission of India has defined entrepreneurship as the 'professional application of knowledge, skills and competencies and/or of monetizing a new idea, by an individual or a set of people by launching an enterprise de novo or diversifying from an existing one', hence emphasis needs to be on growth and development while generating wealth, employment and social good.

In the absence of any detailed empirical studies on entrepreneurial activities of diverse and multiple tribal groups in India, it is difficult to argue on the level of development of each of the group. The fact remains that the Indian tribal population is among the most exploited and poor sections of the society. Moreover, empirical studies of the tribals of the North-East India are not available to have a reasonably accurate picture of entrepreneurship among the tribals in India. Certainly on the basis of available data, it can be suggested that tribal groups of India are a vast reservoir of skills, wisdom and knowledge, which needs to be harnessed. In addition to Government of India's programmes and policies, the voluntary sector, social entrepreneurs, corporates under CSR, and NGOs can empower them, particularly the women through their ethnic entrepreneurship. For the purpose, their training and skill development is necessary for production and marketing the products. Their special needs and interests need to be taken care of through entrepreneurship development programmes. Pal (1999) on the basis of his study suggests that there is a need to approach the problem of marketing of craft-based rural products with a community perspective. Anderson and Giberson (2004) inform that Canadian aboriginal communities adopted and successfully implemented the strategies of promoting the forest and their uses along with entrepreneurship development to enhance their socio-economic condition. Similarly, the tribal groups of India can be mainstreamed through sustainable indigenous entrepreneurship.

Suggested Readings

Bal, G. and Judge, P.S. (2010). Innovation, entrepreneurship and development: A study of scheduled castes in Punjab. *The Journal of Entrepreneurship*, 19(1), 43–62.

Dahiwale, S.M. 1989. *Emerging Entrepreneurship among Scheduled Castes of Contemporary India: A Study of Kolhapur City*. New Delhi: Concept Publishing Company.

Flamant, N. (2003). The employer and his enterprise: International shoemakers in Tamil Nadu. In B. Dorin (ed.) *The Indian Entrepreneur: A Sociological Profile of Businessmen and their Practices* (pp. 101–135). New Delhi: Manohar & Centre De Sciences Humaines.

Judge, P.S. and Bal, G. (2009). *Mapping Dalits: Contemporary Reality and Future Prospects in Punjab*. Jaipur: Rawat Publications.

Khandekar, M. (2013). *Dalit Millionaires*. New Delhi: Penguin.

Rai, Saurbh (2017). Tribal entrepreneurship is booming in India and these 8 start-ups are showing the way. https://yourstory.com/2017/11/tribal-entrepreneurship-india/amp.

Trivedi, M. (1991). *Entrepreneurship among Tribals*. Jaipur: Printwell.

Section IV

Emerging Trends in Entrepreneurship

9

Concept and Process of Rural Entrepreneurship

Rural entrepreneurship may be defined as entrepreneurship taking place at the village level, but it should not be understood in terms of agriculture only. Trade, business and industry are equally important when we examine entrepreneurship at village level. Broadly speaking, rural entrepreneurship may occur in the form of diversification of agriculture, shops, stores and markets catering to the agricultural inputs and changing household needs of the people. The industry can be agro-based, consumer goods, and for agricultural purposes. There is a possibility that government or the big industrialists might have set up an industry on the village land. In this chapter, we do not focus on such kind of entrepreneurship which looks coterminous with the urban landscape. The main focus of this chapter is the activity which has been taken up by the village people by making innovation in their traditional occupations to generate employment and to enhance income levels. In other words, when the village people go beyond traditional pattern of farming and explore new ways of commercialization of the crops and become, as Singh (2013) calls them, 'capitalist farmer entrepreneurs' is what is the focus of discussion. Whereas shops, industry and trade are extensions of the overall pattern of entrepreneurial activities, agricultural related activities are exclusively rural.

Before we focus on entrepreneurs and entrepreneurship in the rural areas of India, it is important to recapitulate the overall concrete social structure of Indian villages, particularly in the context of composition of caste groups and their traditional occupations. Traditionally, every village was considered to be a self-sufficient entity, where its people have interdependent and mutual relationships with each other in terms of their needs. In every village (around 6,49,481 villages according to Census 2011, of these, 5,93,615 are inhabited.) in India, agricultural land is owned by a particular caste known to be the landowning caste. However, castes vary from region to region. This caste group may be high or dominant in the village hierarchy, while at the middle ladder are artisanal groups who are skilful and specialized in certain arts and crafts. The lower castes are dependent upon the upper castes and are landless and usually are agricultural labourers as well as domestic help. Trade and business always remained in the hands of a few middle castes groups, such as Khatri, Baniya, Mahajans from Vaishya *varna*.

Normally the entrepreneurship is associated with business and industrial activity. Just half a century back farmers in India were seldom regarded as entrepreneurs, though the French Physiocrats of the 18th century associated entrepreneurship with agriculture. Over a period of time, agriculture has assumed the character of business in the sense that now a lot of new opportunities and challenges have emerged. Rural entrepreneurship may primarily be understood in terms of the way the farmers are creatively responding to new situations. The attributes required of successful farmers, that is a movement from growing cash crops to agribusiness, are in many ways similar to those commonly associated with industrial entrepreneurs. The traits and characteristics of entrepreneurs apply to the farmers in the same manner. Harper and Vyakarnam (1988) argue that the general belief that farmers and people in rural areas are conservative and that they lack entrepreneurial initiative and managerial capabilities is a myth. Farmers are owners of a business when they have to organize labour and capital for their agriculture. They also take decisions as any manager in an industry would take, and they also demonstrate their capabilities of taking medium and long-term investment decisions especially when deciding on plantation of cash-crops or buying of milch animals. Farmers are also recipients of new technology inputs. In other words, they perform all entrepreneurial functions while engaged in agriculture (c.f. Kanitkar, 1994). Heredero (1979) argues on similar lines when he describes the 'agricultural entrepreneurs', the farmers who adopt better agricultural technology or introduce institutional changes which facilitate absorption of technology. Singh (2002) informs that the training as a strategy to encourage entrepreneurship in collaboration with NGOs have played an increasingly positive role in the process of institutionalizing rural entrepreneurship. Entrepreneurship Development Institute of India has implemented Rural Entrepreneurship Development programmes where training has been imparted in various skills. Pastakia (2012) has suggested various strategies for building pro-poor value chains for rural India.

A study by Singh (1999) reveals a unique experiment in micro enterprise development carried out for three decades on Panchayat Udyog which started in the 1970s in Uttar Pradesh and was inspired by the Gandhian economic philosophy of Gram Swaraj. It created enterprises which were owned and operated by Panchayats. This kind of blend of economic and political structures at the grassroots level can be very meaningful for rural industrialization. Bogaert and Das (1989) favour a 'group approach' by which they mean 'group entrepreneurship'. Based on their field experiences, these researchers suggest that many of the income-generating schemes targeted at the rural poor have failed miserably because the programmes focused on individual beneficiary. They advocate a different strategy, namely, group entrepreneurship that is, inculcating entrepreneurial characteristics among a group of people. Different organizations have developed various strategies for enterprise development out of which group enterprise development is one. Contrary to the above, Kanitkar (1994) suggests that entrepreneurs operating in rural India indicate the 'self-made' characteristics of a large number of individuals, who without proper education and training have ventured into small business. According to Jaisankar and Chandrasekaran (2020), rural industries in India comprise seven different sectors: (a) agriculture allied industries and food processing, (b) bio technology and rural engineering industry, (c) chemical and polymer based industry, (d) forest based industry, (e) fibre industry and handmade paper industry, (f) mineral based industry and (g) service industry.

Nevertheless, the rural entrepreneurship is mainly dependent upon agriculture and allied activities, and other non-agriculture activities which are found to be specific to different regions of the country as per the terrain, climate, water and the crops grown. Rural entrepreneurship through micro, small, and medium enterprises (MSMEs) in these sectors provide ample opportunities to the local people to uplift their socio-economic status. The argument is whether the rural people have been able to avail such avenues. If yes, it is significant to find out the nature and types of entrepreneurial activities of the rural people. It is important to ascertain whether the inhabitants have benefitted as a result of entrepreneurship or such opportunities have been grabbed by the outsiders.

Nearly 62 per cent of the total population is engaged in agricultural activities in India. Agriculture is the sole source of livelihood for nearly 58 per cent population in the country. However, agricultural activities are still performed in traditional ways by a sizeable peasantry. Therefore, the produce is barely enough for subsistence, and it fails to provide gainful employment to the surplus rural population. Even in a state like Punjab where capitalistic development in agriculture due to the green revolution in 1970s occurred, agriculture has started waning out. The overuse of pesticides, chemicals, agro-mechanical technology, monoculture of wheat and paddy have tremendously reduced the fertility of land, as a result of which the production has been increasing at a very high cost of inputs. Adding to it are the unfavourable policies and laws implemented by the Government of India, which are directly responsible for the decline in the benefits of the agriculture to the farmers. Das (2021) informs that during five decades of green revolution that the inverse effect of farm size on productivity is visible at an aggregate level, though the relationship varies across crops. The inverse relationship is even stronger in the eastern and central states for cereals and oilseeds, but the relationship is either neutral or positive for non-grain high value crops in Punjab and Haryana. The inverse relationship between farm size and productivity is not significant in agriculturally advanced states because of the capital intensive use of land by medium and large farmers.

Depeasantization has also emerged as a social reality impacting peasantries of all societies including India. One of the major reasons is that government has taken their land for various development purposes. Moreover, agriculture has progressively become unprofitable, particularly for small and marginal farmers due to costly inputs, low productivity, and fragmentation of land holdings. Over the time, farmers also have sold or mortgaged their land to construct a house, to perform marriage, to buy vehicle, and also for the education of their children. In the process, many landowners have become landless and have joined the service sector doing variety of jobs while some have become workers in the nearby towns or cities. The social impact of depeasantization has been enormous in terms of change or diversification of occupations.

The farming based on high use of pesticides and other chemicals to increase the production has seriously affected the health of the people and has also led to the degradation of environment. The harmful effects on health of the people in general and on women and children in particular in the villages of Punjab (Bal, 2000) raise the concerns to revisit the agricultural practices. Though at one point of time farmers' income increased manifold, but a huge share of it was being spent on medicines for the family. Shiva (1988, 1991) through her studies has shown that green revolution has led to the environmental pollution of Punjab in a big way. The traditional knowledge system has been destroyed, and a monoculture and multi-cropping of wheat and paddy prevails. As a result, the peasant women in particular have lost out in terms of productive work, besides having serious health concerns. The agriculture sector contributes nearly 18 per cent to the GDP of the country for the last many decades.

The resultant prosperity in most of the villages in developed states of India in general and particularly in green revolution areas has resulted into a changed lifestyle of the people. The overall affluence resulted into increasing purchasing power and everyday life of the people has transformed in a noticeable way in the villages. The easy availability and conveniences of modern gadgets, quality goods and luxury items have affected the behaviour, practices, habits and consumption pattern of the rural people. The growing local markets provided a number of opportunities to people from different castes and classes to capture new occupational avenues to meet out the new needs of the rural people. Thus, there is tremendous expansion of trading activities in the local markets catering to the requirements of agricultural inputs and consumption goods.

The high cost of agriculture production, in addition to the changing aspirations of the rural youth, as number of studies have shown that rural indebtedness has increased manifold over the years. All these challenges have also resulted into innumerable social problems like farmers' suicide, alcoholism, drug addiction, dowry problem, honour killings, in addition to show-off of material assets. A number of environmental problems also erupted due to overuse of pesticides and chemical fertilizers, and excessive irrigation has led to overuse and misuse of water resources. Depletion of ground water and scarcity of micronutrients in soil have created an alarming situation in many parts of the country, particularly in green revolution zones.

Nevertheless, the agriculture sector provides vast opportunities for innovations through diversification and by modifying the cultivating patterns and practices. Through the diversification the organic farming, horticulture, floriculture, poly-house farming, mushroom cultivation are becoming increasingly popular with the farmers in a number of developed states of India. These innovative agricultural activities by some enterprising farmers have been identified as agripreneurship. Food-processing industry, and agribusinesses are yet another set of enterprising activities taken over by different sections of the rural society. Rural entrepreneurship, however, is the best strategy for dispersal of industries and removal of rural poverty, as it largely depends upon locally available resources, skills and labour.

A number of measures have been taken by the Government of India over the time to protect the village based artisanal production. Among the rural industries, the agro and food based industries have generated substantial employment. Integrated Rural Development Programmes (IRDP) is one such example of the efforts of the government in this direction. The role of Self-Help Groups and NGOs has also remained crucial in imparting relevant skills and inculcating entrepreneurial capabilities. Some enterprising affluent people are promoting tourism, leisure and cultural activities in the rural areas, who are making efforts at linking the rural business to urban areas. A number of instances are available throughout India which have been developed as tourist spots in the rural areas. For example, Citrus County in central Punjab has been developed for the luxury stay of the tourists in the foothills of Shivalik hills.

With a change in the nature of occupational structure and social and occupational mobility the traditional caste-occupation association has disintegrated to a large extent. Therefore, it is probable that some new groups have emerged as entrepreneurs in the rural areas. Now the question emerges that who are the people who have become rural/agricultural entrepreneurs? To analyse the nature and extent of entrepreneurship in rural areas, we find that it is taking place at the following three levels which have been examined in the proceeding discussion:

1. The owners of land, who have been engaged in traditional agricultural activities are experiencing marginalization and increased inequalities, have moved to agro entrepreneurship or agribusiness. In such a situation, it is significant to examine whether there is still a relationship found between caste and occupation or some new caste groups have entered into agripreneurship.
2. The traditional artisanal groups, such as weavers, potters, leather workers, carpenters, blacksmiths, have become entrepreneurs on the basis of their craftsmanship and hereditary skills by starting cottage, and small-scale handicraft and other micro enterprises.
3. The third group is the one comprising those who have been traditionally controlling the trade, business and market in the villages. It is to be examined whether there is any change in the structure and functioning of the rural market, particularly in the sense when some new groups might have emerged to take up increasing trading activities as a result of surplus generated due to capitalistic development in agriculture.

Agro-based Enterprises

It is an illustration of entrepreneurship directly or indirectly based on the agriculture produce, which covers the manufacturing units processing the oilseeds, paddy milling -popularly known as shellers, cotton ginning mills, food processing units like tomato puree, potato processing. The making of jams from *jamun*, papaya and oranges, poultry farming, dairy farming and handloom industry are not only taken up by the landowning farmers, but also by different castes. Many farmers have diversified to honey farming, pickle making as well. A case of apiculturist from Punjab reveals that he owned 3.5 acres of land which was not sufficient to feed the family. As a result, he started honey farming in 1980s with two boxes after getting training from the Punjab Agriculture University, Ludhiana. At present, he travels to Delhi to sell his honey and is able to earn up to ₹ 25 thousand in a single day at fairs. He has expanded his activities to 550 boxes, his own processing plant, storage and packaging unit. He travels 900 km from his village in search of flowers for good honey. He has become a motivational speaker for others. There are many such instances all over the country where young agriculturists have shifted to such different commercial activities.

Singh (1997), in his study of food processing industry covering oilseed milling and paddy milling in two districts, namely Ludhiana and Bathinda of Punjab, reveals that 60 per cent of rice mills and all except one oil mill are owned by Banias – traditional traders. The study shows that farmers' lack of risk-taking capacity, lack of adequate knowledge about industry and trade and insufficient funds are strong factors hindering them in their endeavour to enter into food processing industries in the state. Thus, it is not the farmers who are becoming industrialists or entering into manufacturing activities, rather people with resources, such as village moneylenders, shopkeepers, traders, and sons of commission agents from the traditional trading castes have shown this kind of mobility. At the same time, however, we may find quite a few studies showing that age-old caste-occupation nexus has been disintegrating even in the rural areas.

Khan and Knight (1997) examine innovations in small farm agriculture by looking at the extent of technological change in the plantation economy of Barbados. They bring out that small farmer innovations are not based on indigenous knowledge, but on improved technology and, as a result, the farming system has moved from a low external input and sustainable agriculture to high external input agriculture. As a result, there is a shift in small farmer entrepreneurship from hawker system towards marketing cooperatives.

The farmers after getting the soil tested and finding conducive weather conditions have ventured into floriculture. The fresh flowers have a great market in India keeping in view the influence of western culture, number of religious places, and consumerism as such. For instance, in a city like Amritsar – a hub of industry, trade and tourism, the wholesale florists have thumping business who get the flowers' imported from foreign countries as well as from different parts of the country to meet the local demand. In the process of development, the lands of many farmers have been acquired by the government for expansion of city limits, road construction and widening. Over the time and particularly around Amritsar, it has been found that many farmers, particularly women landowners, have started growing expensive qualities of flowers largely to cater to the local demand on a small piece of land with which they are left with.

Singh (2019), in his study on agripreneurship in three regions of Punjab, has found that many young farmers (usually less than 40 years of age) have shifted partially or fully to horticulture, floriculture, organic farming and food processing according to the type of soil, water facility and other requirements of the regions. Though there is an overlapping of the agricultural entrepreneurship, but some clear regional variations have been found as in the Malwa region more and more farmers are growing fruits, such as kinnow and grapes. In the Doaba region, poly-house farming has become popular and a number of micro/small food processing units are predominantly located in this area including the famous 'Potato king'. Many mini hubs of floriculture have emerged in addition to mushroom cultivation in the villages of Majha region. With transformation in the cultivating practices the labour process has also undergone change, as there is a growing demand for the skilled labour, which is locally available. The participation of women labourer has gone up. The market for the produce though has widened, but has also become very competitive.

Kaur (2016), in an empirical study of organic farming as a sustainable form of agriculture in Punjab, has found that one quarter of the farmers believe that organic farming is good for health. It will recharge the water table, soil fertility, and the environment, in addition to be cost effective and higher production. The study has revealed that the Punjab government started taking initiative to popularize the organic farming and set up Organic Farming Council in 2006. Farmers were forthcoming, but unfortunately the state government could not sustain the project in the sense that the marketing of the organic produce is a challenge to the extent that, 70 per cent of organic farmers faced marketing problems, but the state agencies failed to provide them assistance. There is a need for improved access to market information, particularly for the rural small-scale initiatives. The agripreneurship in its various forms needs to be supported by the state agencies, as these are innovative ventures of some enterprising farmers. They need to be motivated for sustainable development.

Ideally, it is believed that the liberalization of the economy should enhance the chances for development of rural business. Stein (2007), on the basis of his study of Eastern Indonesia, finds that it has actually not happened. The reasons for their non-entry into business are limited information and knowledge, because still there is concentration and market dominance by powerful business groups. A platform of knowledge as well as an access to information is crucial for picking business opportunities. He concludes that proximity and close neighbourhood relations count for a potential easy spread of information and new business ideas. A number of studies have also depicted the role of social capital through formal and informal network ties, building on trust and sharing a common vision for the performance of small and tiny enterprises, particularly in the context of rural entrepreneurship.

Rural Industry

Rural industry has largely remained significant in the context of micro or small enterprises with a potential to generate wealth and employment. It is not that the rural people have established these enterprises. On the other hand, a number of medium or large industries have been set up by outsiders becoming important in terms of generating employment for the local people, for instance, brick kilns, etc.

The example of an enterprise, namely the Amul, a cooperative of dairy farmers started by Verghese Kurien in 1940s is an extraordinary example of rural poor farmer's entrepreneurship. Every milk producer of the village is a member of the village dairy cooperative society, which provides a stable income to the farmers. It produces a variety of milk products not only for Indian market but also for different countries. The success story of this enterprise has become a case to be studied by business schools. Singh (2013) has provided a few cases of formal agro-industry. The Nijjer Agro Foods, Amritsar, which belongs to an agricultural family, has entered into bulk supply of tomato paste to Nestle and vegetables to National Dairy Development Board (NDDB)'s 'Safal' fruit and vegetable project in Delhi sourcing the raw material from its own farms. It has processing plant for milk and vegetables and undertakes contract farming with farmers in Punjab (ibid.). Also in Punjab, there are cases of the Jat farmers like Rana Gurjeet Singh going into seed production and then they have set up paper plants using agro-residues, later diversifying into sugar and textile (Damodaran, 2008). Damodaran (ibid.) provides an illustration of another Jat, M.S. Bhinder, who started Agro Dutch industries in 1994 for the cultivation, processing and canning of mushrooms making it one of the world's largest integrated mushroom manufacturers. These cases of agripreneurs clearly depict that the young, educated and big farmers have been diversifying in their traditional occupations in the post green revolution period.

Based on the case studies of 86 village-based entrepreneurs drawn from different regions of India, Kanitkar (1994) examines the socio-economic profile of the entrepreneurs, their motivation for shifting from an agriculture-based occupation to a non-farm activity, their approach to raising resources for their enterprises and the factors that facilitated entry of the village-based entrepreneurs into a business activity. The National Bank for Agriculture and Rural Development (NABARD) is one of the important funding agencies promoting rural enterprises. It is a desperate and probably the last resort to survive and earn livelihood for self and the family and that these 86 individuals have been pushed into a difficult option of being one's own master. It is, therefore, significant that almost 90 per cent of the entrepreneurs are first-generation entrepreneur with a clear shift in occupation, as half of them (42 entrepreneurs) were handling activities generally classified as 'service' activity. Fifteen entrepreneurs (19%) were engaged in the manufacturing activity of some product. Ongoing developmental schemes, such as Training of Rural Youth in Self-Employment (TRYSEM) can be reoriented so that a new stream of entrepreneurs are identified and nurtured in the villages.

Rural Market

In rural areas where majority of people live, the trade and business have remained concentrated in the hands of traditional trading caste groups who hereditarily are traders and shopkeepers. They run small shops of grocery or other general items. These shops primarily cater to the household needs of the people. Most of them also work as intermediaries to sell or purchase the food grains of the farmers. They are trading in food grains and have become commission agents. The agricultural inputs like seeds, fertilizers and pesticides are largely met in the village itself. Also small agricultural tools and implements are locally available. It is significant to examine whether some new groups have taken to enhanced trade and business activities in rural areas which earlier were confined only to trading caste groups.

In the post Green Revolution phase, a lot of new lines of trading activities emerged in both the rural and urban areas. Judge and Bal (1996), in a study of Punjab, depict that with the expansion in the volume of trading activities the trading opportunities have been availed by people irrespective of the caste background. Even some of the low castes have also taken to small businesses which led to their social mobility. It is argued that the change in the economic structure has given opportunities to low and backward castes to move up in the social hierarchy by abandoning their traditional occupations.

Owing to change in rural society, people of non-traditional castes have set up micro/small enterprises catering to a variety of needs. The forces of change have been varied ranging from modernization, development, political turbulence to personal initiatives. The structure of the rural markets has undergone a transformation. During the phase (1979–1993) of terrorism in Punjab, the Jats, whose hereditary occupation is agriculture, aspired to become businessmen (as they were of the view that it was relatively more profitable) and they displaced the traditional traders, namely the Khatris and the Banias, and took over many of the businesses. This phenomenon has been observed in a number of villages of Amritsar district. Thus, political instability helped a new set of entrepreneurs belonging to the dominant Jat caste who are largely Sikhs (Bal and Judge, 2001; Bal, 2005). The emerging agripreneurship is not only going to transform the economic structure of the villages, but also the social structure leading to the loosening of the nexus of caste and occupation. The organic farmers have themselves taken to selling their produce in the nearby markets, or by setting up *Hatts* in the villages. Damodaran (2008, pp. 277–278) has found that many Jats in Punjab have entered into *arhat* or grain commission agency (commission agents), and trading in foodgrains in the local *mandis*. He explains that it is the easiest business to enter and manage as they themselves being farmers know the intricacies of the foodgrains and have family relations, and networks with the local farmers. He brings out that 105 out of its 290 licensed that is, 36 per cent of the total licensed commission agents in Asia's largest grain market (Khanna) in 2005–2006 were the Jat Sikhs when there were only 13 in 1985. Out of the 105 *arhatias* from the community, 80 are (more than 75% of these new entrants) farmers-cum-commission agents.

Batthini and Sexena (2017) on the basis of research publications in 50 issues of *Journal of Entrepreneurship* have identified rural entrepreneurship as an emerging area of research citing the need to design strategies for sustainable growth in rural economies. They have highlighted a few areas which either have developed or need to be further explored or ventured into. These are:

1. Application of indigenous technology in rural business for new product development.
2. The role of Self-Help Groups to encourage village people to take up to entrepreneurship.
3. Understanding rural consumer psychology to cater to their new needs.
4. Scope for modernization of agriculture holdings.
5. Promoting tourism, leisure and cultural items of the place.
6. Business innovation in agriculture and food processing sector using modern means of production and marketing.
7. Linking rural businesses to urban areas.

In the context of agricultural entrepreneurship, it is pertinent to emphasize that rural entrepreneurship has a great potential to transform the traditional basis of the society. And if the government so desires, it should promote agripreneurship as a mechanism for bringing about far-reaching changes in the rural social structure where still a majority of the population resides. Now-a-days, social entrepreneurs are primarily focusing their activities on the grass-roots, taking innovative initiatives to develop underdeveloped rural, hilly, and border areas by addressing the issues of social concern, poverty, education, unemployment, and women which will be discussed in detail in the next chapter.

Suggested Readings

Bal, G. and Judge, P.S. (2001). Terrorism and rural entrepreneurship in Punjab. *The Journal of Entrepreneurship*, 10(2), 191–208.

Das, Raya (2021). Farm size and productivity debate in Indian agriculture: Five decades of Green Revolution. *Economic & Political Weekly*, LVI(9), 57–65.

Jaisankar, S. and Chandrasekaran, S. (2020). A study on rural entrepreneurship development through MSME. *International Journal of Advanced Science and Technology*, 29(8), 2580–2584.

Kanitkar, Ajit (1994). Entrepreneurs and micro-enterprises in rural India. *Economic & Political Weekly*, 29(9), M25–M30.

Singh, G. (2019). Changing labour processes through agripreneurship in Punjab. In S. Misra, S. Shukla and G. Batthini (eds), *13th biennial conference on entrepreneurship: conference papers* (pp. 1211–1215). Ahmedabad: EDII.

Singh, Naresh (2002). Institutionalization of rural entrepreneurship through NGOs: Introspection from case studies. *The Journal of Entrepreneurship*, 11(1), 55–73.

Singh, Sukhpal (1997). Aspects of entrepreneurship in primary food-processing industries in Punjab. *The Journal of Entrepreneurship*, 6(2), 223–231.

Singh, Sukhpal (2013). Post-Green Revolution agro-entrepreneurship among capitalist farmers in Indian Punjab and Andhra Pradesh. *The Journal of Entrepreneurship*, 22(2), 161–180.

10

Social Entrepreneurship

Social entrepreneurship has become a buzz word these days in the sense that it is a new generation entrepreneurship with an objective of having social transformation by addressing the social problems. The major motive is to bring positive, equitable and sustainable change by solving the much pending social concerns. This form of entrepreneurship is directly related with the welfare of society which makes it relevant to sociologists. In this context, an entrepreneur applies all his energies and resources to identify, address and resolve the long standing unsolved social problems. One may say that the purpose of social ventures is social welfare, economic sustainability and inclusive growth of the society. It is operationalized at the grassroots level for the socially excluded people, groups, and communities with an aim to create value and impact. Innovation is an underlined current of the social entrepreneurship, though it may be for-profit, not-for-profit/non-profit[1] making businesses.

Concept of Social Entrepreneurship

Social entrepreneurship may be regarded as a new avatar of philanthropy in the modern times to address issues of inequalities, subordination, discrimination and exclusion. In India, philanthropy or charity might have been going on for centuries where the poor were fed good food, given clothes to wear and provided shelter. The rich and well-off people have been giving back to the society or giving charity to the underprivileged, the aim of which is not to uplift them from the misery, rather it was more a show of sympathy for their conditions. Scholars have been arguing that the inadequacy of the state welfare system has stifled initiatives, absolved people of personal responsibility and encouraged dependence (Trivedi and Stokols, 2011). Social entrepreneurship may be similar to charity in certain ways, but it is different in the sense that the concern is on capacity building. Making them to learn the skills and building capacity to do things on their own with a sense of dignity and fulfilment. Making the underprivileged capable to earn living and be self-reliant is the premise of social entrepreneurship. J. Gregory Dees (1998) has researched and written extensively on social entrepreneurship. He maintains a very clear position that recognizes and promotes the role that is, a set of behaviour that are exceptional in the society of the social entrepreneur. He insists that although the name of the role may be recent, the phenomenon is not: there have always been social entrepreneurs, even though they are not called that way, but originally have managed many of the institutions that now exist with social mission. In view of Drayton (2007), the job of the social entrepreneur is to recognize when a part of society is not working and solve the problem by changing the system, spreading solutions, and persuading entire society to take new leaps.

Though the term social entrepreneurship was first used in the literature on social movements, but by 1980s some people and organizations within the broad framework of civil society and international development started using the expression of social entrepreneurship. Soon it got its distinct status, as its concept combines the commercial activities of an entrepreneur with a social responsibility where his economic action carries positive social impact. The income-generating strategies of social entrepreneurs are directly tied to their mission and largely work through the institutional channels. The existing literature on the topic makes us to understand that not-for-profit activity is for creating social value and for-profit are for creating economic value.

Muhammad Yunus (2006) of Bangladesh is rightly acknowledged as the pioneer of social entrepreneurship in South Asia. He changed the lives of rural poor women through micro-credit scheme which later was turned into a Grameen Bank for which he got the Nobel Peace Prize in 2007. He has described two kinds of social business. The first confines to providing social benefits, rather than maximizing profits and may be called as non-profit social enterprise, such as poverty reduction, health care for poor, etc. The second operates in a rather distinct fashion, i.e. profit maximizing businesses owned by the poor or disadvantaged, such as the SEWA (self-employed women's association) formed by Illa Bhatt in 1972 in Ahmedabad helped the poor households to reduce their poverty. In that sense social entrepreneurship may range from starting a bus service to a remote area by a fellowman for the benefit of the community to infrastructural development by the community in an underdeveloped area and helping to eradicate social problems which the state has failed to address.

Alvord, Brown and Letts define, 'Social entrepreneurship is an individual or collective action that attempts to create innovative solutions to immediate social problems as well as to mobilize ideas, capabilities, resources and social arrangements required for long term, sustainable social transformation' (c.f. Vasi, 2009, pp. 160–161). We may define social entrepreneurship as any enterprising activity of an individual or a group of persons with a passion or zeal for welfare of the people and tries to bring long term sustainable transformation in problem areas of social life through innovative ways. Vasi (2009) argues that depending on the type of innovation it promotes, social entrepreneurship can take three distinct forms. First, social entrepreneurship initiatives focus on disseminating a package of innovations needed to solve common problems. For instance, when Mohammad Yunus came up with the idea to provide group based loans without collateral for poor and marginalized Bangladeshi people in late 1970s, the micro credit innovation disseminated so quickly that by 2008, over 4 million families in 27 countries were directly benefitting from it. Second, some forms of social entrepreneurship involve building social capacities or working with marginalized populations to identify capacities needed for self-help. It is based on the assumptions that local groups have best knowledge of the issues and local actors may solve many of their problems. Third, some social entrepreneurship initiatives focus on mobilizing grassroots groups to form alliances against abusive elites or institutions. For instance, the SEWA was formed in early 1970s in order to prevent the exploitation of poor, self-employed women workers and to provide services otherwise unavailable to manual labourers and home-based producers. Success in such social ventures is not measured by financial returns alone as Nicholls (2006) argues, but by tangible improvement to the quality of people's lives.

Light (2008) identifies four different components of social entrepreneurship, that is, entrepreneur, ideas, opportunity and organization. It begins with the novel ideas of social entrepreneur of any neglected, underserved, disadvantaged population. He perceives opportunities as possibilities and carries out to exploit opportunities through some organization. 'Because where others see problems social entrepreneurs see opportunities' (ibid., p. 9); in fact, entrepreneurs are defined partly by their ability to recognize and implacably pursue new opportunities. Since the opportunities also provide resources and potential collaboration, they are key to initiatives' sustainability. This third component is fundamental to the understanding of the concept of social entrepreneurship. The fourth component is the organization, and what is even more important is that these organizations are sustainable ventures. They find a product or service (idea) that matches corporate purpose (opportunity) and generates resources (organizational sustainability). It is important to clarify that social entrepreneurship is not social movement or mechanism to undertake any issue.

Social Entrepreneur

With regard to the origin of the terms social entrepreneur and social entrepreneurship there is an ambiguity. One of the views is that these terms were coined by H. Bowen in 1953 (Kaushik, 2022), while the other is that the term 'social entrepreneur' was first coined by J.A. Banks (1972) in the context of the sociology of social movements (Trivedi, 2010). However, it includes activities of green-root activists, NGOs, policy makers, international institutions, not-for-profit organizations, charities, social purpose businesses and other individuals from civil society, networks and groups that address a range of social and environmental issues in innovative and creative ways. Therefore, social entrepreneurs are catalysts for change, seizing opportunities, inventing new approaches and creating sustainable solutions to transform society for the better (Nicholls and Hyunbae, 2006). Tan at el. (2021), in their study, have found that the personality traits of individuals, who intend to create a social enterprise, are a combination of general entrepreneurial traits, such as pro-activeness and innovativeness, and social entrepreneurial traits namely, empathy and moral obligations.

Though the concept of social entrepreneurs has gained popularity during the last one quarter, yet they are found in all parts of the world. In sociological literature, we find Max Weber's treatment of charismatic leader, that is the individual who has certain extraordinary characteristics and traits that people tend to follow him, forms the essence of social entrepreneur in terms of his leadership role. Drayton (2005) writes that when he traced the change back to its source, he had found an obsessive individual, a person with vision, drive and integrity of purpose, great persuasive power and remarkable stamina. For Light (2008) also the term is very much like leadership. He is of the view that people will make significant changes in their lives if they trust the person asking them to do so. Thus, the social entrepreneur is more like a charismatic leader who is capable of creating followers as well as values among them. Quite similar to entrepreneurial success, we find that in the case of social entrepreneurship, the two basic ingredients of social values are trust in the leader and building a sense of solidarity.

At present, social entrepreneurs constitute a new sector, known as independent sector, non-profit sector, or as Bronstein (2007) mentions, as citizen sector which is growing at a much faster rate. The United Kingdom is the first country in the world to acknowledge the economic and societal importance of the social sector by creating a 'Third Sector' comprising voluntary and community groups, social enterprises, charities, cooperatives and mutuals that share the common characteristics of being non-governmental and value-driven, and principally, reinvesting any financial surpluses to further social, environmental or cultural objectives. In 2006, the British government created the 'Office of the Third Sector' that has the following responsibilities:

1. Work across sectors to provide a supportive environment for a thriving third sector.
2. Enable the sector to campaign for social change.
3. Deliver public services.

4. Promote social enterprises.
5. Strengthen communities. Scholars also argue (c.f. Trivedi and Stokols, 2011) that the very nature of capitalism and repeated government failures to solve the most pressing social problems has led to an increasingly frantic search for a new approach that does not rely solely on the market and/or the state to deal with socio-environmental problems.

Salamon et al. in their work on mapping the third sector in 35 different countries, identified variations between nation-states. In the developed countries, the share of the economically active population employed in the third sector is larger than in developing countries. In their view this does not highlight an absence of these activities in developing countries, as many countries have strong familial, clan and community networks that perform the functions of third sector organizations. Rather, the variations from country to country in the third sector reflect their different cultural, social, political and economic histories (c.f. Doherty et al., 2009, p. 3).

Doppelt argues that due to globalization, there is a significant expansion of world trade resulting in an increase in global per capita wealth. But at the same time there are some negative consequences, such as human rights abuses, environmental degradation, climate change, and public health scares. Civil society has responded to these issues in a number of ways and social entrepreneurship has emerged as a global phenomenon led by social activists and their networks (c.f. Doherty et al.).

Trivedi and Stokols (2011, p. 2) argue that 'the increasing prevalence of the television, internet and wireless technologies has increased people's awareness of the ecological crisis facing our planet and the connections between nations and their people. At the same time, the combined effect of increasing levels of literacy and the spread of information and communication technologies such as computers, fibre-optic cables, fax machines, televisions and satellites have made it far easier for people to organise and mobilise resources to alleviate these problems'. Citizens have now become more conscious of immediate issues and concerns across the world. Social entrepreneurs are demonstrating new approaches to social problems and new models to create wealth, promote social well-being and restore the environment. Every country of the world is facing one or the other pressing social problem which the state tends to address. But there are always some urgent and pressing needs of the people which are not met by the state machinery. There is a boom in social initiatives and a widespread interest in common issues, such as education, health, environment, gender equity and sustainability.

According to Light (2008), social entrepreneur is an individual, group, network, organization, or alliance of organizations that seeks large-scale change through pattern-breaking ideas about how governments, non-profits, and businesses can address significant social processes. Chand (2009) traces the key features of the social entrepreneurial process, that is new ways of solving social problems, resourcefulness, larger scale and wider impact and solutions that are transferable, scalable and cost-effective.

Social Enterprise

Peter Drucker (1979) advocated for the ethical responsibilities of corporations and introduced the concept of social enterprise. An enterprise is social that engages with society. The social objective may vary from providing food, shelter, clothing to education, innovative solutions to social problems by creating a social value. It is also an enterprise which carries economic value, business or trading in goods and services in a market. Thus, social enterprise is a business that trades for a social purpose and is a combination of money (for profit) earned through business model and mission which drives through not-for-profit programme. The distinct feature of social enterprise is that its social mission or social benefit is above the financial benefit. Dees (1998) calls social enterprise as hybrid organization that have mixed characteristics of philanthropy and commercial organization in many ways. He created a social enterprise spectrum, by putting pure philanthropy (non-profit) on the one side of it and a pure commercial purpose (for-profit) on the other end. Somewhere in between these two falls social enterprises. Alter (2006) brings these two together and constructs models, which explain mission and money relationship. Some social enterprises may be mission centric, some mission related and still others unrelated to mission. In mission centric social enterprises, business enterprises are central to parent organizations' social mission. Such social enterprises use self-financing model to advance the mission. In mission-related social enterprises, various business activities are associated with the organization's mission or social services. Income generated through such enterprises help to reduce programme costs or operating expenses, and in the process it creates a social value. Social enterprises unrelated to mission are created with an inspiration to generate profit, though the business activities may have a social content. The income generated is used for organizations' social programmes and operating costs.

In terms of non-profits or not-for-profit and for-profits, social enterprise is conceptualized as occurring along a continuum of organizational settings. At the one end of the spectrum are non-profits relying on philanthropic capital and concerned exclusively with social returns. At the other end are for-profits relying on commercial capital and concerned with financial returns. Between these poles are a range of organizational forms that are concerned with both social and economic returns (Alter, 2006).

These models vary from one country to another. The US model focuses on exceptional individuals aiming at large-scale top down impact, while the UK model is for the mobilization of communities to meet local needs. Nicholls (2006) presents seven models of social entrepreneurship and also informs that non-profit model is typically used in the USA to describe social purpose of organizations that serve the public interest and are registered as tax exempted organizations. While not-for-profit is used commonly in UK for a range of social purpose organizations in which almost every form of for-profit organization, non-profits, and charitable foundations can be classified as a social enterprise. Surely, social enterprises simultaneously possess two attributes, namely trading in goods and services in the market, and the primacy of social objective. Social enterprises are often described as being small and democratic, but many of them are also large.

The cooperatives which have been working in India for long time are also the form of social enterprise. Kaushik (2022) suggests cooperatives that are based on the principle of equity and justice and follow bottom-up approach, as an effective model of social entrepreneurship for development in rural areas. The performance of social enterprises is not necessarily measured in terms of efficiency rather for him social impact is an important parameter for evaluation. He quotes the illustrations of cooperatives like milk cooperative (Amul) and sugar cooperatives which have played significant role to uplift the marginalized sections of the rural society. Therefore, social enterprises, specifically cooperatives in his view need to have efficient and sustainable revenue model to revolve their funds (p. 30). In contrast to the cooperatives the concept of corporate social entrepreneurship is emerging which is more in the sense of social responsibility-inculcating as well as enforcing the big businessmen to give back to the society.

Corporate Entrepreneurship

Entrepreneurship is a phenomenon that can happen in a variety of organizational contexts. Corporate entrepreneurship is a term used to describe entrepreneurial behaviour inside established mid-sized and large organizations. Other popular and related terms are organizational entrepreneurship, entrepreneurship and corporate venturing. Operational definitions of corporate entrepreneurship have evolved over the past thirty years. Corporate entrepreneurship is a process whereby an individual or a group of individuals, in association with an established company, create a new organization or initiate the renewal or innovation within the current organization.

In addition to the individual/group social entrepreneurs, the states tend to inculcate corporate social responsibility (henceforth, CSR) amongst its people who own big businesses so that underprivileged people, excluded groups and social problems are addressed. Corporate Social Responsibility means that various activities carried out by medium to big sized corporate houses, businesses and MNCs for the direct betterment of under-served sections of the society. In almost every country of the world, the corporate houses are encouraged to bear some social responsibility as well. On tracing the history of CSR, its emergence could be traced back to 1950s. The World Business Council for Sustainable Development 2000 has defined CSR as 'Continued commitment by the companies to maintain ethical behaviour and contribute to economic development while improving the quality of life for its staff and their families, the community in which they work and society in general'.

In India, CSR is restricted to a set of mandatory guidelines laid down by the Government of India in the Companies Act, 2013, which any corporation must abide to. Every company having net worth of rupees five hundred crore or more, or turnover of rupees one thousand crore or more or a net profit of rupees five crore or more during any financial year will have to spend at least two per cent of the average net profits of the company made during the three immediately preceding financial years, in pursuance of its Corporate Social Responsibility Policy. To encourage and popularize CSR, the government has instituted an excellence award known as Apex India CSR Excellence Award. In 2021, NTPC, formerly known as National Thermal Power Corporation Ltd. has been awarded this award for its outstanding achievement towards women empowerment. Corporate social responsibility programmes create both social and economic value, whereas government programmes, social movement organizations, and social service organizations create social value (Meyskens et al., 2008).

It is relevant to explain the major differences and similarities between social entrepreneurship and the corporate social responsibility. Andrea Carolina Silva Niño (2015), in her article, draws a comparison between Social Entrepreneurship and Corporate Social Responsibility. There are four points on which they become same, the common points are:

1. Social Welfare: environment, human rights, labour rights, consumer protection and fair trade among others.
2. Development Alliance: State-business-civil society, concern for the future, and to restore social order. While on others they are different: social enterprises are employment generators, and need for work on the concept of social innovation to solve social problems.
3. Prioritize the creation of social value being self-sustaining.
4. Social Enterprises are necessary for a balanced business ecosystem. While CSR focuses on access to investment funds that focus on socially responsible company. Reputation and brand positioning. Guidance toward the values. A strategy that promotes the competitiveness.

Trivedi (2010) outlines four basic themes useful in distinguishing various social enterprises from corporate enterprises: (a) An emphasis on social goals as opposed to economic gains, (b) The social activist role played by the social entrepreneur, (c) Elements of entrepreneurship and innovation, (d) Creating and using economic profit as a means to solve the social problem rather than as an end in itself. To identify which particular values, motives and behavioural repertoires distinguish a social entrepreneur from a corporate entrepreneur, I quote Trivedi and Stokes (2011, p. 3) thus:

> Social entrepreneurs use their entrepreneurial talent to create a positive social change, whereas corporate entrepreneurs use their entrepreneurial finesse to create personal wealth. Generating 'social value' is more important to a social entrepreneur whereas corporate entrepreneurs are more focused on the generation of 'economic value'. A social entrepreneur seeks to invest his or her resources in problems that make more 'social sense'. On the other hand, a corporate entrepreneur seeks to invest in issues that make more 'economic sense'.

Social entrepreneurs combine personal, family and community resources in a new way to provide a better experience to its beneficiaries. Nicholls (2008, p. 12) differentiates social entrepreneurship on the basis of funds, and the funding dimensions of social entrepreneurship reveal it to be a voluntary activism on one side and corporate social innovation on the other end of the continuum. While not-for-profit may be grant funded (grant from government/organization) or partially self-funded, other social enterprises may be fully self-funded.

A Few Cases in the Broad Spectrum of Social Entrepreneurship

The proceeding discussion is based on the empirical studies conducted by Kaur (2016) and Bal (2010) in Punjab in the broader context of social entrepreneurship. These are the illustrations for the spread of education, community development, and women empowerment.

Corporate Social Responsibility

In the era of globalization, corporations have an opportunity to be globally competitive by expanding their production base and market share on the one hand, they are facing great challenge of sustainability and viability on the other hand. They cannot prosper in isolation. These corporations rely on society within which they operate, as they need infrastructure of the society, its source of employees and also the consumers. In return, they are also responsible towards the society. Hence as corporations are created by society, they must therefore serve it, not merely profit from it. This realization led to the new model of business, called as corporate social responsibility. Many corporations like IBM, ICICI, HSBC, Satyam entered into education sector.

Going along with the millennium goal of universalization of primary education with gender equality at all levels of education, the Government of India launched the Sarva Shiksha Abhiyan to address the needs of millions of children across country. Realizing the need, many big corporations of the country entered education sector. One of them is Bharti Foundation set up by Sunil Mittal of Airtel, a philanthropic branch of Bharti enterprises, started Satya Bharti School programme aiming to deliver quality education to underprivileged children across rural India under three models of implementation, namely green field schools, adopted government schools and public-private partnership. With this objective they entered six states with a wide spread of districts in each. In Punjab, it started 95 schools in three categories, namely primary schools, senior secondary schools and elementary schools. Kaur (2016) carried out a detailed empirical study on its contribution to spread education, particularly in the border villages of Amritsar district. It was found that most of the children studying in these schools are from under privileged sections of the society, from lower castes and also girls are in predominance. The responses of the community revealed benefits at the level of knowledge, gaining confidence, satisfactory teaching methods and mid-day meal scheme. Parents found an improvement at the behavioural level of the children, and the practice of good habits among the students. Children were keeping cleanliness of themselves as well as the surroundings. The researcher also visited the schools after three years and found that they were growing and expanding their activities. The Bharti Foundation presents a case of success and sustainability by reaching the remote, excluded areas and deprived sections of the society.

Social Enterprise for Women Empowerment

This case is an illustration of women empowerment which happens when women across caste class, age, and education status joined together to create a social enterprise called Shri Mahila Griha Udyog Lijjat Papad, popularly known as Lijjat – a for-profit organization with social goals. The Lijjat was formally registered in 1966 with its head office in Mumbai. At present, it has branches throughout India in different states. An empirical research was carried out by Amrit Preet Kaur (2016) in Sarabha Nagar branch of Ludhiana of Punjab state. This centre was set up in 1988 and it has 577 members with its own building having nine rooms. The centre is headed by a *Sanchalika* and co-*Sanchalika* who is production in-charge, besides the cashier, storekeeper, etc. They are primarily engaged in *papad* making. Women collectively participate with division of work activities, such as making of dough, distributing dough, receiving *papad*, packing *papad*. The women work from their homes. At home they prepare *papads* by getting dough from the centre and after completion of work they either come to the centre to give and get the payment or the member-in-charge collects it from their houses. The study reveals that through this project women are able to financially support their families. This organization has helped the unskilled, illiterate, and poor women to be self-reliant. Lijjat has empowered women by harnessing their entrepreneurial abilities and also provided financial security. Over the time, it has grown much bigger, and is found to be sustainable as it has formalized its structure and functioning. Women from underprivileged sections are being motivated to get engaged in its activities. Through their earnings at Lijjat, women were able to provide education and solemnize the marriage of their children, and were able to participate in the decision-making of the family affairs.

Village Life Improvement Programme

Trivedi (2010) argues that most of the attempts to define social entrepreneurship are individualistic in their conception and fail to acknowledge collective forms of social entrepreneurship which faces variety of challenges. An illustration of diaspora of Punjab being exposed to the popular concept of corporate social responsibility in their developed countries got enthused to do something for the development of their ancestral villages during the last two decades. It is well known that Punjabi diaspora found world over has stories of success to narrate and more significant is that their ties with their homeland have become multi-layered or as Thandi (2010) calls them transnational where they circulate within the transnational space through telecom, tourism, transport, trade and transfer. But over the years, they did not experience much change in their villages, thus they took the initiative to improve the lives of their fellow beings in the villages. A project of 17 different villages was prepared providing the blueprint for the development of all the villages of Punjab subsequently. The total cost was calculated and they made efforts to generate funds. To ensure the sustainability of the projects, they focussed on education, sanitation, self-governance, infrastructure and income generating activities.

The case of one village, Khroudi in Hoshiarpur district of Punjab depicts the development process initiated through the social entrepreneurship of two prominent NRIs of the village as the change agents. It is significant to present this case to also underline the issues related to its sustainability and also the reasons for lack of sustainability of the project (Bal, 2012). Before they took up the project there were shabby streets, open sewers, a polluted pond and stinking marsh in the middle of the village, besides the unsafe drinking water. The daily life of the villagers was marked by inadequate defecation facilities, unsafe disposal of waste water, stinking village ponds, a lot of bio waste scattered all around as a result of which there used to be frequent spread of water borne diseases. With the consultation of the village people they prepared a project, got it approved from the Government of Punjab under dollar for dollar scheme. The funds were collected with the help of diasporic community and even a Canada-based Indo-Canadian friendship society got involved. A meagre amount was also contributed by the village residents. They established a Village Life Improvement Foundation and started developing infrastructure, concrete streets with sidewalks, solar street lights, and underground sanitation opening into sewerage treatment plant, regular water supply, and sewer connection to each household. Parks were developed in the village and construction of crematorium, a community centre, guest house, computer education facility were carried out along with the tree plantation drive. A corpus fund of rupees ten thousand was also created to meet the day-to day needs and maintenance of the provisions. It became so famous that *India Today* magazine covered a story of the model village and the then President Abdul Kalam visited the village.

However, it is important to raise questions with regard to its sustainability. Is this type of social change sustainable? What may be the long-term effects for the welfare of the people? The amenities under the project could sustain only seven to eight years. Gradually the things started coming back to the original. The solar lights got damaged, stagnant water was seen in the streets and parks. Waste was littering all around. The seepage pit was blocked and water was flowing sideways. Treated water was stagnating in the pond. Swings and benches were broken. In a nutshell, the village was more like any other ordinary village in less than a decade. One of the major reason for the lapses was lack of proper estimate for maintenance. In addition to the underestimation of the recurring expenditure, the most significant is the emotional and economic involvement of the community in the project.

On the basis of empirical observations of Khroudi village, it is relevant to add some nuances which are purely social to the concept of social entrepreneur and social entrepreneurship. Following two aspects are essential for a social entrepreneur: First, he/she must win the confidence of all individuals for whom some welfare or change is being undertaken. The role of cultural capital of the social entrepreneur is real game changer. First motivate the people and make each of them to participate in the collective work. In this particular case, though the social entrepreneurs had clear and pious intentions to bring transformation in the lives of the village mates, but they could not apprehend the heterogeneity of the village community in terms of caste, class, factionalism and individual interests. Second, so far as sustainability of any such social welfare activity is concerned, it is essential to have regenerative capacity of the project. We have illustrations of the Government of India adopting welfare model for the development of the villages, but the welfare model to bring gender equality failed miserably as the beneficiaries could not develop collective feeling from which the collective responsibility was to emerge. The effectiveness of the role of social entrepreneur should be evaluated in long terms, because his/her social entrepreneurship may start from dependency of others on him, but it must move on to self-sufficiency to self-sustainability. Social entrepreneurship can be successful only when it creates long-term solutions to social problems by building local capacities. Therefore, the efforts aiming at change and development should be carried out as a social enterprise and not as a charity or philanthropy by making the other party a stakeholder. As in the beginning it has been stressed that there is a very thin line between philanthropy and social entrepreneurship. Peredo and

Chrisman (2006) have emphasized the importance of inclusiveness. They argue that lack of ownership is the main reason that many poverty alleviation programmes have devolved into global charity since most projects are conceived and managed by development agencies rather than members of community.

Reputation or credibility is vital for social entrepreneurs to be able to tap into their social networks to garner and mobilize resources in terms of their ability to assemble and effectively utilize many resources. The ability to develop a network of relationships is a hallmark of visionary social entrepreneurs as emphasized by Trivedi and Stokes (2011). Credibility is the key factor for social entrepreneurs, as it also helps to maximize others' commitment to the collective purpose championed by the leader. It is precisely the leader's credibility that helps social entrepreneurs to maintain a clear focus on the overarching goals (or vision) of the organization.

Social entrepreneurs are usually supported by volunteers who share a common vision of mitigating socio-environmental problems. As profit generation or maximization is not at the centre of such ventures, resource mobilization for social enterprise is very different compared with traditional business. Social entrepreneurs are the main propellers of resource generation in their organizations. Along with their personal wealth, they rely heavily on their social networks to carry forward their mission. They understand the necessity of being inclusive to generate a feeling of ownership and sense of value-added participation.

After having an exhaustive understanding of various dimensions of social entrepreneurship, it may be summed up by commenting that the future belongs to social entrepreneurship, though one may start as commercial entrepreneur but to sustain and spread the business, it is very important to create social value. One may go along with Kaur's (2016, p. 186) views that 'private-not-for-profit partnership, employment, fee-for-service and market intermediary models proposed by Alter (2006) may yield the best results if followed scrupulously'. To make these models clearer in the context of India, I quote the illustrations (Kaushik, 2022) of Self-Employed Women's Association (SEWA) – a support model, Pipal Tree Foundation for employment, online Bookshare as fee-for-service, and Amul as employment model can create an alternative system to redress the social issues. However, it is important to keep in mind that for social entrepreneurship to sustain, there has to be some capital generation, because in a capitalist society the uninterrupted flow in and out of capital is indispensable, which has to be done by keeping in mind the positive social functions it performs.

Note

1. Not-for-profit and non-profit have been used interchangeably in the existing literature.

Suggested Readings

Bronstein, David (ed.) (2007). *How to Change the World: Social Entrepreneurs and the Power of New Ideas*. New York: Oxford University Press.

Dees, Gregory (1998). Enterprising nonprofits. *Harvard Business Review*, 76(1), 55–67.

Doherty, Bob et al. (2009). *Management for Social Enterprise*. New Delhi: Sage Publications.

Kaur, Amrit Preet (2016). Changing contours of entrepreneurship: A study of social entrepreneurship in Punjab. PhD thesis, Guru Nanak Dev University, Amritsar.

Light, Paul C. (2008). *The Search for Entrepreneurship*. Washington, DC: Brookings Institution Press.

Nicholls, Alex (ed.) (2006). *Social Entrepreneurship: New Models of Sustainable Social Change*. New York: Oxford University Press.

Trivedi, Chitvan (2010). A social entrepreneurship bibliography. *The Journal of Entrepreneurship*, 19(1), 81–85.

Trivedi, Chitvan (2010). Towards a social ecological framework for social entrepreneurship. *The Journal of Entrepreneurship*, 19(1), 63–80.

Trivedi, Chitvan and Stokols, Daniel (2011). Social enterprises and corporate enterprises: Fundamental differences and defining features. *The Journal of Entrepreneurship*, 20(1): 1–32.

11

Indian Diaspora in Entrepreneurship

Indian diaspora in entrepreneurship is an umbrella term for the Non-Resident Indians (NRIs) and People of Indian Origin (PIOs), who established themselves as entrepreneurs in foreign lands. Deciding to take up to business instead of going into salaried job is a major issue for an immigrant. For some it might be due to unemployment, whereas for others it might be self-employment and for some others perhaps there is no other option but to take up to business of some kind. The economic might of the Indian diaspora has become conspicuous mainly in the late 20th and early 21st century. The globalization of the economic activities has witnessed the emergence of the Indian diaspora as a key player on the world stage is what Rai (2007) opines. Rai categorizes the Indian diaspora turned into entrepreneurship into three: first, Indian professionals turned entrepreneurs like Sabeer Bhatia and Vinod Khosla are primarily venture capitalists; second, the NRI business icons notable among them, Lakshmi Mittal and Lord Swraj Paul have more diversified industry; and third the PIO business people are most diverse and are found in broad range of industries – at cutting edge of technology to traditional enterprises.

The intensification of migration flows and the emergence of a transnational economy have led to a growth in immigrant business activity. As a result, the entrepreneurial activity of immigrants is gaining the attention of the increasing number of scholars across the countries. Irastorza and Pena (2014) inform that recent findings of the studies also show that immigrants are more prone to becoming entrepreneurs than natives. They, in their study of immigrants in Spain, reveal that the self-employed immigrants' income exceeds that of salaried workers. The human capital and location related environmental variables were found to be the best predictors of both self-employed and salaried immigrants' earnings.

To understand the dynamics of entrepreneurship among the immigrants, it is significant to take note of the conditions that influence the self-employment process which Roger Waldinger, Howard Aldrich and Robin Ward (2000, p. 377) have separated into three categories, namely: (a) pre-migration characteristics, (b) the circumstances of migration and their evolution, and (c) post-migration characteristics. First, pre-migration attributes include skill, language, business experiences, kinship patterns, and exposure to conditions (such as a high level of urbanization and industrialization) that would foster entrepreneurial attitudes. Second, the circumstances of migration are the conditions under which the immigrants move, whether as temporary workers or as permanent settlers, as well as the factors influencing their settlement type. Third, characteristics such as economic and occupational position and discrimination (or the lack thereof) would fall under the post-migration rubric. The present chapter is an attempt to outline how these factors interact with one another and with the local available opportunities. Therefore, the chapter has two parts. The first part primarily focuses on the pre-migration attributes of the immigrant entrepreneurs. Prominent among them are from Gujarati community, specifically the Patidars whose hereditary occupation has been business and trade and they have exceptional skills, capabilities, experiences and family and kinship network to establish a business. The second part deals mainly with the post-migration features, that is, new generation entrepreneurs across religion, caste and regions on the basis of their economic and occupational position who have set up businesses in the host country. A number of successful Indian entrepreneurs are in the US, particularly in IT sector. These young entrepreneurs are different from the earlier business entrepreneurs endowed with hereditary business skills for whose success the social capital remained the major determinant. Both pre-migration and post-migration characteristics interact in the context of immigrants' settlement conditions, whether they are permanent settlers or temporary migrants. The temporary migrants may not be interested in setting up business, as they intend to go back to their own country after accumulating some money through low level, dead-end jobs. However, the permanent settlers have high ambitions extending to the positions occupied by the natives as well as the rewards generated by these positions. The lack of occupational mobility, experiences of discrimination, glass ceiling, and unequal salaries prompting the permanent settlers to be self-employed has been examined in the second part.

The economic sociology of immigrants reveals various trends, processes and patterns of their entrepreneurial activities. Usually, immigrants tend to get concentrated at few places as they share language, dress, food and almost similar life chances with each other. As the immigrants tend to hail from a particular region in India with kinship network, distant family ties and commonality of practices, customs and rituals provide them a sense of solidarity and feeling of trust. They tend to settle in particular areas forming a community having specific needs. For instance, we find most of the Indians, particularly Punjabis settled in Brampton, Surrey in Canada, Southall in England and Yuba City in America. Their specific needs contribute to the emergence of entrepreneurship amongst some innovative persons either from the same community or by some others in the same locality. Studies have shown that immigrants largely tend to land up in small-scale entrepreneurship by adopting family based strategies of economic adjustment. Family members are the most trustworthy and least costly collaborators in business. The initial market for immigrant entrepreneurs emerges within the immigrant community, for they serve their special needs and preferences. The young entrepreneurs are more extrovert in the sense that they have contacts beyond their own Indian community.

The available theoretical perspectives on immigrant entrepreneurship raise the question on the conditions, both economic and social, which are responsible for the emergence of entrepreneurship amongst the communities. Light and Rosenstein (1995) reveal that ethnic resources like families, enforceable trust, multiplex social networks and ideologies, rotating credit associations and religion encourage and support the founding of new business firms. In addition to such social factors, the economic conditions are equally important. For a business to emerge and sustain there must be a demand for the goods. As per their interaction theory, the interplay of the demand and supply is crucial to examine the diasporic entrepreneurship. In the initial stages of the business, demand comes mainly from immigrant community itself. Their cultural needs and items of consumption are best served by the businessmen of their own community. Immigrants' special needs, such as permanent settlement, citizenship, work permit, passport and visa extensions are also best understood and worked upon by the immigrant law firms, travel agents and accountants. However, this kind of community demand and supply also becomes a hurdle in their growth process in the long run. Such enterprises tend to remain small-scale, financially constrained and limited to the street corners. If they need to expand their businesses, then they have to shift to a market place where there is open competition. An entrepreneur has to work very hard and for longer hours and keep the prices lower. The economy is embedded in the society and the society constraints it as well as makes it feasible.

Waldinger, Aldrich and Ward (2000) emphasize the interaction between opportunity structure of the host society and the group characteristics and social structure of the immigrant community to provide an explanation for immigrant enterprise. Small-scale enterprises lower the entry barriers to immigrants with limited capital and technical resources. They note that it is common for members of a particular ethnic group, which has just moved to a new locality, to try to buy up the businesses of an older ethnic group. Opportunities for ownership result from the process of ethnic succession, and vacancies for new business owners arise as the older group that previously dominated small businesses moves to higher social positions.

Bal (2006) argues that the policy of multiculturalism, particularly in Canada, the USA and UK, helps us to understand the nature and type of entrepreneurship among diasporic communities, as the policy gives the right to every ethnic community in these countries to maintain its identity in terms of dressing, food habits, language, practice of religion and entertainment to preserve its cultural heritage. Multiculturalism with its underlying policy of equality with difference gives space to each ethnic group to maintain its identity in the host society (Judge, 1994). Ethnic entrepreneurs fulfilled such needs in a way that it helped to fulfil the needs of the diverse communities as well as popularized the policy of multiculturalism. The needs of the community and the recognition of their needs under the policy of multiculturalism encouraged some enterprising people to venture into business. We may say that the policy of multiculturalism provided opportunities to enterprising persons to cater to the new demands, and at the same time by fulfilling local needs of the people, it proved to be a success, hence mutually benefitting.

I: Pre-migration Attributes

Gujarati Entrepreneurs

Gujarati as a word signifies the inhabitants of a region that is, Gujarat state of India. Because of their unparalleled skills of doing business, the Gujarati and the business have become synonymous. When we refer to Gujarati, it is generally understood in terms of business and trade. Among the Gujarati, the Patidars are the most prominent businessmen. They include three sub-castes or groups, namely Patel, Desai and Amins. The Patidars are primarily landowners and farmers. As agriculturists, they had been growing commercial or cash crops like indigo, cotton and sometimes jute, which they were carrying at far off places to sell. Trade has been the basis of their travel to far and wide and by 18th century, the Gujarati trading capital had extended to many African countries. During the 19th century, they settled in East Africa, learnt their language, customs, developed land and business and became influential. In addition to their domination in ginning industry in many African countries, they took diverse forms of retail and wholesale business.

Towards the end of the 19th century, the Gujarati started as small entrepreneurs in South Africa, East Africa, and Pacific Islands, like Fiji in the East as well as in the Caribbean Countries. From there many Patidars, due to their exodus from Kenya, Uganda and Tanzania, migrated to Britain. A study of London Patidars (Tambs and Lyche, 1980) informs that in England, they are mainly concentrated in London and Leicester. They are the best of the shopkeepers selling Indian goods ranging from handicraft products, books, newspapers, to cloth and sarees. Besides the shops, they are house owners giving it on rent, moneylenders, wholesalers, agents and brokers, etc.

After the recession years of 1970s in American economy, many educated immigrant Gujarati lost their jobs and at this juncture many of them decided to invest their savings to start businesses again in mid-1980s. Among the Indian Americans, the first two moteliers in America happened to be Gujarati. They purchased a 100 room hotel, a monastery on lease. A Gujarati would start with a modest and old motel, and with his hard work, business skill and risk taking aptitude would change it into a decent multi-room motel. They maintained the community tradition of supporting a new entrant with capital and networks to start his own business. By 1990s Gujarati were deep into hospitality industry comprising hotels and motels. Motels also solved the problem of housing and commuting for the new immigrants, as the migrant family was easily accommodated in the motel itself doing house-keeping jobs, etc. Another cultural characteristic of the Patels is intensely woven with the economy of the motel industry. If a Patel wants to buy a motel, he can rely upon the guidance and financial support of his relatives and friends. They will buy land cheap in commercially undeveloped areas and then build motels on it (Sheth, 2001). There have been waves of Gujarati immigrants to American cities like New York, San Francisco, New Jersey and to Canadian cities and their chain migration continues till date. In addition to running retail and wholesale businesses, at one point of time the whole New York newspaper stands were with the Gujarati. The gas stations, jewellery business, and also providing various cultural items like Bollywood music cassettes, Gujarati ethnic goods, such as dresses, food items and even *dandia* stores.

In the mid-1970s, a variety of Indians joined the life in Canada. The Gujarati started many small and big businesses in Toronto. Milton Israel (1994) mentions that about fifty thousand Gujarati living in Ontario have East African roots. He narrates a case of a Gujarati businessman, who imported fish, vegetables and fruits by air directly from India and supplied it to other stores, besides his own. Martin Merger (c.f. Isreal, 1994), who studied Indian entrepreneurship in Toronto, found that they arrived in 1970s with substantial prior business experience, depended on family sources of capital, living in suburbs and were educated, whose customers were primarily the Indians. Bipin Patel, a Patidar developed overhead signs which he markets across Canada, the US and Europe. Similarly the donut business of Shreyas and

Sohan Azmera grew into the largest supplier of dough to bakeries in North America.

What might have been the reasons for their success as entrepreneurs and becoming synonymous with business in developed foreign countries is an issue for exploration. It may be stated that primarily it is their capitalist orientation that helped them to establish themselves. The social capital was available in the form of financial support, networks, guidance, trust and family and community solidarity. Rutten (2001) writes that Patidars are more prone to partnership within family and kinship than others. They have the strongest sense of togetherness and family feelings, and such characteristics are most conducive to doing business. Metcalf, Modood and Virdee (1996) compared four subcategories of South Asian ethnic businesses: Indians (Hindus and Sikhs), African Asians, Pakistanis and Bangladeshis, and then used cultural attributes to explain different performance of these ethnic minority groups. Their study found that business practices and attitudes among Indian, Pakistani and East African Asians were different whereby self-employed women were keen to stress the importance of family cohesion and men were happier if 'their women' worked in the family business rather than elsewhere (Metcalf et al., 1996).

II: Circumstances and Conditions of Migration

We may begin by referring to a study conducted by Archana Verma (2002) in this context. It examines the migration of a dominant in numbers, low-status caste group Mehton from Paldi village in the Hoshiarpur district of Punjab to the settlement at Paldi on Vancouver Island in British Columbia at the turn of the 20th century. A number of unfavourable circumstances back at home and opportunities (affluence) available in far off Canada were the reasons for them to migrate. In Canada, they took up jobs on farms, fruit ranches, in canneries, sawmills and clearing land. They also entered into lumber industry as workers in a big way. But their cultural symbols, racial bias on one side and their hard work and success on the other created hostile feelings amongst the Whites. Later, the community members along with Jats from the native area took a lumber company on lease and soon in 1916 they formed their own companies – The Pacific Lumber company and Mayo Lumber company. Maiya Singh and Dhumman Singh by all standards could be called as pioneer entrepreneurs in Canada whose conditions of living and working there created circumstances which led them to owning a mill. Mayo Mill flourished through their collective hard work and became a successful venture. Through their entrepreneurship they gained economic and social mobility though their point of reference was always the family and kin in Punjab. The status of Paldi Mehton immigrants improved further as they successfully created a 'Little Punjab' at their mill site which provided opportunities for their familial kins and village brethren to raise their status as a group.

III: Post-Migration Characteristics

A new generation of entrepreneurs (intrapreneurs/professionals) from India is sought after worldwide, especially in the US when India does not restrict migration out of the country. Indian immigrants in the United States are highly successful in entrepreneurship. While working in the US, several Indian professionals with degrees in engineering, management and science gain confidence in their business skills and have information about business opportunities. They also have know-how needed to run a business acquired through on-the-job training, besides the English language fluency and the contacts needed to start business. Generally, unemployment, economic downturns, recession faced by the economies lead immigrants to give up their jobs to start their own companies. The rapidly changing Information Technology (IT) industry provides ample opportunities. In 1998, an estimated 775 companies in California's Silicon Valley were run by entrepreneurs of Indian origin. In a study of 2000 for the Indian Government, it was estimated that over 300 Indian-born entrepreneurs in the US had a personal net worth of more than 5 million dollars each. They are first generation business men and women, coming from non-business families and often from outside the traditional business and caste communities of India (Chithelen and Souza, 2005). They have their professional degrees from IITs, IIMs but due to high level of unemployment in India and lack of job mobility in addition to low salaries they have moved to the developed countries. To begin with, they took up jobs in their IT industry and gradually after accumulation of some capital decided to have their own enterprise, generally two or three professionals got together and launched their own companies.

Already in India they had learnt to work very hard for getting education and doing well in the examinations as a result of which they could easily cope up with the demands of the jobs in developed countries. They raise their initial capital in stages and from a variety of sources including family and friends.

Another study by Varma and Varma (2009) on the Indian immigrant entrepreneurs in the US has identified six features of their success in the science and engineering sectors. One, the US immigration policy gives preference to professionals, scientists, engineers and skilled workers. Most of them have come for higher studies in science or engineering after getting education from top Indian institutes like IITs. After finishing education they are offered jobs in the universities or in the industry, hence get their student visas converted into permanent residents. Indian immigrant scientists and engineers tend to be mathematically minded, analytical, and are good at diagnosing technical problems. Two, being raised in India, in middle class families, they have learnt to do hard work and have determination to overcome obstacles. Three, due to subtle obstacles, like glass ceiling, immigrant status, and racial prejudices operating on the way to promotion to higher ranks in jobs, these scientists and engineers are compelled to launch their own companies by using their personal funds or borrowing from family members, friends and colleagues. Four, after working for a decade or so, they become more confident of their skills and are not reluctant to launch and manage companies. Though in the beginning, very few investors were willing to give seed money to Indians for their business plans and I quote authors (ibid., p. 67) 'Since the mid-1990s, there has been a sea change in the mindsets of Indian scientists and engineers and a new Indian entrepreneurial culture has emerged. As a result, successful Indian Immigrant entrepreneurs have become role models and opened the doors for the next generation'. Five, they have developed a strong community around entrepreneurship by forming business organizations where they meet, exchange ideas and experiences, share solutions and expertise. For instance, the Silicon Valley Indian Professionals Association, and the Indus Entrepreneur founded in 1980s and 1990s have been playing a significant role in the emergence of new entrepreneurial culture. Through these associations, they are able to find investors and acquire resources. Six, the prevailing American entrepreneurial culture gives Indian entrepreneurs a confidence as it provides encouragement to private enterprise. In addition to it, the political stability, appropriate business policies, legal protection for intellectual property, easy access to financial and human capital, and support system for start-ups creates a favourable environment for entrepreneurship.

In case of individual entrepreneurs, it is the social capital which helped them in India to acquire education and also to study in foreign country. In order to become entrepreneurs in foreign countries, it is the human capital in the form of education, knowledge and skills that helped them directly. Though in post-migration attributes it is mainly the role of human capital, but to succeed as entrepreneurs it is the interplay of social and human capital. Granovetter (1985) argued that social networks were key determinants of economic action for ethnic businesses, which is true even in modern capitalist societies. Social embeddedness implied that entrepreneurial behaviours were constrained by ongoing social relations, and therefore, the degree of embeddedness was an important resource influencing an ethnic enterprise's future capability and performance. Portes and Sensenbrenner (1993) suggested that human capital and market capital, which included both tangible material goods and social capital that fosters group solidarity, and trust and reciprocal obligations combined to facilitate ethnic entrepreneurial activities.

There are several instances of Indian immigrant women who emerged as transnational entrepreneurs. On the basis of personal observations and contacts it is very interesting to find that a large number of Punjabi immigrant women have been doing business of ethnic goods in England, the US and Canada. The detailed study of Parminder Bhachu entitled *Dangerous Designs* (2004) carried out in England reveals how Asian women fashion influence the diaspora economies. It is about an ethnic dress, the Punjabi suit worn by women of north India and Pakistan and their diaspora counterparts. The Punjabi suit has traversed generations of taunts and labelling to resurface as modified version when Lady Diana is shown as wearing one and the top brands selling the suits. The different interpretations of the suit created by second generation Bubby Mahil and other hybrid designers tend to transcend the ethnic boundaries to become part of the British mainstream. Geeta Sarin, a pioneering fashion entrepreneur, who opened a boutique in

London, has developed an alternative market, namely the first Asian mail-order catalogues of ready-made Indian clothes, fusion clothing and innovative mix of fabrics, also hybridized cuts are her interventions. Many women entrepreneurs in the US as well as ones like Bubby and Damini in UK tend to send the sketch of the dress through internet, frequent phone calls and visits to India where the customized outfit is made and then sent back through courier within a month which is sold at exorbitant rates. Bhachu (ibid., p. 57) explains, 'With all this riveting interaction and dialogue of discussing and drawing outfit, they come up with a new design, dialogically produced'. There are wholesalers of suits like Komal Singh and Mala Rastogi based in South Hall, London, who import readymade suits at a wholesale level from India and sell locally among their own communities. The Punjabi community has grown much in size over the time and has its ethnic needs, particularly women. A number of enterprising women of the community have been fulfilling their need for fashion clothing, art clothes and artefacts in addition to accessories, pashmina stoles, and jewellery through transnational consumption narratives.

Alongside these detailed studies, we have cases of young immigrant entrepreneurs, who became millionaires, and are living in different countries of the world. Ravi Gehlot, at the age of 23 years, was one of the UK's youngest self-made millionaires. He is of the view, 'It is not difficult to make a million pounds out of a business, as long as you are dedicated and persistent, it's very achievable' (BBC NEWS/Business/young Asians playing and working Hard, p. 1). Another is Dheeraj Pandey who arrived in America from Bihar in 1997 to pursue a PhD in computer science at the University of Texas. In his second year, Pandey dropped out to become an engineer instead. After nine years in Silicon Valley, including nearly five at Oracle – and surviving the bursting of the tech bubble in 2000 – Pandey decided to venture into his own business. With his green card and no more than $1,00,000 in savings, Pandey started Nutanix in San Jose in 2009, with a goal to make IT infrastructure simple and elegant, folds computing, storage, and virtualization resources. He has more than 2,000 employees in 40 countries.

Spinder Dhaliwal, on the basis of her study, informed in an interview (Asian Network Report, 2006) how the attitudes of today's young business entrepreneurs differ from the first generation immigrant business people from South Asia. Young people are more willing to make contacts outside the community and unlike their parents, they are more likely to trust non-family and friends for advice and financial backing. Their work ethic is different too. Young people want to work smart rather than do hard work. The first generation looked at enterprise as a survival strategy. They never spent their money recklessly. They pooled money from the community to start their businesses.

A number of studies reveal that entrepreneurship and business ownership are important aspects of the economic contribution of immigrants. Immigrants are usually found to have higher business ownership rates than the native born population. Canadian research shows that economic class immigrants are more likely to own technology based companies than Canadian born business owners, possibly because they are considerably more likely to have a science, technology, engineering or mathematics (STEM) University degree (Picot and Ostrovsky, 2017).

Fairlie et al. (2010) examine the performance of Indian entrepreneurs and cause of their success in the US, Canada and UK. As per 2000 Census, more than one million immigrants from India reside in the United States. Some 10.9 per cent of the Indian immigrant workforce owns a business in the US who are also the highest earning entrepreneurs from any country in Asia. In UK, the Indian entrepreneurs are highly concentrated in wholesale and retail trade with 41.9 per cent in this industry. Indian firms are also more concentrated in transport, storage and communication, health and social work than the national average. In Canada 48.4 per cent of Indian entrepreneurs hire employees.

To sum up the discussion, it may be argued that immigrant entrepreneurs play a vital role in disseminating the ideas, products and processes that capitalist societies need to advance. Ensign and Robinson (2011, p. 48) emphasize that 'Immigrant enterprises can only succeed by entering mainstream markets catering to mainstream customer bases it is notable that often the market itself begins to assimilate immigrant introduced innovations. Superior products and processes gain acceptance by the dominant community and are then labelled as belonging to 'us' and are no longer foreign by definition'.

Using citation and co-citation data from Social Sciences Citation Index between 1965 and 2008, Ma, Wang and Lee (2012, pp. 192–193) investigated international ethnic entrepreneurship research and identified the invisible network of knowledge production in ethnic entrepreneurship field. The co-citation analysis reveals and I quote thus:

The field was organized around five different research clusters in 1965–1998, namely, ethnic-immigrant enclaves, ethnic minority, immigrant entrepreneurship, immigrant adjustment and ethnic resources; and around another five different research themes in 1999–2003, namely, ethnic-immigrant enclaves, ethnic-minority business, constraints for ethnic enterprise, social embeddedness and ethnic entrepreneurs; and concentrated on four core research themes in 2004–2008, namely, ethnic-immigrant enclaves, growth of ethnic enterprises, immigrant self-employment and ethnic networks. The changing pattern of international ethnic entrepreneurship studies showed that researchers in this field had shifted their foci from exploring ethnic-immigrant enclaves to studying immigrant business and self-employment as well as social embeddedness in ethnic business and ethnic networks over the past four decades. Future research can be derived from this invisible knowledge network to focus on such topics as ethnic resources, ethnic enclaves, social embeddedness and transnational entrepreneurship activities.

Their advice to policy makers is that immigrants should seriously be taken into account as an important target group for the promotion of entrepreneurship. Schlosser (2012) has highlighted the challenges to access resources experienced by immigrant entrepreneurs and has developed mentoring programmes for nascent entrepreneurs to resolve the challenges which may be utilized by the policy makers.

Suggested Readings

Alejandro, Portes (ed.) (1995). *The Economic Sociology of Immigration: Essays on Networks, Ethnicity, and Entrepreneurship*. New York: Russell Sage Foundation.

Bal, Gurpreet (2006). Entrepreneurship among Diasporic communities: A comparative examination of Patidars of Gujarat and Jats of Punjab. *The Journal of Entrepreneurship*, 15(2), 181–203.

Chithelen, I. and Souza, Val. (2005). Public capital markets and new generation of entrepreneurs: success of Indians in the US and potential in India. *Economic & Political Weekly*, XL(40), 4373–4377.

Fairlie, R.W., Krashinsky, H., Zissimopoulos and Kumar, K.B. (2009). Indian entrepreneurial success in the United States, Canada and United Kingdom, RAND labour and Population Working paper series.

Rai, Rajesh (2007). Business and Entrepreneurship. In B.V. Lal, Peter Reeves and Rajesh Rajesh, *The Encyclopaedia of the Indian Diaspora* (pp. 77–79). New Delhi: Oxford University Press.

Rutten, M. (2001). Family enterprises and business partnership: Rural entrepreneurs in India, Malaysia, and Indonesia. *The Journal of Entrepreneurship*, 10(2), 165–89.

Tambs-Lyche, H. (1980). *London Patidars: A Case Study in Urban Ethnicity*. London: Routledge & Kegan Paul.

Varma, Roli and Varma, Daya R. (2009). The making of Indian immigrant entrepreneurs in the US. *Economic & Political Weekly*, XLIV(3), 64–69.

Verma, Archana B. (2002). *The Making of Little Punjab in Canada*. New Delhi: Sage Publications.

Section V

Role of State in Entrepreneurship Development

12

Government Initiatives for Entrepreneurship Development

The postcolonial India faced the mammoth challenges of poverty, unemployment and regional disparities to handle which it brought in the interventionist strategy in a big way. To boost the economic growth in the country, it was relevant for the state machinery to intervene decisively. The first Prime Minister of India, Jawaharlal Nehru, also underlined that it was the duty of the state to bring about equality of opportunity and diminish the tremendous differences which exist between various groups. In doing so the state naturally had the tendency to interfere, which it had to. To make India economically self-reliant the government of independent India decided to have planned growth with a socialistic perspective in the light of which the Five-Year Plans were launched in 1951. In every Five-Year Plan, the policies and programmes were laid down for industrial development, primarily for the promotion of small-scale industry to generate employment in the early phases of plans. The main objective of the third Five-Year Plan was to improve the productivity by improving the skills, supplying technical advice, better equipment, credit facilities to promote growth of industry by organizing the artisans and craftsmen. By the fourth Five-Year Plan the emphasis on self-reliance paved the way for entrepreneurship development. Ever increasing rate of unemployment even after almost two decades since Independence of the country made the Government of India take initiatives to develop entrepreneurship through planned efforts. The primary objective was that entrepreneurs could be created through training, which was contrary to the view hitherto held that entrepreneurs are born in certain families and communities. The Government of India intervened to inculcate entrepreneurial attributes through planned programmes for entrepreneurship development in India. In 1962, the Small Industry Extension and Training Institute (SIET) was established in Hyderabad, which with the support from Harvard University's Professor David C. McClelland conducted training and research programmes for five years in Rajamundi, Kakinanda and Vellur of Andhra Pradesh and Tamil Nadu. These experiments proved that through training and education the need for achievement (n/ach) as a trait of an entrepreneur could be developed. The success of these experiments further strengthened the emphasis on developing entrepreneurship through training known as entrepreneurship development programmes (henceforth, EDP). To carry out the training at regional levels, technical consultancy organizations (TCOs) started organizing EDPs. TCOs, such as North India Industrial and Technical Consultancy Organization (NITCON), North Eastern Industrial and Technical Consultancy Organization (NEITCO), were established.

The discussion on government initiatives in this chapter has been divided under three parts. Part I traces the initial efforts of the government soon after India achieved independence, i.e. 1960s to 1990. In other words, these initiatives continued till the country opted for liberalization of the economy. Part II deals with the nature and extent of entrepreneurship from July 1991 to 2014 in the light of the liberalization policy adopted by the Government of India and the impact of the policy on different dimensions of the economy. Part III takes note of the policies and programmes launched by the present government since 2014 and assessment of the present scenario of entrepreneurship development.

Creating Entrepreneurs through Training and Education

I must begin the discussion from the pioneering initiatives taken by the Gujarat Industrial Investment Corporation in late-1960s in Gujarat in coordination with some state agencies and a three-months-long EDP was launched as a result. It was meant for new and selected entrepreneurs who had latent entrepreneurial potential and the purpose was to train them to manifest their capabilities. The emphasis was on setting up a small venture, managing it and making it a success by way of earning profits. The 1970s witnessed the emergence of varieties of strategies and models of developing entrepreneurship. Various training programmes were designed for the development of entrepreneurship in the light of the model based on need for achievement and the experiments carried out by McClelland where the focus was to increase the level of need for achievement. In addition, the model based on management skills, where the emphasis was laid on learning the essentials of business management, was used. The programmes were designed to equip persons to set up the unit and manage it. It also helped them to prepare projects and give them information about institutional infrastructure available. Most of the training programmes conducted by various organizations followed this model with some inputs of achievement motivation. Akhouri (1988, p. 6) shed light on these efforts in the following manner:

> Two major factors have played significant role in developing entrepreneurship. One is the development of human factor – the entrepreneur himself, another major factor is the development of environment where entrepreneurial activities can flourish and grow. The human factor refers to the attitude, desire and motivation of individual, his capability to perceive, the environment change and opportunities as well as his ability to solve problem which entrepreneur is likely to face. The training is effective in developing all these aspects of human factor, provided it is planned well with balanced emphasis on all aspects.

Yet another model, namely Entrepreneurial Index proposed by Nadkarni and his associates, who have been actively engaged in designing and organizing programmes for the development of entrepreneurship, was also used. Entrepreneurial Index model emphasizes the development of self as well as development of abilities necessary for enterprise building. The mixed design model of the National Institute of Motivational and Institutional Development and its modifications were used by technical consultancy organizations. Here one needs a team of trainers to manage the training activity. Training is responsible for generating awareness, developing attributes and providing the necessary linkages (Krishna, 2003). The entrepreneurship development programmes were largely knowledge dominated, as these were largely imparting knowledge about how to prepare the proposal, manage it and market it, etc. A large number of institutions and organizations were engaged in a variety of training and research activities for entrepreneurship development.

In 1979, the Centre for Entrepreneurship Development in Ahmedabad was established and it was upgraded to the Entrepreneurship Development Institute of India in 1983. It was entrusted with the task of spreading and institutionalizing the entrepreneurship development activities in the country. The following diagram shows the institutions, organizations which got involved in Entrepreneurship Development in India in 1980 till the new economic policy was introduced. There were nearly 686 organizations participating in the development of entrepreneurship in India towards the end of 1980s. All India Financial Institutes, namely IDBI (Industrial Development Bank of India), IFCI (Industrial Finance Corporation of India), ICICI (Industrial Credit and Investment Corporation of India) and SBI (State Bank of India) besides the Government of India's DST (Department of Science and Technology) and at state level, commercial banks were funding, supporting and organizing entrepreneurship development programmes. Awasthi and Sebastian (1996) inform that as per the IDBI information, 1,170 EDPs for various target groups, namely general, women, science and technology, and ex-servicemen have been sponsored by all India financial institutions between 1978–1988–89. During this period, 31,000 entrepreneurs were trained at the cost of 521.72 lakh.

It can be discerned from the diagram that six different Union Ministries at the national level in addition to voluntary organizations, seven state level departments and institutions were involved. Corporations, centres and agencies had percolated to the district level. This was the extent of efforts made by government directly and also through other voluntary organizations in the country. One may casually ask then why still the country is lagging behind in entrepreneurial development. It is relevant to mention that sixteen evaluation studies, as mentioned by Awasthi and Sebastian (ibid.), varied in the objectives, coverage and content have been carried out

Institutions/Organizations Involved in Entrepreneurship

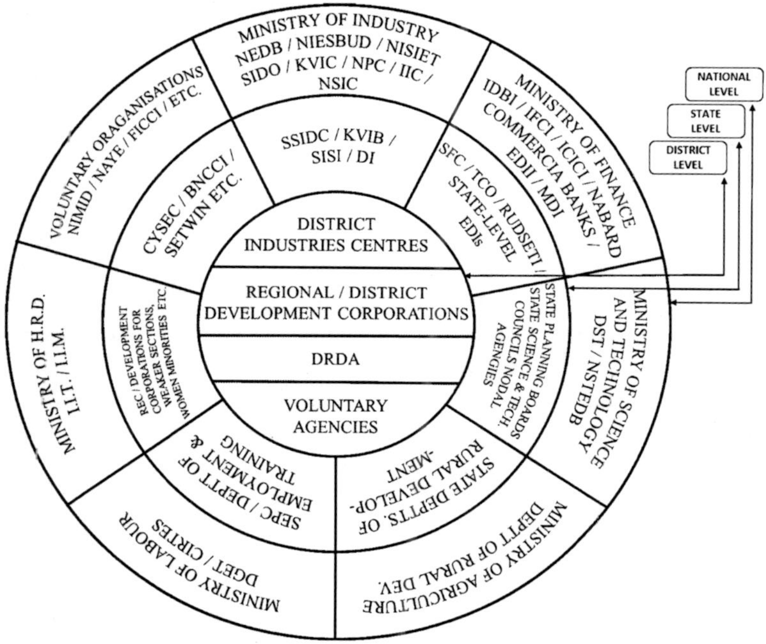

Source: M.M.P. Akhouri, Entrepreneurship Development, 2 April 1988, p. 6.

to assess the impact of these training programmes. EDP being dynamic activity, needs to be renewed and restructured to meet the changing needs of the potential entrepreneurs. The country, out of its scarce resources, has spent huge money on this initiative. Whether these programmes were cost effective and have they been able to meet their objectives, are some of the significant issues raised by Awasthi and Sebastian (ibid.) with regard to the impact of the EDPs. They carried out a comprehensive study at all the four levels to have an in-depth exploration of the EDPs. The data were collected from trainers, trainees and control group of non-trainees, support system and sponsors using two approaches: Enterprise Building Activity and Human Resource Development Strategy. The study brought out that the ideal age for becoming an entrepreneur is thirty plus irrespective of their education, but have some work experience with a middle class family background and have clarity of objectives. The persons with practical experience and knowledge of business manage the ventures better. Though there are inter-state and inter-organization variations in the performance of EDPs in the enterprise set-up rates, yet EDPs have diversified the base of entrepreneurship, as two-third of the trainees belong to non-business families and nearly 90 per cent joined EDPs at a pre-preparatory stage, that is, either they did not have any business idea or had a raw idea. The number of EDPs conducted in each state and number of EDP locations within each state indicate the regional spread of the programme over the time. A major portion of women trainees consisted of housewives and all those who could start their ventures were running them successfully. The study (ibid., p. 68) has also calculated that by spending ₹ 1 on training leads to the mobilization of ₹ 27.56 worth investment and ₹ 19.45 worth output in the initial year itself, for it helps in creating full time regular employment for approximately five persons per venture in addition to the trained entrepreneur at a cost of ₹ 1,795 per person employed. Thus, EDPs were found to be cost effective. Nearly 75 per cent of the total trainees felt that the EDPs have made a large to moderate impact on them in promoting their entrepreneurial career. The EDP as a developmental strategy has had shown 27 per cent success rate. It all depends upon whether you see the glass half full or half empty. A number of suggestions were also made for the improvement of the EDPs. For instance, the trainees must be selected having good knowledge of the subject and the use of appropriate methodology. The post-programme follow-up support must be given. The training in management skills also needs to be strengthened. Krishna (2003) argues that upgrading of the concepts is a necessary condition for increasing the effectiveness of training. The bureaucratic procedures in sanctioning loans, getting NOCs, shortage of raw material, delay in getting water and power connections, and discouraging attitude of the support system were identified as major hurdles. Chandra (1996), on the basis of a micro-level study of Karnataka state, argues that an entrepreneur's practical experience in or exposure to entrepreneurial activities is important for the success of small ventures.

Overall, the implementation of EDPs remained the major weakness of the strategy. To begin with, these training programmes were fully financed along with some stipend. Gradually, the subsidy was reduced and by mid-1990s a small amount of ₹ 500 (₹ 250/for SC/PH) as course fee was charged for one-month course. Usually, the advertisement was published in the newspapers and banners were put at strategic places to motivate the people to avail opportunity for self-employment. One might have come across such advertisements which read as 'that Small Industries Service Institute are organizing Product cum Process oriented EDP for women entrepreneurs specifically on hosiery and readymade garments industry'.

After adopting the Economic Liberalization Policy in 1991 by the Government of India, the entrepreneurship development programmes also underwent a qualitative change, though they continued to exist with the changed rules and regulations. The state sponsorship was reduced to the extent that even most of the financial institutions, and banks withdrew from it. At present, only small-scale industry department as per the needs and relevance for a particular state, arranges the training programmes. A study by Bodha (2017) of J&K state shows that in order to promote entrepreneurship amongst the people of Jammu & Kashmir, many state initiatives have been carried out through the Jammu & Kashmir Entrepreneurship Development Institute (JKEDI). The JKEDI conducts EDPs from time to time, but there has been a paradigm shift. The JKEDI began its regular activities in 2004 and it runs four projects, namely the seed capital fund scheme (most popular scheme), youth start-up loan scheme, National minorities development finance corporation (working for the benefit of minorities), and the Himayat (a skill training scheme for low income and less educated youth). The JKEDI runs programmes to create awareness about its activities. An aspiring entrepreneur submits his proposal, and if it is approved, loan is sanctioned by the J&K Bank which is the only debt syndicator bank under various schemes. The person before launching the venture undergoes the relevant training in capacity building imparted by the JKEDI. The study reveals that the assistance given by the JKEDI to the beneficiaries has become a primary source of motivation for them. However, to switch to entrepreneurship, (though the training modules suffers from a number of shortcomings, for instance), there is no adequate follow-up of the ventures and no assistance to find out the market. Overall, the major weakness of the EDPs in general has been the way training is imparted. Emphasis remained more on knowledge, rather it should have been less academic and more practical.

Economic Liberalization Policy

The persisting large-scale accumulated economic crisis led to the macro-economic imbalances of the Indian economy in terms of fiscal deficit, imbalance of payments and huge foreign debt. A gradual liberalization of the industrial policy had to be undertaken in July 1991 by the then Government of India. Already in the middle of the 1980s the savings and the affluence of the upper middle class in India had created favourable conditions for industrial investments on the one hand and for a consumerist boom for domestic industrial production on the other. Under the pressure of a consumer demand, new industrial entrants and the changing global trade regime and industries' manufacturing consumer durables rapidly increased their capacities owing to which many new products were introduced in the market. Even the old firms which did not produce goods of international quality for decades, marketed new improved products. In a way, India had started slowly opening up its markets. Maruti Udyog (A Government of India undertaking) had collaborated with Suzuki of Japan for manufacturing of cars with 51–49 per cent share in 1985 during the times of the Prime Minister, Rajiv Gandhi. Critics argued that the policy makers at that time set wrong priorities and it accelerated the economic crisis to a point of no return but to seek help from International Monetary Fund (IMF) under whose directions new economic policy had to be adopted.

What is the new economic policy? It is basically opening up of the Indian economy which earlier was closely guarded with restrictions of all sorts. The basic parameters were making the Indian economy a market economy where there is free competition, efficiency, and thus integration with the world economy. The shift from public enterprises to privatization required denationalization and deregulation. Denationalization involved changing the ownership of public sector assets to private sector. Deregulation is basically liberalization or opening up of the areas or sectors which were hitherto reserved exclusively for public sector, whereas globalization meant to bring more Foreign Direct Investment (FDI) into the industrial sector. For the purpose, the rules for Non-Resident Indians were changed. The restrictions imposed earlier were removed and the logic for this move depended upon three reasons: (a) FDI would bring attendant advantages of technology transfer, marketing expertise and introduction of modern managerial techniques. (b) FDI would bring in new possibilities for promotion of exports. (c) FDI would bring substantial investments. Thus, the liberalization policy had covered a wide spectrum of policies including fiscal, industrial, trade and labour policies. In a nutshell, we can say that economic liberalization policy was aimed at globalizing the Indian economy; and the Dunkel draft dealt with the conditions under which such globalization could take place. India approved this trade treaty and General Agreement on Tariffs and Trade (GATT) was signed in April 1994. All member countries of GATT were required to first replace all types of non-tariff barriers with tariff and second to reduce the levels of tariff under a time-bound programme. The rules regarding domestic support and also for export competition were framed which were to be fully implemented within ten years (Judge and Bal, 1996).

With the implementation of the new economic policy there was lot of hue and cry in different departments and organizations of India fearing deadly consequences. Nevertheless, policies never have had a uniform impact. Different people are affected differently. In other words, this was a structural adjustment programme and it was very likely to entail sacrifices by all sections of the society. Though losses of the short term could be the gains of the longer period, but it was not likely that the looser would be the gainers. A number of studies were published calculating the impact of the economic policy which argued that the poor working class, women and rural people would suffer the major brunt of the new policy. The basis of the arguments were that the expenditure on poverty alleviation programmes, particularly for rural poor and women, would be curtailed and also the subsidies provided on various goods and services were to be withdrawn in a phased manner. Thus, it directly affected the programmes like, EDPs, and the credit squeeze affected adversely the small-scale industries and the labour.

With the liberalization of the economy many new entrepreneurs from within and outside the country entered into the Indian business. Foreign direct investments increased in the very first year of the introduction of the new policy to 569 from 151 the previous year. Investments also increased from 160 crore in 1990–91 to 1950 crore in 1991–92 and 7,220 crore in 1992–93 where up to 51 per cent of the total equity was allowed without any prior permission (Davala, 1994.). Under the new industrial policy some of the major industries in the public sector were deregulated, thus reducing the number of reserved industries to eight from seventeen earlier with the hope that deregulation would increase competition and hence there would occur improvement in production, quality of production and efficiency. The monopoly restriction on trade practices (MRTP) Act was repealed with the hope that foreign collaborations and privatization would prevent concentration of economic power with big business houses. Most of the deregulated industries were delicensed and opened up for FDI. At the same time it gave impetus to exports of certain products like textile, leather and precious stones, etc.

Soon after the pressure from international companies began to mount on the Government of India to open up the service sector as well. Liberalization of trade in services began and General Agreement on Trade and Services (GATS) came into effect in 1995 with a set of rules and disciplines to promote orderly and transparent trade and investment liberalization in services. To begin with, it was open only in cash-and-carry wholesale formats with 100 FDI. Sharma (2015) informs that FDI in retail trade may create job losses and displacement of traditional supply chain due to which the Indian government opened the retail hesitantly. Until 2011, the Indian government denied Foreign Direct Investment (FDI) in multi-brand retail, forbidding foreign groups from any ownership stake in supermarkets, convenience stores or other retail outlets. Even single-brand retail was limited to 51 per cent shareholding and subjected to a bureaucratic processing. In September 2012, the Government of India unveiled a Foreign Direct Investment Policy allowing foreign retailers to own up to 51 per cent in multi-brand retail and 100 per cent in single brand retail. With the opening of the retail businesses a large number of global multinationals extended their retail activities in India though quite a number of them were already running businesses in partnership with prominent business houses of India. These retailers entered into a variety of formats ranging from mono/exclusive branded retail shops to multi-brand retail shops and to convergence retail outlets.

With the opening of the service sector, particularly the retail formats, there were lot of anticipations with regard to its negative impact on the traditional traders both in rural and urban areas, though quite a few studies also depicted its brighter side as well. The contribution of retail trading to Gross Domestic Product (GDP), by which we mean the total value of all the services and goods that are manufactured within the territory of the nation during the specified period of time, of the country steadily increased from 8 per cent in 2006–07 to 26.60 per cent in 2011–12. Since an exhaustive discussion on the social consequences of economic liberalization policy would be made in the next chapter on globalization and entrepreneurship, we may just continue with the growth of the GDP. Within less than a decade, the GDP of India started growing at a higher rate. In 2000, it was 3.8 per cent, in 2003 it was 7.86 per cent, in 2004 and 2005 it remained almost the same at 7.92 per cent, but in 2006 it was 8.06, and then in 2007 it slightly reduced to 7.66. After its steep fall in 2008, it again rose to 7.86 in 2009 which rose to its all-time high in 2010 that is, 8.49 per cent. After a slight downward leap in 2011 and 2012, India started recovery in 2013–14 when the GDP growth rate accelerated to 6.4 per cent from the previous year's 5.5 per cent. The contribution of manufacturing to GDP steadily increased from 15.9 per cent in 1999–00 to 24.3 per cent in 2011–12. The service sector also started growing gradually during these years. In 2021 the service sector accounted for 53.89 per cent of Indian GVA (Gross value added) of 179.15 lakh crore. The industry sector lags behind it with 25.92 per cent contribution and the agriculture sector is at the third place with 20.19 per cent contribution. Sharma (2015, p. 231) on the basis of an empirical study concludes that 'retail globalization policy is going to radically alter social relations, special expression, traditional markets, lifestyles and consumption patterns of people and employment trend … . Hence, a balanced regulatory framework and competition policy is a must for traditional formats and the modern formats to co-exist'.

Decade of Innovations, Century of Entrepreneurs

The economic self-sufficiency of families, groups and communities is essential condition for the economic development of the country for which innovations are an indispensable condition. Innovations in the areas of business, trade and entrepreneurship are always being viewed as significant strategy for all-inclusive growth of the country. India being a young country has more than 62 per cent of its population in the age group of 15–59 years and more than 54 per cent of its total population below 25 years of age. Such a demographic feature provides ample opportunities for entrepreneurial activities. Taking innovations as the only way out of the persisting issues of socio-economic inequalities, the President of India declared 2010–20 as the 'Decade of Innovations', with the idea to create an indigenous model of development suited to Indian issues and challenges. Several converging factors suggest that 21st century will be century of entrepreneurs. Entrepreneurs innovate and can act as agents of change.

In 2014, Narendra Modi took over the reins from a technocratic Prime Minister Manmohan Singh. Narendra Modi had remained Chief Minister of Gujarat state for two terms and that state was adjudged as the best performing state attaining the first rank in 2015, third in 2016 in terms of ease of doing business state ranking. When he took over as the Prime Minister, he brought the model of Gujarat for the whole country. He started a number of programmes and took many initiatives to start and sustain the businesses. The Ministry of Skill Development and Entrepreneurship was set up in November 2014. Soon 'Make in India' and 'Skill India' was set up in 2014. Thereafter, 'Startup India', 'Stand up India' schemes were launched on 16 January 2016. Entrepreneurial education, training and development were emphasized through the Startup India Action Plan, particularly aiming to promote entrepreneurship among educated youth including agriculture, manufacturing, social sector, health care, education, etc. in tier 2 and tier 3 cities and rural areas. Startup means an entity in India not prior to five years with annual turnover not exceeding ₹ 25 crore in any preceding financial year, working towards innovation, development, deployment or commercialization of new products, processes or services driven by technology or intellectual property. The compliance was made possible through self-certification, and making registration process easy and timely. Norms were further relaxed for public procurement for startups. In order to catalyse entrepreneurship, diverse initiatives, such as credit guarantee fund, tax exemption for first three years, launch of Atal Innovation Mission, and building innovation centres at national institutes like IITs, NIT, IIMs, were undertaken. Under the Startup India plan, startups were to be promoted in the biotechnology sector to facilitate bio-entrepreneurs, besides supporting the creation of world class incubators.

While addressing at the Startup India Innovation week on 16 January 2022, the Prime Minister announced that January 16 would be celebrated as National Startup Day (*The Tribune*, 16 January 2022, p. 16) in order to spread the culture of startups in every nook and corner of the country. He said 'Today there is at least one startup in 625 districts of the country. Of them, half are in tier 2 and 3 cities where youth from poor and ordinary families are engaged in developing startups, As a result lakhs of people are getting employment'. He said that as against 4,000 patents registered in 2013–14, in 2020–21 the comparative figures was 28,000. To have a cursory view of the impact of the above mentioned plan, it is found that the Startup India scheme was launched in Punjab in 2016, but only 408 startups were set up in the entire state till 2021 which is less than 1 per cent of the national average, where 46,042 startups were established. For instance, Amritsar district, a boarder district has so far recorded only 21 startup entries under the flagship of this scheme (Bagga, *Amritsar Tribune*, 17 January 2022, p. 1.). It may be the result of Punjab state lagging behind in innovations or it may be the result of half-hearted implementation of the programme.

India jumped 17 positions in the World Bank's Ease of Doing Business Index in 2020 and was ranked 63, whereas in 2019, it ranked 77 out of 190 countries. It was a development that could help the country attract more foreign investments. It was ranked 100 in 2018, making a leap of 30 places from its 130 placement in the world ranking in 2017. India has improved its rank by 53 positions in the last two years and 65 positions in the last four years. The Doing Business assessment provides a measure of business regulations and their enforcement across 190 economies on ten parameters affecting a business through its life cycle. India has improved its rank in six out of ten indicators.[1] The improvements were registered in the indicators related to getting electricity, registration of property and trading across borders, and enforcing contracts. In grant of construction permits, India's rank improved from 181 in 2017 to 52 in 2018, an improvement of 129 ranks in a single year. In 'Trading across Borders', India's rank improved by 66 positions moving from 146 in 2017 to 80 in 2018. It is relevant to mention that New Zealand topped the list of 190 countries in ease of doing business, followed by Singapore, Denmark, and Hong Kong.

The acceleration continued through 2014–15 and 2015–16 with growth rates of 7.5 per cent and 8.0 per cent respectively. However, in November 2016, due to demonetization and soon after the implementation of Goods and Services Tax (GST), though the biggest reform in the history of indirect taxes in India, the growth process of Indian economy got disrupted and it went down from 7.1 per cent in 2016–17 to 6.6 per cent in 2017–18. Later in the year 2019, Covid-19 pandemic led the Indian economy to a nose dive which at present seems to be extremely difficult to turn around unless the country has a very brilliant public policy design. As the state has gradually withdrawn itself from welfarism and public sector is slowly being handed over to a few big capitalists, the small and medium entrepreneurs have been left to fend for themselves in the sea of sharks.

Note

1. These parameters include ease of starting a business, construction permits, getting electricity, registration of property, getting credit, promoting minority investor, paying taxes, trade across borders, enforcing contracts and resolving insolvency.

Suggested Readings

Awasthi, Dinesh N. and Sebastian, Jose (1996). *Evaluation of Entrepreneurship Development Programmes*. New Delhi: Sage Publications.

Bodha, Irm Jalali (2017). *Entrepreneurship and Development: Examining State Initiatives in Jammu & Kashmir*. PhD thesis, Guru Nanak Dev University, Amritsar

Judge, P.S. and Bal, Gurpreet (1996). *Strategies of Social Change in India*. New Delhi: MD Publications Pvt. Ltd.

Krishna, K.V.S.M. (2003). Bridging the Gap: Conceptual paradigms and training for entrepreneurship development. *The Journal of Entrepreneurship*, 12(1), 92–116.

Sharma, Rachana (2015). *Shops and the Malls: A Sociological Exploration of Indian Retail Business*. Delhi: Kalpaz Publications.

13

Globalization and Entrepreneurship

I begin this chapter with the following quote from Morris, Kuratko and Covin, (2008: 15):

> We live in a time of a global entrepreneurial revolution. In virtually every nation, every industry and every market, entrepreneurs are challenging existing assumptions and creating value in novel ways. It is not that venture start-ups are at all-time high. The rate of new product and service introduction is at record levels in most industries. The same can be said for patents issued and new products and processes licensed. The development, application, and enhancement of new technologies are occurring at a breathtaking pace. New forms of business organization and business relationships are appearing almost daily. Entrepreneurial thinking and acting is changing the way business is conducted at every level. It does not matter where you live/placed and what you do-entrepreneurship is redefining what you make, how you make it, where you sell it, and how you distribute it.

The above quote clearly depicts that the process of globalization has actually revolutionized the entrepreneurial ecosystem. As the number of new ventures, products, technologies, and patents literally explode worldwide, established companies are faced with a fundamental choice. They can either become victims of this revolution as a result of aggressive and upstart firms moving quickly by undermining their positions in the existing markets and also by creating whole new markets, or they can join the revolution. Companies cannot be static, for they must continually adjust, adapt, and redefine themselves. This is the fundamental principal of free market economy. However, in this entrepreneurial age, the rate at which companies must transform themselves is accelerating. Many of the conventional rules of business no longer apply. Fundamental assumptions about employees, products, control of resources, technologies, and markets have been challenged and in some cases discarded altogether (ibid.).

Castells (1996), a Spanish sociologist has argued that ITC (information, technology, communication) is leading to the formation of a global network society in which organizational and national borders dissolve. Thus, globalization is a process through which the people across physical boundaries simultaneously experience certain forms of culture, information, entertainment, and market. The simultaneity of the market experiences is fundamental in the context of entrepreneurship, as there is an increased international flow of capital, goods, services, people, and information. India set the process of globalization due to new economic policy which was adopted in 1991. The policy laid down that the Foreign Direct Investment (henceforth FDI) in industrial sector would attract investors for investments with offers of low taxes on businesses and presence of labour that is highly qualified, skilled, compliant and cheap. Rules for NRI investments also changed, as earlier imposed restrictions were removed. Assuming that there would be promotion of exports with FDI, it was understood that it would bring advantages of technology transfer, marketing expertise and introduction of modern managerial techniques. Globalization set in the growth of transnational corporations that can base certain operations in countries where labour is the cheapest and take profits where taxes are the lowest. India's concern is even if they take back their profits, but employment would be generated. The Dunkel draft laid down the conditions under which trade would take place. With the change in various rules and regulations under GATT (April 1994) and GATS (January 1995) of trade and business, there is an impact of globalization on business entrepreneurship, both wholesale and retail, trade in the traditional set-up like shops, and industrial entrepreneurship.

India emerged as a favourite destination for business because of the ever growing affluent middle class, high consumer population, vibrant stock model, stable democracy and world's largest young workforce base, as 40 per cent of its population is under the age of 35 years. Over the next two decades since the adoption of liberalization policy of Indian economy in 1991, a number of conditions with regard to prior approvals, NOCs, norms for overseas investment in production and development were liberalized. Thus, the FDI policy was gradually liberalized to boost inflows. With globalization, marketization and privatization, a new entrepreneurial ecosystem started emerging in India. As a result, the lives of entrepreneurs, their entrepreneurship on the one hand and consumption pattern of the people of India on the other have undergone considerable change. India in 2020 had a 21.6 trillion rupees consumer market. The present chapter is in continuation of the previous chapter and it primarily aims at examining the new issues and challenges which have emerged as a result of globalization for entrepreneurship development in India.

New Entrepreneurial Culture

With the onset of globalization, a new era of entrepreneurship has been ushered in. New entrepreneurs from within and outside the country started entering the arena. Following the terms and conditions of GATT, there was a commitment to withdraw all subsidies, special concession and protection to small enterprises from internal competition of medium and large industry and market protection to large enterprises in a phased manner which has shaken the Indian entrepreneurship from its very roots. Fearing a fierce competition, soon a new trend of closing down or dying out or giving up of the enterprises began. At the same time, some entrepreneurs using their long industrial and entrepreneurial experiences found out new strategies for survival and growth through mergers, collaborations and partnerships to face the competition from within and outside.

One aspect of globalization has been the growth of transnational corporations that can base certain operations in countries wherever they could get cheap labour, low taxes, and more profits. Multinational Corporations (MNCs) could enter the Indian economy in different formats which are as follows:

1. Through franchise, which is a process by which MNC gives the brand name to the entrepreneur in host country against

loyalty. For example, Subway, McDonald and Pizza Hut swept away the Indian market within no time.

2. Through partnerships and joint ventures, which means by collaborating with the company in the host country by putting some share which is less than 50 per cent. For instance, Suzuki ventured with 49 per cent share with Maruti Udyog.
3. The MNCs create the whole set-up of the enterprise for the entrepreneur in the host country and with the start of business hand over the business key to the host to conduct it. Most of the Highway projects fall in this category.
4. Indian entrepreneur can have an agency or be a distributor of an MNC in the country.
5. MNC can directly own and operate the outlet. That is with 100 per cent FDI engagement the example of which is IKEA, a Swedish furniture manufacturer which opened its first store in Hyderabad.

The Multinational Corporations not only posed the major challenge in the bigger segment but also the medium and small enterprises which were threatened by their invasion with capital. While the Hyundai, Honda, Ford, LG and Samsung vigorously introduced new marketing strategies in India, the Cartoon network, National Geographic, Discovery, BBC World, and MTV provided new ways of giving information and entertainment to the people of India. Pepsi and Coca Cola entered India and captured even the rural market to the extent that Ramesh Chohan gave up the fight and sold his Thums Up to Coca Cola. Nevertheless, Indian Tupperware, Mittal Steels, Tata Motors, Reliance and others also set in the same process of entries, takeovers, and buying in the USA, UK, Europe, and other developed countries of the world. In 2016, there were over 800 Indian companies in the UK. Indian market became so volatile within its two decades of globalization that many concerns could not survive in this turmoil, and some car companies, such as Cielo, Peugeot left India.

As explained in the earlier chapters, Indian entrepreneurial movement has moved from trade to moneylending to manufacturing in the case of Marwaris and from agriculture to trade to manufacturing was the path for Gujaratis. But with globalization, the technical skills, commercial knowledge, management skills began to dominate. A new breed of entrepreneurs has emerged, who are educated, technocrats, and professionals. They are setting up micro, small and medium enterprises. In a way, the very profile of entrepreneurs who earlier were from business castes, artisans, and craftsmen have been undergoing change. The predominance of entrepreneurs from traditional business communities has started waning. This new generation of entrepreneurs belongs to diverse caste groups, regional background, young, educated and are professionals. The earlier concentration of industry has also started dispersing. New centres of manufacturing and services have emerged. Now Bangalore is popularly known as Silicon Valley of India and has emerged as Information and Technology hub. It is getting lots of work on outsourcing from countries like America where a large chunk of educated IT professionals are employed; similarly, Hyderabad, Chennai and Pune have emerged as new centres of entrepreneurial activities.

Automatic transition from grandfather to father, father to son of businesses became very hard to sustain. In the emerging entrepreneurial ecosystem in India, the traditional business knowledge, styles, and structure would not work. Now new products, new technology, new capital sources and new markets require new knowledge, new technical skills and different management skills. The son has to learn new soft skills where the arrogance of the families will not work. Before the liberalization of the Indian economy, a few business families were dominating and the success in business, assured profits, brand name and fame made them sluggish or less innovative. Patel (2007) labels it as prosperity crisis due to complacency of many owner-entrepreneurs of new small-scale business units. They attain their affluence after a hard uphill struggle and then they are eager to enjoy their new-found wealth.

In the emerging scenario, succession has to be planned by selecting and grooming a successor and building a team of competent persons has turned out to be a serious concern. The management-succession crisis (ibid., 2007) may descend on the firm when the founder-owner dies, remains ill for long time or get incapacitated. In India, we have a number of illustrations like Ranbaxy, where the sudden death of the family monarch led to the crisis of leadership. Delegation of power to young members led to serious crisis in such cases. The monopolies, overconfidence, over ambitious expansions, and success become major causes of downfall.

The new rules of international trade, patent registration, and highly competitive markets have created what Morris, Kuratko and Covin (2008: 16) called the global environment, which is characterized by real time communication, production and distribution virtually anywhere in the world having more sophisticated suppliers, customers and competitors located virtually anywhere in the world with competitive advantage through global outsourcing and international strategic alliances in entrepreneurship.

The Foreign Direct Investments invited the Non-Resident Indians to return to India and invest in business. To begin with, prominent NRIs like Lord Swaraj Paul and Vithalbhai showed a great interest by submitting proposals to set up refineries from their own resources in India. But soon the uncertain policy environment and lengthy bureaucratic procedures to do business in India discouraged them. During the first two years, there was a rapid growth of foreign direct investment in India. The number of proposals cleared had gone up from 151 during the year preceding the announcement of the new policy to 569 during the first year and to 726 in the second year. Deregulation of industries increased competition and to combat competition, companies had to be efficient and innovative. The repealing of certain provisions of the MRTP (monopoly restrictions on trade practices) Act, which deals with the growth of large business houses, was supposed to prevent concentration of economic power by keeping a check on the relative growth of MRTP practices. This was done through foreign collaborations and privatization. The new industrial policy had simplified various regulations by publishing a list of 34 broad industrial groups covering over 160 industries where FDI upto 51 per cent of the total equity was allowed without any prior permission.

India emerged as a knowledge economy where there is growth of ICT, IT and service sector. The developed countries depended upon outsourcing to India. India also became a major source of suppliers of technical professionals. Entrepreneurship has successfully emerged in IT and service sectors as a result of which GDP started growing steadily, and number of billionaires have gone up by ten times, but the number of poor also has increased tremendously. In addition, the gap between the economic and the social growth started widening. The social sector, particularly health and education, started getting marginalized for the common people. Highways, infrastructural development helped the entrepreneurs to enter the market, but there is no focus on the development of city lanes.

The process of globalization has also made MSMEs more prominent, though the big have become bigger and many small units have been reduced to micro-level catering to the local markets and low cost needs of the people. Small-scale industries and small entrepreneurs faced credit squeeze due to withdrawal of subsidies and they could not raise equity in capital market. Their social capital became a way to cooperate, trust and coordinate their activities with others in the highly competitive market to survive. Even traditional business castes and communities depended upon family, kinship and caste and other primordial ties for sustenance (Bal, 1996).

Traditional industries like food and textile have deteriorated. The share of chemicals, machinery, and electrical has increased. Indian engineering grew at a faster rate. Now more and more capital intensive techniques are used in Indian manufacturing owing to which employment generating capacity has come down. There is an increase in production, employment in small-scale sector and export of small industrial products which does not fetch much of a foreign currency. The policy had far reaching implications for labour and trade unions. The working class has been robbed of their bargaining power due to shift in management strategies, such as employing casual contractual labour, job insecurity and getting bulk of their production done through ancillary units. Management techniques have changed. Now there is a demand for MBAs, intrapreneurs,[1] rather than pure managers. Process of industrial democracy and participatory management has been introduced by the Japanese MNCs, but the Koreans have implemented their own strategies of doing business. Now there is a clear-cut separation of management from ownership and decision-making ability has less significance, thus, the very concept of entrepreneur has undergone a change.

Women Entrepreneurship

Due to globalization, there is much scope for women entrepreneurship. On the basis of data from Global Entrepreneurship Monitor, Jorge (2017) informs that there is an emerging trend in the feminization of entrepreneurship in developing countries.

Though in India such a trend has not yet set in, yet more and more women are becoming entrepreneurs across caste, class, religion, region and age. Women, who are capable of striking balance between family and work, tend to venture into business while bringing up the children and taking care of the elderly. Majority of them gave up their lucrative jobs in corporate sector and entered into the world of business by operating from home. One of the entrepreneurs from Jammu, who earlier was a cabin crew member of an aviation company, left her job to start her unique startup wherein she trains people in etiquettes, body language and table manners. She has given online training to people in nearly 36 countries and also in-person training in schools, hotels and other institutions (Sharma, 2022). Catering to the emerging needs of the middle class in India, a gymnast started a gym after her marriage exclusively for women in a mid-sized city. Many other women have started small, online retail businesses like tour and travel business, boutiques, and beauty products, make-up studios, etc. Also, there are many organizations emerging which help these businesses in selling and promoting their products and services. Similarly, the ethnic products of artisans and tribal goods have a global market. A number of voluntary organizations, cooperatives and social enterprises, like Rangsutra, are working to help the rural artisans to find the global market for their products and also facilitating the sale of the items.

Environmental Concerns

Presently, environmental issues in entrepreneurship or for entrepreneurship have become significant. Therefore, we need more of ecopreneurs who take care of the environmental issues in production process and at the same time they also get a lot of new ideas and opportunities to manufacture and safeguard the environment as well. As a matter of fact, the entrepreneurs have more responsibility to control emissions to air, water and soil. There are new legislative rules and regulations. The concept of environmental social responsibility has been extended to all manufacturing companies under the Environment Protection Act, 1986. The concept of green entrepreneurship has been emerging in both rural and urban areas. Products also have to comply with a large number of international and national guidelines and standards to survive in the market. If it fails to comply, the product would be unsalable. At the same time the consumers have also become more conscious of environmental effects making an impact on their purchasing decisions. For instance, there is more emphasis on green products, organics, etc. against the use of polythene. Therefore, the issues of environment have given opportunities of new market and commercial benefits. Business activities to benefit from environmental revolution are in the areas of supply of goods, equipment and services aimed at solving the problems of pollution and, as a result, the trend towards adopting nano-technology and molecular manufacturing could be observed among entrepreneurs. So far, in India, we have failed to address the issue of garbage management, which gives a lot of opportunities to innovate the ways of its management. There have been many protests against the violation of all those activities which are negatively impacting the social and environmental aspects in our quest towards sustainable development of MNCs in India.

Business Ethics

Certain virtues and values constitute an entrepreneurial code for business ethics. A strong view of our traditional society was that business is amoral and ethics is something that has to be imported or grafted onto it. In other words, business is inherently immoral and the purpose of ethics is to restrain business. Hicks (2009: 56) comments that entrepreneurship is a particular vehicle for moral activity. Entrepreneurial success is not the whole of ethics, but it is a good start for business ethics. Ethical codes matter socially and moral codes are crucial personally. Hicks (ibid., p. 57) concludes, 'That the key thesis of an entrepreneurial code of ethics is that business ethics should focus on creativity, productivity, and trade. Creative, productive traders are highly-realized moral individuals. Thus, business ethics should take entrepreneurship seriously and foundationally as a moral phenomenon'. To elaborate the point further, we can take the examples of Ambani and Tata groups. When AirIndia was deregulated and sold to Tatas, nobody made a negative comment, rather people opined that now AirIndia is in the right hands. On the contrary, whenever the Ambani group expanded, the Modi government was targeted and accused of helping him. The personality traits and value producing activities of Mukesh Ambani, Adani, and Rattan Tata as entrepreneurs implicitly inform an ethic. Putting in the categories given by Hicks (ibid.), Ratan Tata is the prototypical entrepreneur who creates value, trades with others and lives his dream and largely remains invisible, whereas many top-most businessmen represent predatory ethic, and do not hesitate to harm others and use the proceeds to benefit themselves and become representatives of zero-sum gain. Gain-at-the-expense-of-others practices are widely condemned in business ethics.

Human Right Issues

After the advent of globalization, the concerns for human rights have come up in a big way. The UN Guiding Principles on Business and Human Rights (UNGPs) call upon businesses to respect human rights. Countries are obligated under international human rights law to protect human rights abuse within their territories, including business enterprises. It is the rights of the workers and the employees, which have turned out to be the major concerns. Whether they get safe working conditions and good quality of work life is an issue. The abuse of child labour is yet another serious concern. Whether the online business companies are protecting the people's right to privacy and upholding the data protection laws? It also includes the rights of the customers. Studies have found human rights positively associated with social entrepreneurship. Gender justice is still another issue to be addressed by an entrepreneur. Do the entrepreneurs provide for the safety and security of women employees? Are they getting equal wages for equal work? Do they follow the rules and regulations laid down by the ILO? The digital, artificial intelligence, automation and robotics raise serious concerns about the impact on human rights. Vulnerability to human right offences gets much serious in countries like India where poverty and unemployment are of great concerns.

New Trends

We are witnessing a plethora of new trends emerging in the globalized age. The rise of consumerism on the one side and multinational enterprises on the other end have created new concepts of market places, the multiplex shopping, trading malls, the entertainment cum business arcades, high definition convention centres, teleconferencing, on-line shopping while sitting at home, and e-commerce have given opportunity to new, self-financed, modest entrepreneurs. These modern marketing strategies have high degree of professionalism and the prices are fixed according to the demand of the products.

The demand for certain products have increased manifold. Global market increased exports from India to the tune of USD 528.45 billons during 2019–2020 in textiles, leather goods, jewellery, precious stones, health care and beauty products. During the last three decades, the Indian economy has been changing at a much faster rate than the earlier decades. Indian market is able to fulfil the needs across the classes of the people. With the opening up of new export opportunities interaction with foreign entrepreneurs has been mutually benefitting. The import of raw material has increased. A new breed of social entrepreneurs has emerged. India has also achieved excellence in corporate entrepreneurship.

The changing industrial environment of 1980s started the initiation of corporate culture in India. The instant success of Maruti Suzuki in late 1980s may be accounted for Japanese corporate culture. Japanese industrial corporations institutionalized elements of their culture, such as strong sense of solidarity and trust amongst its all stakeholders. Panini (1988) calls that a modern corporation is really a collective entrepreneurship venture. Big entrepreneurs are setting up large enterprises requiring huge capital and so they have started going public and are launching shares in the market with which the corporate culture has emerged in a big way in India. When Dhirubhai Ambani launched his first petro-chemical unit in late-1980s, it was noticed that it was all public money collected through the share market. Presently, it is the stock market – Bombay Stock Exchange (BSE) and National Stock Exchange (NSE) where NIFTY and SENSEX are stock market indices.[2] On the basis of the performance of the companies, the value of the shares is determined. To fulfil the needs of the capital for nascent entrepreneurs, venture capitalists are also playing a vital role in entrepreneurship development. Thus, the requirement of having money to start any business is being fulfilled by going public. Families need not raise capital.

In the age of globalization, 'soft skills competencies', that is combining knowledge, skill and right kind of attitude/motivation are determining the success and higher achievements of new entrepreneurs (Jain, 1998). An international study in three continents and three cultures, including India, has identified 13 soft skill competencies[3] the possession of which distinguishes high performers from low performers in business.

To sum up the discussion, it may be argued that the process of globalization in the context of entrepreneurship cannot be examined through SWOT (strengths, weakness, opportunity and threats), though it may be a useful exercise. It is very clear that in the globalized era, the attributes of an entrepreneur and the whole entrepreneurship ecosystem have undergone a transformation in which entrepreneurs require emotional intelligence, or in other words, social intelligence or social acumen to acquire business acumen. Goleman (2007) propagates social intelligence as the new science of human relationships in modern organizations. The development of non-cognitive capacities like empathy, concern and the impulse for compassion, that is social cognition, connects us with other people and are most required from new age entrepreneurs.

Notes

1. Who possess certain striking personal qualities – these attributes are adventurer, innovator, designer, leader, entrepreneur, change agent, and animateur (Sayeed and Gazdar, 2003).
2. The performance of the enterprises, that is top 50 in case of Nifty that are traded in National Stock Exchange (NSE) and top 30 companies in Sensex trading in Bombay Stock Exchange (BSE) speaks of the economy.
3. Important soft skills include: communication abilities, listening skills, team work, networking, critical thinking, attitude, interpersonal skills, personal attributes, personality traits, etc.

Suggested Readings

Hicks, Stephen R.C. (2009). What business ethics can learn from entrepreneurship? *The Journal of Private Enterprise*, 24(2), 49–57.

Jain, P.C. (1998) (ed.). *Handbook of New Entrepreneurs*. New Delhi: Oxford University Press.

Morris, M.H., Kuratko, D.F. and Covin, J.G. (2008). *Entrepreneurship and Innovation in Corporations*. New Delhi: Cengage Learning India Private Limited.

Panini, M.N. (1988). Corporate culture in India. *Economic & Political Weekly*, M-86–M-94. 27 August.

Patel, V.G. (2007). *When the Going gets Tough: Strategic Responses to Business Crises*. New Delhi: Tata McGraw-Hill Publishing Company limited.

14

Challenges and Constraints for Entrepreneurship Development in India

After having an overall view of various dimensions of entrepreneurship development in the country, there is a need to ponder over the issues and challenges which entrepreneurial development in India have been encountering. To explore the relatively recent phenomena of entrepreneurship development, data presented in Global Entrepreneurship Monitor[1] (GEM) India Reports have been examined for this purpose. GEM researchers and experts collect primary data and reports are prepared on entrepreneurship dynamics each year which are significant to understand global entrepreneurial activity. On an average, 75 countries[2] of the world are part of the GEM consortium, which have been collecting and presenting data since 1997. The GEM India Reports are prepared by scholars from EDII, Ahmedabad, though for data collection other Entrepreneurship Development Institutes of India are also involved.

The broad objective of the present chapter is to assess quantitative data collected through empirical study of all regions of the country presented in the GEM India Reports on various parameters of entrepreneurship development in India during the last one decade. Exploring the data on India for the decade 2010–2020 (declared as the decade of Innovations), it was found that the GEM India study was not undertaken in 2010 and 2011, as India started participating for GEM study in 2012 which was published next year. Therefore, the analysis is based on the reports from 2013 to 2020. Though the parameters and their nomenclatures to collect data did not remain constant over the time, yet we find some consistency. Each report is based on data collected from 3,000 to 4,000 plus adult population. It is also assumed that during this decade the renewed government initiatives might have taken the country to newer heights of development. Also, the level of entrepreneurship development would provide insights to the extent of innovations carried out during the phase.

The World Economic Forum develops Global Competitive Index every year and classifies economies of the world in three broad categories, which are: first stage–factor-driven, second stage–efficiency-driven, and third stage–innovation-driven. Indian economy is classified under the first stage, i.e. factor-driven by which it means that economies compete on the basis of their unskilled labour and natural resources. Thus, economy focuses on public and private institutions, well developed infrastructure, a stable macro environment and healthy workforce that has at least received basic or primary education. It may be argued that there is still a need for development of social and public institutions, infrastructure for growth of business and entrepreneurs, introduction of policies related to entrepreneurship and business development, and basic surety of health and education for every resident in the country (GEM 2014: India Report). The latest GEM report 2020–21 also places India in the low income economy group alongside Angola, Burkina Faso, Egypt, Morocco, and Togo.

A number of government regulations, policy programmes and reforms were made to create a favourable entrepreneurial ecosystem in the country. The entrepreneurial ecosystem is relatively a newer concept which shows a shift from the individualistic, personality based research towards a broader perspective that incorporates the role of social, cultural and economic forces in the process. Dodd and Anderson (2007) have defined an entrepreneurial ecosystem as a set of interdependent actors and factors coordinated in such a way that they enable productive entrepreneurship within a particular region. In the light of tall political claims made by the Indian government over the last few years, it is relevant to assess the empirical reality of entrepreneurial ecosystem in India.

During the decade 2010–2020, Indian economy has passed through great turmoil. In 2010, the GDP growth was 8.50 per cent but next year it dropped to 5.24 per cent. India started recovery in 2013 when the GDP growth rate accelerated to 6.4 per cent from the previous year's 5.5 per cent. The acceleration continued through 2014–15 and 2015–16 with growth rates of 7.4 per cent and 8.0 per cent respectively. However, in November 2016 with the announcement of demonetization, the economic growth of the country took a deep downward plunge. Before the economy could spin over, the Goods and Services Tax (GST) was implemented irrationally and erratically in the country which further disrupted the growth process of Indian economy. The GDP in 2018 was 6.53 per cent which came down to 4.04 per cent in 2019. Unfortunately, COVID-19 pandemic, coupled with wrong decision of complete lockdown shattered the Indian economy to negative growth, that is, –7.96 per cent in 2020, a 12 per cent steep fall from the previous year, which in the history of independent India had never happened. In the backdrop of such a scenario, it is not only a serious challenge for policy makers, but also for economists and sociologists as well to address the development of entrepreneurship in the country.

Taking Initiative to Start Business

Let us begin with the process when one decides to start some business in India, that is the number of days it takes to register the company. The data reveal that still it takes long, in 2014 it took 27 days, in 2015 slightly reduced to 26 days. Somehow, in 2016 it increased to 29 days and in 2017 it again has come down to 26 days to get the company registered. Out of the factor-driven economies of these years, Russia comes second but there also it takes only 10 days. Despite computerization, it takes relatively very long to get-set and go in India. There are 13 different bureaucratic procedures involved which are the highest in the case of India in comparison to other countries. In factor-driven economies, India takes maximum number of days. Even in 2018 and in later years as compared to BRIC countries, India has the highest number of bureaucratic procedures (13) to comply before starting a business.

Values Attached to Entrepreneurship

Further, it is relevant to examine how other people perceive entrepreneurship as a desirable career choice when they decide to take it as a career. Data reveal that still in India it is a less desirable career choice. India stands at the lowest amongst the BRIC countries and also in factor-driven economies. India also occupies the lowest rank so far as high status to successful entrepreneurship is concerned. Therefore, besides a change in prevalent cultural values, the country needs to speed up its economic reforms agenda to overcome hurdles. The regional variations in terms of entrepreneurship development have been shifting each year. Sometimes it is western India having more positive attitude towards entrepreneurship in general as compared to the northern regions. In 2017, a major regional shift took place, when societal values towards entrepreneurship were higher in northern and southern regions than in eastern and western India.

Besides the prevalent social values, it is significant to explore how our young population perceive the prevailing business opportunities. Do they believe in their own capabilities to take up business? Or they still have fears of failure to take up business?

Table 1

Self-Perceptions of the Adult Population with Regard to Business

Years	*Adult Perceive Good Opportunities to Start Business*	*Adult Believe to have Capabilities to Start Business*	*Having the Fear of Failure*
2014–15	39%	37%	38%
2015–16	38%	38%	44%
2016–17	44.3%	44%	37.5%
2017–18	44.9%	42.1%	39.6%
2018–19	49.8%	52.2%	50%
2019–20	83.14%	85.15%	62%
2020–21	82.45%	81.65%	56.8%

Source: Data compiled from GEM India Reports.

It is clear from Table 1 that the opportunities available to start some business have picked up gradually, primarily from the second half of the previous decade, i.e. 2016 onwards. The youth have also started believing in their capabilities to start business, though the data show flexible trends in terms of having fear of failure. Looking at the opportunities and considering their capabilities or skill know how, till 2018 nearly 40 per cent persons have had the fear of failure in business if they start it due to many policy formulations. But in 2019, suddenly the fear of failure increased and continued to be so till 2021. But at the same time their perception with regard to opportunities available for business has increased tremendously. Moreover, the proportion of persons believing that they possess skills and knowledge to start business has suddenly increased to 80 per cent and above. It is significant to remind that during the Covid-19 phase due to repeated lockdowns a lot of people lost their jobs. In the absence of creation of new jobs, people started looking forward to taking up some kind of business, believing in themselves to start business to earn livelihood, but at the same time also had high fear of failing in business. This sudden jump largely shows people's resilience to counter the economic crisis in their lives.

Total Early-Stage Entrepreneurial Activities (TEA)

Total early-stage entrepreneurial activity means the percentage of working population about to start an entrepreneurial activity as well those who have started one from a maximum of three and a half years. It is relevant to mention that in India quite a sizeable proportion of people tend to start enterprise out of opportunity, that is taking advantage of opportunity to do some business. It is significant to add that India has the high percentage of improvement drive for the purpose of increasing income. Also nearly one-third of the aspiring entrepreneurs took up business out of necessity, as they did not have any better choice of occupation.

Table 2 depicts the percentage of the population that is either about to begin, or has already established an entrepreneurial activity, for a maximum of 42 months. Data depict that a very nominal proportion of persons have become entrepreneurs, though it was gradually picked up for three years but suddenly TEA has fallen down. It may be argued that among the adult population only 10.8 per cent persons were engaged in some aspect of Total Entrepreneurial Activity (TEA) in 2015 which was showing encouraging trends, but the TEA has continuously declined between 2015 and 2017. One may say that after demonetization, becoming entrepreneur has also become difficult. Entrepreneurship coupled with

Table 2
Total Early-Stage Entrepreneurial Activity (TEA)

Years	*Nascent Entrepreneur (Setting up a business 0–6 years)*	*New Business Owner (In operation for more than 3 months but less than 42 months)*	*Total Early-stage Entrepreneurial Activity (TEA) Value %*
2014–15	4.1%	2.5%	6.6
2015–16	3.2%	7%	10.8
2016–17	3.9%	6.8%	10.6
2017–18	–	–	9.3
2018–19	8.8%	–	11.4
2019–20	9.4%	2.27%	15.0
2020–21	3.2%	5.90%	5.34

Source: Data compiled from GEM India Reports.

innovation is considered to be the foundation of any economy. However, we are performing badly, as the established business rate in India, that is, the percentage of the adult population, which is owner/manager of businesses in operation for more than 42 months, is contributing to the economy and employment by 6.8 per cent in 2016–17 which is the lowest among the other factor-driven economies. The data for 2017–18 are not available except for the TEA percentage. The nascent entrepreneurship prevalence rates are the highest in 25–34 years of age group, though only 5–6 per cent of the youth have access to any kind of skills. The region-wise TEA rate for 2019–20 is the highest in the northern region, followed by southern, eastern and is the lowest in western India. Bengaluru has been adjudged as world's strongest startup city. During the pandemic, businesses that were 42 months old have decreased by 50 per cent. TEA in case of males decreased by 53 per cent and females 79 per cent. Pandemic has a significant impact on entrepreneurial activities and women entrepreneurial activity rate has been affected severely.

Table 3 shows that the probability of being an early stage entrepreneur is the highest amongst the age categories of 25 to 54 years of age. The middle of the 20s in India is the time when young persons have finished the studies and it is the right time to choose the occupation. Therefore, we need to target the middle age groups,

Table 3
Total Entrepreneurial Activity (TEA) by Age of Entrepreneurs

Age Categories (years)	*2015–16*	*2016–17*	*2017–18*	*2018–19*	*2019–20*	*2020–21*
18–24	8.7	9.9	9.2	12.3	14.5	4.2
25–34	11.5	11.1	8.5	13.3	16.9	6.6
35–44	12.2	11.6	11.5	9.5	15.28	5.8
45–54	12.1	10.4	7.9	12.6	11.94	4.6
55–64	9.3	9.4	9.1	7.0	14.66	4.6

Source: GEM India Reports.

neither too young nor too old people, to take up to entrepreneurial activities. The latest GEM India Report 2020–21, published in 2022 clearly depicts the devastating impact of Covid-19 on entrepreneurial activities across age groups which has reduced to a single digit, though it could sustain itself in the initial phases of pandemic.

Total Entrepreneurial Activities by Gender

The ratio of females to males in the TEA is 0.6. Overall, in all factor-driven economies ratio is 0.8. Male-female ratio tends to be higher in countries with high overall business activity. In the year 2016, 7.6 per cent Indian women were engaged in early stage entrepreneurship when it was 13.5 for men in the same year. In 2018–19, TEA for males was 14 per cent and for women it was 8.7 per cent, for 2019–20, TEA for males was 17.1 per cent and for females it increased to 12.7 per cent. In 2020–21, the TEA reduced tremendously, male TEA was 7.9 per cent, while women's TEA stood at 2.6 per cent. Now women in general are participating less in entrepreneurial activities. Women respondents have lower scores on Perceived Capabilities (43% in 2014, which further dipped to 31% in 2015 and in 2016 it gained back at 41%) and in Perceived Opportunities (41% in 2014, 28% in 2015, 40% in 2016) than their male counterpart. Paradoxically, the fear of failure rate is much more in the case of men as compared to women. In 2016, for men it was 61 per cent and in case of women it was 39 per cent; however, in 2015 and 2014 the difference between the two is not so much. A study conducted by Jorge (2017) based on GEM data from 2009 to 2014 brings out the fact that in Europe, men are or have become entrepreneurs at a rate that is slightly, but significantly, higher than women, while the opposite happens in Latin American countries where it is in favour of women. No significant gaps were found in Asia and Africa. Beyond doubt, feminization of entrepreneurship has not yet happened in India and it is still a long way to go. About one-third (34%) of early stage entrepreneurs are women in India. Women start business more out of necessity when no other option for work is available. In the country, there are 58.5 million entrepreneurs out of which only 8.05 million are women, which accounts for 14 per cent of the total entrepreneurs in India. It is further found that out of the total 8.05 million women entrepreneurs, 79 per cent businesses are self-financed and are of small size. Therefore, the contribution of women entrepreneurs to GDP of India is very low, that is, 17 per cent as compared to global average which stands at 39 per cent (GEM India Report, 2020–21).

Challenges for Innovative Entrepreneurship

After having an empirical view of the entrepreneurship development, there is a need to ponder over the challenges which have become hindrance or constrains against the entrepreneurial activities in India. The GEM India Report 2019–20 identifies five major constrains in terms of financial support 37.5 per cent, government policy 37.5 per cent, cultural and social norms 26.35 per cent, political institutional and social context at 26.75 per cent and the prevailing economic climate counts for 15.4 per cent. In order to improve the entrepreneurial activity in India, 55.5 per cent recommended that government policy needs to be reviewed, other 38.8 per cent are for improvements in education and training and still other 27.7 per cent ask for financial support to improve entrepreneurial activity in India. These three major recommendations encompass a lot many issues, such as technology transfer and commercialization are the most important issues in the development. Taking the innovations as the base, there is a need to strengthen the Research and Development (R&D) in India. The Indian state has withdrawn from it in a big way, rather R&D has been handed over to the private players whose main interest is profit generation. Unless we take R&D seriously we cannot move forward. The model of China's part of cultural revolution may be adopted in this case when they asked all their people to fulfil their daily needs through innovations. In the process, people came with a number of innovative thoughts, ideas, and goods.

India is much behind in the development of institutions of innovations. Literature on entrepreneurship also reveals that in developing countries we have more of imitating entrepreneurs as these countries do not have enough resources to spend on research and development. Besides this, the policies of the government do not aim at encouraging innovation. The question is why it is not happening. The rigid regulations and complex tax structure, particularly, VAT and then implementing half-baked GST, fiscal bungling and corruption are greatly impacting the system. Moreover, the institutions of higher learning, research and training are facing serious financial crunch. There is no substantial effort or policy in place to encourage young minds to create something new.

One of the major issues for startups is policy uncertainty. The GEM data clearly depict that the entrepreneurial ecosystem is not investor friendly. The ecosystem of India is comfortable for existing businesses, but a bit tedious for the startups (GEM India, 2019–20). The politicization of the economic issues is a threatening challenge which India faces. Also there is lack of adequate infrastructure for supporting startups. Starting a business ranking of India in 2019 was 136 out of 190 countries. Industry sector participation percentage of TEA in India on the basis of adult population survey of 2016 revealed that nearly 71 per cent of the early stage entrepreneurs are involved in wholesale/retail activities. There is a sharp decline in agricultural activities. Only 12 per cent took up agriculture, while mining, manufacturing and transport activities had 42 per cent share in 2015. Health, education, government and social service had only 9.3 per cent share, ICT and finance had 4.5 per cent activities, besides 3.3 per cent in other activities. In 2019–20, 61 per cent of the total entrepreneurial activity is engaged in wholesale and retail business, 11.9 per cent in manufacturing sector, followed by health, education, government and social sectors (11%). The share of manufacturing in GDP is stagnating around 16 per cent despite Make in India initiatives. If there is no innovation, then the exports would also not rise.

Employment projections for the next five years also show a dismal picture. The GEM data show that 51 per cent have mentioned that they will not employ any worker in the coming five years. Other 44 per cent may employ 1–5 employees and only 5 per cent may provide employment to 6 or more number of persons. The GEM data for 2016–17 and 2017–2018 show that 60 per cent of the people did not employ any person in the last year which means that they did not expand their business, whereas 37 per cent did generate employment for 1 to 5 persons and only 3.5 per cent having big enterprises created 6 or more jobs. This shows a very low growth rate of development. Data from GEM 2019–20 reveals that 7 per cent Indians will not add any new employee to their business, only 6.4 per cent are planning to engage 1 to 5 new employees.

Even though a big amount of FDI, $208.99 billion, since 2014–17 has come, it has not led to much job creation. Acquiring of skills by the youth has also not led to an increase in jobs. Automation and digitalization is taking place in big industries. A Reserve Bank of India study (2018) has revealed that manufacturing jobs grew only by 2.1 per cent and total employment fell by 0.1 per cent in 2015–16 and 0.2 per cent in 2014–15. The GEM (2017) data clearly indicate that the unemployment rate has been the highest in the past two years.

The business discontinuation rate in the adult population (18–64 years) is the highest in India at 26.4 per cent compared to all factor driven economies where it is 6 per cent. It came down to 4.6 per cent in 2018–19 and 2.9 per cent in 2019–20. The reasons identified are lack of profitability (17%), problem of accessing finance and running out of capital, and bureaucracy, but more than 50 per cent discontinue as they sell, retire, exit or find some other opportunity.

Finally, it is important to know the innovation orientation in India in view of the fact that innovation has a long-term impact. On the basis of GEM data, 2016, which has used innovativeness of the product or service and novelty of technology used, the rate of innovation in India was 28 per cent which rose to 46.9 per cent in 2018–19. India's ranking on the Global Innovation Index (out of 141 counties) had come down from 66 in 2013–14 to 81 in 2014–15. However, in 2018–19, the ranking stood at 57, which in 2020–21 has entered in the top 50 countries on Global Innovation

Index by getting at 48 position out of 190 countries. Who is reaping the benefits of innovation? It is India's Information Technology sector which has grown at 15.5 per cent in 2021–22. Software and services exports account for nearly half of India's overall exports. They are delivering IT solutions and also consultancy services, besides delivering innovations through startups. Presently, India has 100 Unicons,[3] most of which are in service sector with a total valuation of $ 333 billion. Of these, as many as 44 have been added in 2021, and 16 have been created in 2022 so far. India now comes third after US and China in hosting the largest number of Unicorns in the world. Though it points towards growth, but what about majority of MSMEs in the country.

The startups have gone up from over 700 in 2016–17 to over 14,000 in 2020–21. Roy (2022) informs that venture capital funds worth over $6 billion were launched in India in 2021. More than $39 billion have been invested in Indian startups in 2021 alone. This sharp rise has been driven by the recent success of public issues of startups and the pandemic pushing digital adoption. The young entrepreneurs register their entities with the department of Industrial Policy and Promotion. In December 2018, it released data of state-startup ranking of 27 states and three Union Territories over three dozen action points under seven broad categories, which shows that northern states are lagging much behind, as they lack startup ecosystems and the state of Gujarat is the best performer. Punjab occupies 20th place with only 100 startups, though the policy was also started late in September 2017. Once again there is a high concentration of entrepreneurship in only five states, as 60 per cent of the enterprises are concentrated in Maharashtra, Karnataka, Delhi, UP and Telangana. Punjab and other northern states could not even develop entrepreneurial culture. Despite the best of the plans, getting funding is a herculean task in the region. National expert survey of GEM 2016–17 indicates that the level of entrepreneurial traits like creativity, self-sufficiency and the personal initiative has decreased. No doubt, entrepreneurial agent is shaped by the society, but in turn he also employs his agency to change the structure (Dodd and Anderson, 2007). We need to shift focus from individual to society.

Considering these challenges we may say that Indian economy is unique in the sense that it incorporates the features of each stage of development. For instance, India shows signs of post-industrial society where the share of service sector has increased over the time. The contribution of services to gross domestic product is 54 per cent while industry has 29 per cent share and agriculture is just 17 per cent. Even with limited knowledge of economics one may say that for a factor-driven economy like India this points towards a dangerous trend. The entrepreneurial intentions rate in India in 2015–2016 was at 15 per cent, in 2016–17, 14.9 and in 2017–18 it came down to 10.3 per cent and in 2018–19 rose to 20.6 and in 2019–20 it became 33.3 per cent. Investments were fine in 2015–16 but at present these have almost stopped. Furthermore, unofficial sources reveal that the unemployment rate has gone up from 9 in 2019 to 12 per cent in 2021 (any number above 5% is considered bad) which further gives dismal picture of the public policy.

Where are the opportunities? The Centre for Monitoring Indian Economy (CMIE) reveals that unemployment is on the rise with the rate of 7.4 per cent in December 2018, the retrenched workforce, estimated to be 11 million between December 2017 and 2018, and the incidence of joblessness is the highest amongst the vulnerable sections and sectors. For instance, 82 per cent of the jobs lost are in the rural sector and 80 per cent of the joblessness is borne by women. More importantly, the issue of underemployment is crucial as two-fifth perceive themselves as underpaid. An ILO Report in 2018 on World Employment and Social Outlook has classified almost four-fifth of the employment in India as 'vulnerable', only a less than one-fifth being regular salaried employees. A report, State of Working India, 2018, released by Azim Premji University found low wage employment to be a problem even in the organized sector, which earlier was a problem in the informal sector only. For instance, labour productivity in organized manufacturing is estimated to have increased by 6 times over the past three decades, whereas wages increased by only 1.5 times (c.f. *EPW* editorial, 2019: p. 7). The data based on these reports reveal that the government has failed to generate employment, which is a necessary condition for inclusive growth.

To improve the business sustainability, emphasis must also be laid on entrepreneurship education and training. Youth needs to be motivated to choose entrepreneurship as a preferred career. Still in India it is a less desirable career choice which is lowest amongst

BRIC countries. In factor driven economies, India comes at the lowest rank as far as high status to successful entrepreneur is concerned. In India about one-third (34%) of early stage entrepreneurs are women. And women start business more out of necessity (means when no other option for work is available). They also have a higher rate of fear of failure in business. The celebration of the so-called decade of innovations has been eclipsed more by faulty policy making and less by natural calamities. To sum up the discussion, we may say that still India has to go a long way to create an entrepreneurial ecosystem.

Notes

1. Global Entrepreneurship Monitor project was initiated in 1999 by London Business School, UK and Babson College, USA.
2. In 2014 GEM survey 73 countries participated which represents 72.4 per cent of the world's population and 90 per cent of the world's GDP.
3. Unicorn is startup company which has achieved a value more than $ 1 billion. The top 10 Unicorns of India, 2020–21 are Paytm, OYO rooms, Byju's, OLA Cabs, Swiggy, Zomato, Paytm Mall, Renew Power, Big Basket, and Udaan. India already has a few decacorns, means startup with a valuation of $ 10 billion, namely Flipkart, Nykaa, Swiggy, Byju's.

Suggested Readings

Global Entrepreneurship Monitor 2014: India Report.

Global Entrepreneurship Monitor 2015–16: India Report.

Global Entrepreneurship Monitor 2016–17: India Report.

Global Entrepreneurship Monitor 2017–18: India Report.

Global Entrepreneurship Monitor 2018–19: India Report.

Global Entrepreneurship Monitor 2019–20: India Report.

Global Entrepreneurship Monitor 2020–21: India Report.

15

Conclusion

It has routinely been presented that the Indian economy is one of the fastest growing economies of the world. No doubt Indian economy is dynamic, bold and overall business opportunities are good. India has a large young population, huge middle class consumers, skilled workers, and quite a well-entrenched ecosystem of business and trade. The nature and character of Indian entrepreneurship have largely been determined by certain castes, communities and families as an outcome of their relationships, interactions, networks, and mutual bonds. Alongside them, there always were some young, educated and innovative individuals across the assigned attributes who took risk, made critical decisions, provided leadership and gave a boost to entrepreneurship development. In other words, the social capital and cultural capital have been reinforcing each other resulting into entrepreneurial growth.

As the Indian economy is dynamic and overall business environment is good, there is a need to inculcate the entrepreneurial spirit amongst the masses, particularly amongst the marginalized communities and groups to achieve inclusive growth. Normally, it is the responsibility of the state for creating an entrepreneurial environment, providing the infrastructure, easing out the procedures to carry out business, and formulating the simple, transparent terms and conditions of doing business. Inconsistent, irrational and inflexible decisions of the government usually do not create an ecosystem where people across classes, regions and castes could be benefitted. A substantial proportion of the people are living on the margins of the society having tremendous hidden entrepreneurial talent where the state needed to intervene. Even in the cases of tribal and Dalits entrepreneurs, there is a very little visibility of the state functionaries including banks. They lack resources to initiate some business, while banks can let go of the lengthy procedures and formalities for big businesses, but not for the poor. The micro businesses need support and reassurance from the government rather than eliminating them with bulldozers. Asit Banerji, in the study (Entrepreneurship at the Grassroots, *EPW*, LVII, 2022) of poor rural migrants engaged in businesses at the grassroots level in urban spaces, rightly suggests that their micro enterprises should not be mixed up with the vastness and variety of MSME[1] sector. The study further illustrates the cases of Japan, South Korea, China and other several South-East Asian countries which greatly depended upon their micro business sector in the early stages of their industrialization. 'This not only generated employment on a mass scale but also enhanced productivity and product quality, pushing up labour-intensive exports' (p. 62). The neo liberal era has provided opportunities particularly to micro and small entrepreneurs. Even though they produce goods of low quality and quantity of low value, yet they cater to the needs of lower classes which is again a substantial proportion of Indian population. Encouraging micro and small enterprises would play not only a significant role in the dispersal of entrepreneurship across region, place, caste and class, but also for generating employment and equitable entrepreneurial growth.

To improve the business sustainability, the training and development must be put in place. The entrepreneurship development programmes (EDPs) have their relevance to impart knowledge and training, but follow-up of the nascent enterprises is not in place to restore the confidence of the entrepreneurs to take risk and to invest capital. The policymakers need to be working more sincerely and rigorously with innovative public policy to achieve inclusive, sustainable growth.

Ramachandran (2022) is of the view that unicorns are the future of business and trade in India as the case have been around the world. There is a surge in unicorns in India during the pandemic years largely due to change in the work environment. The work from home culture has driven innovations towards the internet and digital platforms that is, digital payments and e-commerce even in class 2 and 3 cities. The question is whether these unicorns and decacorns will solve the problem of unemployment? The answer is in negative, however, it may bridge the rural-urban, town-city digital divide.

Despite so much talk about starting businesses in India, there are two major drawbacks in doing so. First, doing business in India involves maximum procedures, and formalities. It relatively takes longer time which has not been adequately curtailed to win the confidence of the businessmen. Second, the sustainability of the enterprises is a serious challenge. There are a number of startups, nascent entrepreneurs, and unicorns in India, who could do fairly well for some time, but the speed with which they came up, they closed down or surrendered because of hasty, unfavourable policies of the government. The case of CCD (Coffee Café Day) is an eye opener. The unexpected success led to the unrealistic expansion, diversification coupled with unfavourable excise and taxation policy of the state which contributed to its ultimate steep fall and exit.

For any country to develop an entrepreneurial culture it has to ensure internal harmony, consistent and uniform implementation of political decisions, which in the case of India is seriously lacking. Instability, political turmoil, and promotion of caste and religion based ideology certainly proves detrimental to the economic development. Understanding entrepreneurship from the political economy point of view has become all the more relevant during the present times. To foster new enterprises and sustainable growth there is an urgent need to improve entrepreneurial culture in India. The prevalent sociocultural norms and values carrying a bias against doing business also need to be reoriented.

There is a common consensus that the study of entrepreneurship for long has become multidisciplinary covering sociology, psychology, economics, management, commerce, financial and business studies. Though each of the disciplines tries to understand the phenomenon of entrepreneurship by drawing its boundaries, yet we cannot move further without the interdisciplinary approach. In addition to entrepreneurship being multidisciplinary and interdisciplinary in its approach, it has become an octopus shaped over the time. The word entrepreneur[2] has been split into two – entre and preneur. More than affix, the suffix has become more prevalent and widespread which signifies the essence of entrepreneur, for instance we commonly use edupreneur, ecopreneur, agripreneur, infopreneur, etc. which refers to a person who is earning money by doing business in education, environment, agriculture, and information sector respectively. Nevertheless the changing contours of entrepreneurship point towards its continuous growth.

Various governments in the past and present have been making attempts to promote entrepreneurship for the well-being of its people as well as for the health of the economy. During the last two or more decades it has been time and again announced that entrepreneurship as a subject would be introduced in the mainstream education by introducing a compulsory paper on entrepreneurship at the undergraduate level in all educational institutions. It is only in Business schools and Technology institutes that the course is part of the curriculum design, whereas there is a need to bring it at grassroots levels. The Hindi translation of an entrepreneur is 'uddami'. Teaching the essence of an *uddami* and his *'uddmikta'* are actually what we Indians need to learn at a very early stage. I always realize that the Hindi word (though very lately coined) encompasses more a socio-psychological dimension of an entrepreneur. The subject of entrepreneurship is still largely unexplored. Katz (c.f. Batthini, 2017), while guiding core publications in entrepreneurship and related fields, informs that the Social Science Citation Index (SSCI) and other major indexing services show that entrepreneurship is growing as a field of study. In order to introduce and increase entrepreneurship education and research, there is a dire need to increase financial support.

Sociology of entrepreneurship may be regarded as the approach which apparently analyses the way a capitalist emerged in a capitalist society. Sociology has a rich discipline of labour studies, whereas management sciences have been regarded by many as the discipline which teaches how to control and regulate labour. On the other hand, understanding the nature of entrepreneurship in any capitalist society does not only help in making sense of why some enterprises succeed, whereas others fail. It situates innovation in the centre of the discourse of making a successful entrepreneur. We are used to emphasizing the role of innovation in technology and it is clear enough that humanity has been amply benefitted by various technological innovations. However, it hardly crosses a layman's mind that innovation is not the monopoly of technology. Innovating in any sphere of life generally pays dividends. After all innovation is nothing but doing things in a new way. In other words, finding new ways of doing the same thing is an ability which is not generally found for which, as the phenomenologist would say, is a result of the fact that most of the individuals live a routinised life and they keep on doing what they have been doing for years, decades or centuries. The everyday life reality in its routinized form gave advantage to those castes and communities, which had already been engaged in business.

One of the challenges of the Indian society has been that the castes and communities engaged with machines and tools known as artisan classes occupied lower caste position and they continued to work in their traditional settings meeting the demands of the upper castes. The needs of the upper castes which created demand were also routinized by virtue of which the artisan classes remained poor, low paid and dependent on upper classes. In the same, the businesses did not get much challenges for a long time despite the fact that there have been evidences of Indian traders engaged in international trade. However, the finished goods which were merchandized could be produced by the local artisans, who never faced challenge of changing technique to increase production. As a result, secured in their routinized world, the Indian trader never felt threatened till the arrival of capitalism in the form of British rule. Thus, we begin to observe changes taking place in Indian businesses in terms of the volume of trade and the multiplicity of commodities to be circulated within the country as well internationally. Adaptation to the new circumstances required not only adaptive measures but also innovations in business practices.

Owing to the nascent stage of capitalism, the traditional business communities' social capital played major role in establishing and continuing the enterprises, but the opening of new businesses and services in the form of manufacturing of goods and providing of services, new modes of transportation and communication, etc. offered opportunities to the emergence of more and more entrepreneurs, but since there was a need for capital to start businesses in new areas opened by Raj, the reinforcement of the power of the traditionally rich and trading castes took place.

In the post-Independence period, the situation continued for a reasonably long period, but we still see the emergence of new entrepreneurs. More and more diversification in the caste and communities began to occur in the entrepreneurial activities. With the banks becoming more and more liberal in giving loans to the new entrants, changes took place in the business and industrial environments. It could be noticed within a decade of the green revolution in agriculture when capital accumulation occurred in the 1970s, which was also helped by the remittances from the Indian diaspora, the new entrepreneurs began to emerge. The link between the diaspora Indians and the entrepreneurship became pronounced after the introduction of the new economic policy in 1991, when India announced the beginning of an end of license raj and began to open its economy for the foreign capital. Certain sectors, which might not have been even imagined except in the stories of Asimov in the 1970s, came up and the notable among them was IT sector. Information Technology changed everything about and of business and it paved the way for innovation and starting a new enterprise. Though the relevance of social capital has still remained, but the crucial role of cultural capital in the form of skill aided by innovation became the mantra for success of entrepreneur. Unfortunately, as mentioned earlier, the Indian state has failed to keep pace with the new environment.

Since 2014, the Government of India has turned to corporate capitalist development on the model of the US, but it has seriously ignored the most important condition for such a development, namely keeping balance of trade. Both China and the Western world have heavily invested in the production of knowledge, which has been adequately linked with its industrial and business needs. Despite the fact that India had constituted a commission on it, nothing has been done so far. What we are witnessing is largely the decline in the field of education and knowledge production with strongly established Research and Development as a part of the industrial needs. Policies as such may not bring anything good until the well developed knowledge producing institutions are not adequately funded. For India, to compete in the world market, it is indispensable that its entrepreneurs have the requisite environment and capacity to negotiate at the world level.

Notes

1. Micro, small, medium enterprises (MSME) in a country like India with so much of vastness and diversity is too broad in scope. Banerji (2022, p. 58) informs that 'it includes industrial and service units that differ from each other in terms of size, structure and the resources employed. Medium and small industries generally belong to organized industrial sector as they function in a formal legal framework. While micro units are mostly unorganized and operate without much constraint'. He gives illustration of micro/petty businesses such as vegetable and fruit stalls, small shops and wayside eateries that are usually run by individuals of small means with very limited capital and human resources. There is a need to address the issues and challenges of each of them separately as they have their distinctness.
2. The normal dictionary meaning of the word entrepreneur is a person who makes money by starting new business.

Bibliography

Aga, Anu (2012). Women in India: From shadows to excellence. In Ashok S. Kolaskar and Motilal Dash (eds), *Women and Society: The Road to Change* (pp. 12–18). New Delhi: Oxford University Press.

Agarwal, Bina (1994). *A Field of One's Own: Gender and Land Rights in South Asia.* Delhi: Cambridge University Press.

Aggarwal, Saaz (2012). *Sindhi: Stories from a Vanished Homeland*. Pune: Black-and-White Fountain.

Akhouri, M.M.P. (1988). Entrepreneurship development. *Employment News*, Anniversary Number, 2 April, pp. 4, 6–7.

Aldrich, Howard E. (2005). Entrepreneurship. In Neil J. Smelser and Richard Swedberg (eds), *The Handbook of Economic Sociology* (pp. 451–477). New York: Russell Sage Foundation.

Alter, S.K. (2006). Social enterprise models and their mission and money relationships. In Alex Nicholls (ed.), *Social Entrepreneurship: New Models of Sustainable Social Change* (pp. 205–232). New York: Oxford University Press.

Anderson, R.B. and Giberson R.J. (2004). Aboriginal entrepreneurship and economic development in Canada: Thoughts on current theory and practice. *International Research in the Business Disciplines*, 4, 141–167.

Andrea Carolina Silva Niño (2015). Social entrepreneurship and corporate social responsibility: Differences and points in common. *Journal of Business & Economic Policy,* 2(2), 85–93.

Aron, Raymond. (1967). *Main Currents in Sociological Thought*. 2. Harmondsworth, Middlesex: Penguin Books.

Awasthi, Dinesh N. and Sebastian, Jose. (1996). *Evaluation of Entrepreneurship Development Programmes*. New Delhi: Sage Publications.

Bagga, Neeraj (2022). *Amritsar Tribune*, 17 January, p. 1.

Bal, Gurpreet (1995). *Development and Change in Punjab*. New Delhi: National Book Organization.

Bal, Gurpreet (1997). Women entrepreneurs: Emerging trends and issues. In Paramjit S. Judge and Satish K. Sharma (eds). *Dimensions of Social Change: Essays in Honour of Professor P.N. Pimpley* (pp. 169–188). Jaipur: Rawat Publications.

Bal, Gurpreet (1998). Communities and culture in entrepreneurship development in India. *The Journal of Entrepreneurship*, 7(2), 171–182.

Bal, Gurpreet (2000). Development and women's health: A sociological study of a Punjab village. *Guru Nanak Journal of Sociology*, 21(1), 67–87.

Bal, Gurpreet (2005). Violence, migration and entrepreneurship: Punjab during the Khalistan movement. *Economic & Political Weekly*, 36(3), 3978–3986.

Bal, Gurpreet (2006). Entrepreneurship among diasporic communities: A comparative examination of Patidars of Gujarat and Jats of Punjab. *The Journal of Entrepreneurship*, 15(2), 181–203.

Bal, Gurpreet (2012). Understanding failure of diaspora development initiatives in rural Punjab: Towards social entrepreneurship as an alternative model. *Guru Nanak Journal of Sociology*, 33(1 and 2), 1–18.

Bal, Gurpreet (2017). City, caste and business: A study of Khatris in Amritsar. In Sasi Misra, Sunil Shukla and G. Batthini (eds), *12th Biennial Conference on Entrepreneurship* (Conference Papers), Vol. 11, pp. 1119–1127, Delhi: Bookwell & EDII Ahmedabad.

Bal, Gurpreet and Judge, P.S. (2001). Terrorism and rural entrepreneurship in Punjab. *The Journal of Entrepreneurship*, 10(2), 191–208.

Bal, Gurpreet and Judge, P.S. (2010). Innovation, entrepreneurship and development: A study of scheduled castes in Punjab. *The Journal of Entrepreneurship*, 19(1), 43–62.

Banerjee, Chandrajit (2020). Financing innovation in India. In Soumitra Dutta, Bruno Lanvin and Sacha Wunsch-Vincent (eds), *Global Innovation Index 2020: Who will Finance Innovation*? New Delhi: Confederation of Indian Industry.

Banerji, Asit (2022). Entrepreneurship at the grassroots. *Economic & Political Weekly*, LVII(11), 57–63.

Banks, J.A. (1972). *The Sociology of Social Movements*. London: Macmillan.

Banker, Feroze (ed.) (2000). *Progressive Entrepreneur: Managing Firm and Factory as Profit Centres*. New Delhi: Kanishka Publishers, Distributors.

Barnouw, Victor (1978). 'The Sindhis, mercantile refugees in India: Problems of their assimilation'. In by Sylvia Vatuk (ed.), *American Studies in the Anthropology of India* (pp. 447–459). New Delhi: Manohar.

Batthini, G. and Saxena, K. (2017). *Emerging Trends in Entrepreneurship Research: Review of the Journal of Entrepreneurship*. Delhi: Bookwell.

Batthini, G., Bhatt, V. and Joshi, R. (2014). *Thematic & Analysis: The Journal of Entrepreneurship Articles*. Delhi: Bookwell.

Beaumont, S., Singh, K. and Ramachandran, K. (eds) (1992). *Development of Microenterprises by Women*. Ahmedabad: British Council and Indian Institute of Management.

Bhachu, Parminder (2004). *Dangerous Designs: Asian Women Fashion the Diaspora Economies*. New York and London: Routledge.

Bodha, Irm Jalali (2017). *Entrepreneurship and Development: Examining State Initiatives in Jammu and Kashmir*. PhD thesis, Guru Nanak Dev University, Amritsar.

Bogaert, M.V.D. and Das, S.P. (1989). *Group Entrepreneurship with the Rural Poor: An Idea, Whose Time has Come*. New Delhi: Indian Social Institute.

Bourdieu, Pierre (1986). The Forms of Capital. In J.G. Richardson (ed.), *Handbook of Theory and Research for the Sociology of Education* (pp. 241–258). New York: Greenwood Press.

Bronstein, David (2007). *How to Change the World: Social Entrepreneurs and the Power of New Ideas*. New York: Oxford University Press.

Buchanan, D.H. (1934). *Development of Capitalistic Enterprise in India*. New York: Macmillan.

Burt, Ronald S. (2000). The network entrepreneur. In Richard Swedberg (ed.) *Entrepreneurship: The Social Science View* (pp 281–307). New Delhi: Oxford University Press.

Caputo, Richard K. and Dolinsky, Arthur (1998). Women's choice to pursue self-employment: The role of financial and human capital of household members. *The Journal of small Business Management*, 36(3), 8–17.

Castells, Manuel (1996). *The Rise of the Network Society, The Information Age: Economy, Society and Culture*, Vol. I. Oxford: Blackwell.

Chakraborty, Vinamrta and Kumar, Utpal (2020). Opportunities for tribal entrepreneurship development in Jharkhand to combat post

COVID-19 challenges. *Parikalpana-KIIT Journal of Management*, 150–163.

Chand, Vijaya Sherry (2009). Beyond non-governmental development action into social entrepreneurship. *The Journal of Entrepreneurship*, 18(2), 139–166.

Chandra, P.M. (1996). What creates an entrepreneur? Some observations from a micro study. *The Journal of Entrepreneurship*, 5(2), 253–260.

Chithelen, I. and Souza, Val (2005). Public capital markets and new generation of entrepreneurs: Success of Indians in the US and potential in India. *Economic & Political Weekly*, 40(40), 4373–4377.

Coleman, James S. (1988). Social capital in the creation of human capital. *American Journal of Sociology*, Vol. 94, Supplement: Organizations and Institutions: Sociological and Economic Approaches to the Analysis of Social Structure, S95–S120.

Dahiwale, S.M. (1989). *Emerging Entrepreneurship Among Scheduled Castes of Contemporary India: A Study of Kolhapur City*. New Delhi: Concept Publishing Company.

Damodaran, Harish (2008). *India's New Capitalists: Caste, Business and Industry in a Modern Nation*. Ranikhet: Permanent Black.

Dana, Leo Paul (1998). Models for entrepreneurship: Towards cultural sensitivity. In R.K. Kanungo (ed.), *Entrepreneurship and Innovation: Models for Development* (pp. 64–77). New Delhi: Sage Publications.

Das, G. (2014). Introduction. In T.A. Timberg, *The Marwaris: From JagatSeth to the Birlas* (pp. xi–xxx). New Delhi: Penguin Books.

Das, Raya (2021). Farm size and productivity debate in Indian agriculture: Five decades of Green Revolution. *Economic & Political Weekly*, LVI(9), 57–65.

Davala, Sarath (1994). New economic policy and trade union response. *Economic & Political Weekly*, XXIX(8), 406–408.

De, Arup (1995). Transformation of the Marwari. *Mainstream*, 29 July, 25–30.

Dees, Gregory (1998). Enterprising nonprofits. *Harvard Business Review*, 76(1), 55–67.

Desai, Ashok V. (1994). The Origins of Parsi Enterprise. In Rajat Kanta Ray (ed.), *Entrepreneurship and Industry in India 1800–1947* (pp. 99–108). New Delhi: Oxford University Press.

Dix, Carol (1991). *Enterprising Women: The Lives of Successful Business Women*. London: Bantam Press.

Dobb, Maurice (1976). From feudalism to capitalism. In Rodney Hilton (ed.) *The Transition from Feudalism to Capitalism* (pp. 21–29). Verso: London.

Dodd, D.S. and Anderson, A.R. (2007). 'Mumpsimus and the Mything of the Individualistic entrepreneur', *International Small Business Journal,* 25(4), 336–341.

Doherty, Bob et al. (2009). *Management for Social Enterprise*. New Delhi: Sage Publications.

Dorin, B. (2003). *The Indian Entrepreneur: A Sociological Profile of Businessmen and Their Practices*. New Delhi: Manohar & Centre De Sciences Humaines.

Drayton, Bill (2007). The citizen sector transformed. In D. Bornstein (ed.) *How to Change the World: Social Entrepreneurs and the Power of New Ideas* (pp. 48–61). New York: Oxford University Press.

Drucker, P.F. (1979). *Adventures of a Bystander*. London: Heinemann.

Drucker, P.F. (1985). *Innovation and Entrepreneurship: Practice and Principles.* New York: Harper & Row.

Dumas, Colette (2001). Micro enterprise training for low income women: The case of the community entrepreneurs programme, *The Journal of Entrepreneurship*, 10(1), 17–42.

Durkheim, Emile (1964). *The Division of Labour in Society*. New York: Free Press.

Dutta, Sudipt (1997). *Family Business in India*. New Delhi: Sage Publication.

Editorial (2019). Where will the 10% be employed? *Economic & Political Weekly*, LIV(2), 7–8.

Ensign, Prescott C. and Robinson, Nicholas P. (2011). Entrepreneurs because they are immigrants or immigrants because they are entrepreneurs? A critical examination of the relationship between the newcomers and the establishment. *The Journal of Entrepreneurship*, 20(1), 33–53.

Ettlie, John E. and O'Keefe, Robert D. (1982). Innovation attitudes, values, and intentions in organization. *Journal of Management Studies*, 19(2), 162–182.

Fairlie, R.W., Krashinsky, H., Zissimopoulos and Kumar, K.B. (2010). Indian entrepreneurial success in the United States, Canada and United Kingdom, RAND labour and Population Working paper series.

Feldmann, Horst (2007). Protestantism, labour force participation, and employment across countries. *American Journal of Economics and Sociology*, 66(4), 795–816.

Fisher, M.P. (1980). *The Indians of New York City: A Study of Immigrants from India*. New Delhi: Heritage Publishers.

Flamant, N. (2003). The employer and his enterprise: International shoemakers in Tamil Nadu. In B. Dorin (ed.) *The Indian Entrepreneur: A Sociological Profile of Businessmen and their Practices* (pp. 101–135). New Delhi: Manohar& Centre De Sciences Humaines.

Gadgil, D.R. (1971). *The Industrial Evolution of India in Recent Times, 1860–1939*. Delhi: Oxford University Press.

Gartner, W.B. (1988). Who is an entrepreneur? Is the wrong question. *American Journal of Small Business*, 12(4), 11–32.

Goleman, Daniel (2007). *Social Intelligence: The New Science of Human Relationships*. New York: Bantam Books.

Gopakumar, K. (1995). The entrepreneur in economic thought: A thematic overview. *The Journal of Entrepreneurship,* 4(1), 1–17

Gopalakrishnan, R. (2014). Foreword. In Shyamal Majumdar, *Business Battles: Family Feuds that Changed Indian Industry* (pp. vii–ix). New Delhi: Business Standard Books.

Goswami, A., Dalmia, N. and Pradhan, M. (2008). Entrepreneurship National Knowledge Commission, Government of India Publication.

Granovetter, Mark (1992). Economic action and social structure: The problem of embeddedness. In Mark Granovetter and Richard Swedberg (eds), *The Sociology of Economic Life* (pp. 53–81). San Francisco: Westview Press.

Guha, Amalendu (1970). ParsiSeth as entrepreneurs 1750–1850. *Economic & Political Weekly*, 5(35), 107–115.

Guha, Amalendu (1970). The comprador role of ParsiSeths 1750–1850, *Economic & Political Weekly*, 5(48), 1933–36.

Guha, Amalendu (1984). More about ParsiSeths: Their roots, entrepreneurship and comprador role, 1650–1918, *Economic & Political Weekly*, 19(3), 117–132.

Guillen, M.F., Collins, R., England, P. and Meyer, M. (2002). *The New Economic Sociology: Developments in an Emerging Field*. New York: Russell Sage Foundation.

Hagen, E.E. (1962). *On The Theory of Social Change: How Economic Growth Begins*. Homewood, IL: Dorsey Press.

Harper, M. and Vyakarnam, S. (1988). *Rural Enterprise: Case Studies from Developing Countries*. London: Intermediate Technology Publications.

Heredero, J. M. (1979). Agricultural Entrepreneurship. In T.V. Rao and T.K. Moulik (eds), *Identification and Selection of Small Scale Entrepreneurs* (pp. 151–159). Ahmedabad: Indian Institute of Management.

Hicks, Stephen R.C. (2009). What business ethics can learn from entrepreneurship. *The Journal of Private Enterprise*, 24(2), 49–57.

Hilton, Rodney (1978). *The Transition from Feudalism to Capitalism*. London: Verso Editions.

Hisrich, R.D. (1985). *The Women Entrepreneurs versus Male Entrepreneurs*. Toronto: Lexington Books.

Hoselitz, Bert F. (1960). *Sociological Aspects of Economic Growth*. New York: Feffer and Simons Inc.

Huntington, Samuel P. (1968). *Political Order in Changing Societies*. New York: Feffer and Simons Inc.

Indira, K. (1990). Women entrepreneurs in the slums of Hyderabad and Secunderabad. *Social Change,* 20(2), 82–89.

Irastorza, Nahikari and Peña, Iñaki (2014) Earnings of immigrants: Does entrepreneurship matter? *The Journal of Entrepreneurship*, 23(1), 35–56.

Israel, Milton (1994). *In the Further Soil: A Social History of Indo-Canadians in Ontario.* Toronto: Toronto Organization for the promotion of Indian culture.

Iyengar, Sudarshan (1998). Voluntary initiatives for tribal development in Gujarat. *The Journal of Entrepreneurship*, 7(2), 211–235.

Iyer, Lalitha (1991). *Women Entrepreneurs: Challenges and Strategies*, New Delhi: Friedrich Ebert Stiftung.

Jain, P.C. (ed.) (1998). *Handbook for New Entrepreneurs*. New Delhi: Oxford University Press.

Jaisankar, S. and Chandrasekaran, S. (2020). A study on rural entrepreneurship development through MSME. *International Journal of Advanced Science and Technology*, 29(8), 2580–2584.

Jorge, Velilla (2017). Feminization of Entrepreneurship in Developing countries? Evidence from GEM data. https://mpra.ub.uni-muenchen.de/79997/accessed on 27/6/2022

Judge, P.S. (1994). *Punjabis in Canada: A Study of Formation of An Ethnic Community*. Delhi: Chankaya Publications.

Judge, P.S. (2012). *Foundations of Classical Sociological Theory: Functionalism, Conflict and Action*. New Delhi: Pearson.

Judge, P.S. and Bal, Gurpreet (1996). *Strategies of Social Change in India*. New Delhi: MD Publications.

Judge, P.S. and Bal, Gurpreet (2009). *Mapping Dalits: Contemporary Reality and Future Prospects in Punjab*. Jaipur: Rawat Publications.

Kanitkar, Ajit (1994). Entrepreneurs and micro-enterprises in rural India. *Economic & Political Weekly,* 29(9), M25–M30.

Kanitkar, Ajit and Contractor, Nalini (1992). *In Search of Identity: Women Entrepreneurs of India*. Ahmedabad: Entrepreneurship Development Institute of India.

Kanungo, Rabindra N. (ed.) (1998). *Entrepreneurship and Innovation: Models for Development*. New Delhi: Sage Publications.

Kaur, Amritpreet (2016). Changing contours of entrepreneurship: A study of social entrepreneurship in Punjab. PhD thesis, Guru Nanak Dev University, Amritsar.

Kaur, Kiranpreet (2007). Role of social structural variables in entrepreneurial orientation: A study of women entrepreneurs in Punjab. *Social Change*, 37(1), 77–97.

Kaushik, Roopesh (2022). Understanding cooperatives as social enterprises. *Economic & Political Weekly*, LVII(5), 24–30.

Khakhalary, B. (2017). Tribal entrepreneurship: A case study on Dhaba business in Rajapara locality of Kamrup district. *EPRA International Journal of Economic and Business Review,* 5(8).

Khan, Jamal and Knight, Richard B. (1997). Innovations in a plantation economy: A study of barbadian small farmer. *The Journal of Entrepreneurship*, 6(1), 87–98.

Khandekar, M. (2013). *Dalit Millionaires*. New Delhi: Penguin.

Kilby, Peter (1971). Hunting the Heffalump. In P. Kilby (ed.), *Entrepreneurship and Economic Development* (pp. 1–40). New York: The Free Press.

Krishna, K.V.S.M. (2003). Bridging the gap: Conceptual paradigms and training for entrepreneurship development. *The Journal of Entrepreneurship*, 12(1), 92–116.

Kudaisya, M.M. (2003). *The Life and Times of G.D. Birla*. New Delhi: Oxford University Press.

Levkovsky, A.I. (1972). *Capitalism in India: Basic Trends in its Development*. New Delhi: People's Publishing House.

Light, Ivan and Rosenstein, C. (1995). Expanding the interaction theory of entrepreneurship. In Alejandro Portes (ed.), *The Economic Sociology of Immigration: Essays on Networks, Ethnicity, and Entrepreneurship* (pp. 166–212). New York: Russell Sage Foundation.

Light, Paul C. (2008). *The Search for Entrepreneurship*. Washington, D.C.: Brookings Institution Press.

Ma, Zhenzhong, Wang, Tangting and Lee, Yender (2012). The status of international ethnic entrepreneurship studies: A co-citation analysis, *The Journal of Entrepreneurship*, 21(2), 173–199.

Majumdar, Shyamal (2014). *Business Battles: Family Feuds that Changed Indian Industry*. New Delhi: Business Standard Books.

Malinowski, B. (1978). *Argonauts of the Western Pacific*. London: Routledge.

Markovits, Claude (2008). *The Global World of Indian Merchants 1750–1947: Traders of Sindh from Bukhara to Panama*. New Delhi: Cambridge University Press.

Mathew, Ashlin (2019). Making it in India. *Finance & Development*. https://www.imf.org/Publications/fandd/issues/2019/03/womens-entrepreneurship-in-India-mathew.

Mattis, Mary C. (2000). Women entrepreneurs in the United States. In Ronald J. Burke and Marilyn J. Davidson (eds), *Women in Management: Current Research Issues* (Vol. II, pp. 53–68). New Delhi: Sage Publications.

McClelland, D.C. (1961). *The Achieving Society*. Princeton: D. Van Nostrand Co.

McClelland, D.C. (1965). Achievement motivation can be developed. *Harvard Business Review*, 41, 6–24, 178.

Meeta and Rajivlochan (2020). *Making India Great Again: Learning from Our History*. New Delhi: Manohar Publishers.

Meredith, G.G., Nelson, R.F. and Neck, P.A. (1982). *The Practice of Entrepreneurship*. Geneva: ILO.

Metcalf, H., Modood, T. and Virdee, S. (1996). *The Asian Self-employment: The Interaction of Culture and Economics in England*. London: Policy Studies Institute.

Meyskens et al. (2008). The impact of resources on social entrepreneurship organizations: The symbiosis of entities in the social engagement network. http://usasbe.org/knowledge/proceedings/pproceedingsDocs/2008/paperID219.pdf. (Accessed on 3.7. 2011).

Mittal, Akhilesh. https://www.cii.in/sectors.aspx?enc=prvePUj2bdMtgTmvPwvisYH+5EnGjyGXO9hLECvTuNt8Yt8MGwm3xV7pjS9tGblw

Morris, M.H. and Lewis, P.S. (1993). Entrepreneurship as a significant factor in societal quality of life, *Journal of Business Research*, 13(1), 21–36.

Morris, M.H., Kuratko, D.F. and Covin, J.G. (2008). *Entrepreneurship and Innovation in Corporations*. New Delhi: Cengage Learning India Private Limited.

Nadel, S.F. (1957). *The Theory of Social Structure*. London: Cohen and West Ltd.

Nafziger, E.W. (1971). Indian entrepreneurship: A survey. In Peter Kilby (ed.), *Entrepreneurship and Economic Development* (pp. 287–316). New York: The Free Press.

Nair, M.R. (2017). Can 100 births stop the decline in Parsi population, *Hindustan Times,* July, 319 hindustantimes.com/Mumbai-news/can-a-100-births-stop-the-decline-in-parsi-population/story-sq4u4kbgjfho1qLYi0aePK.html

Nicholls, Alex and Hyunbae, A. Cho (2006). Social entrepreneurship: The structuration of a field. In Alex Nicholls (ed.), *Social Entrepreneurship: New Models of Sustainable Social Change* (pp. 99–118). New York: Oxford University Press.

Pal, Sanjay (1999). Producers and markets in rural Bihar: A case of tribal handicrafts. *The Journal of Entrepreneurship*, 8(1), 79–91.

Panigrahi, N. and Panda, P. (2000). *Trading Community of India: An Anthropological Study of Ethnicity*. Jaipur: Rawat Publications.

Panini, M.N. (1988). Corporate culture in India. *Economic & Political Weekly*, 23(35), M-86–M-94, 27 August.

Pareto, Vilfredo (1935). *The Mind and Society: A Treatise on General Sociology*. New York: Dover Publications.

Parsons, Talcott (1972). *The Social System*. New Delhi: Amerind.

Pastakia, Astad (2012). Building pro-poor value chains: Experiences from rural India, *The Journal of Entrepreneurship*, 21(2), 269–288.

Patel, V.G. (2007). *When the Going gets Tough: Strategic Responses to Business Crises*. New Delhi: Tata McGraw-Hill Publishing Company Limited.

Patvardhan, V.S. (1990). *Growth of Indigenous Entrepreneurship: The House of Garwares*. Bombay: Popular Prakashan.

Patvardhan, V.S. (1995). *Growth of Indigenous Entrepreneurship: Enterprises of Dahanukar, Apte, Dandekar, Sathe and Parkhe*. Bombay: Popular Prakashan.

Peredo, A.M. and Chrisman, J.J. (2006). Toward a theory of community based enterprise. *Academy of Management Review*, 31(2), 309–28.

Peter, Rosa, Carter, Sara and Hamilton, Daphne (1996). Gender as a determinant of small business performance: Insights from a British Study. *International Journal of Small Business Economics,* 8(6), 463–78.

Picot, G. and Ostrovsky, Y. Immigrant and second-generation entrepreneurs in Canada: An intergenerational comparison of business ownership. *Statistics Canada*. https://doi.org/10.25318/36280001202100900003-eng. accessed on 27/6/2022

Pocock, D. (1972). *Kunbi and Patidars: A Study of the Patidar Community of Gujarat*. Oxford: Oxford University Press.

Portes, A. (1995). Economic sociology and the sociology of immigration: A conceptual overview. In Alejandro Portes (ed.), *The Economic Sociology of Immigration: Essays on Networks, Ethnicity, and Entrepreneurship* (pp. 1–41). New York: Russell Sage Foundation.

Portes, A. and Sensenbrenner, J. (1993) Embeddedness and immigration: Notes on the social determinants of economic action. *American Journal of Sociology*, 98, (May), 1320–1350.

PTI News. *The Tribune*, 16 January 2022, p. 16.

Putnam, Robert D. and Kristin A. Goss. (2002). Introduction. In Robert D. Putnam (ed.), *Democracies in Flux: The Evolution of Social Capital in Contemporary Society* (pp. 3–20). New York: Oxford University Press.

Radcliffe-Brown, A.R. (1952). *Structure and Function in Primitive Society: Essays and Addresses.* Glencoe: The Free Press.

Rai, Rajesh (2007). Business and entrepreneurship. In B.V. Lal, Peter Reeves and Rajesh Rai, *The Encyclopaedia of the Indian Diaspora* (pp. 77–79). New Delhi: Oxford University Press.

Rai, Saurbh (2017). Tribal entrepreneurship is booming in India and these 8start-ups are showing the way. https://yourstory.com/2017/11/tribal-entrepreneurship-india/amp. accessed on 27/6/2022

Ramachandran, Sushma (2022). Unicorn universe expanding in tough times. *The Tribune*, Jalandhar, 23 June, p. 7.

Ray, R.K. (1994). Introduction. In R.K. Ray (ed.), *Entrepreneurship and Industry in India 1800–1947* (pp. 1–69). New Delhi: Oxford University Press.

Richardsen, A.M. and Burke, R.J. (2000). Women entrepreneurs and small business owners in Norway and Canada. In M.J. Davidson and R.J. Burke (eds), *Women in Management, Current Research Issues* (Vol. II, pp. 69–83). New Delhi: Sage Publications.

Robins, Nick (2006). *The Corporation that Changed the World: How the East India Company Shaped the Modern Multinational*. New Delhi: Orient Longman.

Roy, Subir (2022). IT sector reaping dividends of Innovation. *The Tribune*, 24 February, p. 7.

Roy, V.C. (2019). Northern States among the Laggards, *The Tribune*, Jalandhar, 4 February, p. 16.

Rutten, Mario (2001). Family enterprises and business partnership: Rural entrepreneurs in India, Malaysia, and Indonesia. *The Journal of Entrepreneurship*, 10(2), 165–189.

Sayeed, O.B. and Gazdar, M.K. (2003). Intrapreneurship: assessing and defining attributes of Intrapreneurs. *The Journal of Entrepreneurship*, 12(1), 75–89.

Schlosser, Francine (2012). Taking an active approach in entrepreneurial mentoring programmes geared towards immigrants. *The Journal of Entrepreneurship*, 21(2), 201–221.

Schumpeter, J.A. (2000). Entrepreneurship as innovation. In R. Swedberg (ed.), *Entrepreneurship: The Social Science View* (pp. 51–75). New Delhi: Oxford University Press.

Shah, T.M. (2018). 'Hand'made in India: Tribal sustainopreneurs of change and prosperity. In Entrepreneurship and the sustainable development goals. Retrieved from https://doi.org/10.1108/S 2040: 69–83.

Sharma, Arjun (2022). Youth shouldn't rely on government jobs. *The Tribune*. 22 February, p. 9.

Sharma, K.L. and Singh, H. (1980). *Entrepreneurial Growth and Development Programmes in Northern India: A Sociological Analysis*. New Delhi: Abhinav Publications.

Sharma, Rachana (2015). *Shops and the Malls: A Sociological Exploration of Indian Retail Business*. Delhi: Kalpaz Publications.

Sheth, P. (2001). *Indians in America: One Stream, Two Waves, Three Generations*. Jaipur: Rawat Publications.

Shirokov, G.K. (1980). *Industrialization of India*. New Delhi: People's Publishing House.

Shiva, Vandana (1988). *Staying Alive: Women, Ecology and Survival in India*. New Delhi: Zed Books.

Shiva, Vandana (1991). *Ecology and Politics of Survival: Conflicts Over Natural Resources in India.* Thousand Oaks: Sage Publications.

Singer, Milton (1972). Industrial Leadership: The Hindu ethic, and the spirit of Socialism. In *When a Great Tradition Modernizes: An Anthropological Approach to Indian Civilization* (pp. 342–357). New York: Praeger Publishers.

Singh, G. (2019). Changing labour processes through Agripreneurship in Punjab. In S. Misra, S. Shukla and G. Batthini (eds), *13th Biennial Conference on Entrepreneurship: Conference Papers* (Vol. 11, pp. 1211–1215). Delhi: Bookwell & Ahmedabad: EDII.

Singh, K.P. (1993). Women entrepreneurs: Their profile and motivation. *The Journal of Entrepreneurship*, 2(1), 47–58.

Singh, Kamla (1992). *Women Entrepreneurs*. New Delhi: Ashish Publishing House.

Singh, Naresh (2002). Institutionalization of Rural Entrepreneurship through NGOs: Introspection from Case Studies. *The Journal of Entrepreneurship*, 11(1), 55–73.

Singh, S.K. (1999). Panchyat Udyog in Uttar Pradesh: A democratic experiment in micro enterprise development, *The Journal of Entrepreneurship*, 8(2), 207–217.

Singh, Sheobahal (1985). *Entrepreneurship and Social Change*. Jaipur: Rawat Publications.

Singh, Sukhpal (1994). Refugees as entrepreneurs: The case of the Indian bicycle Industry. *The Journal of Entrepreneurship*, 3(1), 81–96.

Singh, Sukhpal (1997). Aspects of Entrepreneurship in Primary food-processing industries in Punjab. *The Journal of Entrepreneurship,* 6(2), 223–231.

Singh, Sukhpal (2013). Post-Green Revolution Agro-entrepreneurship among Capitalist Farmers in Indian Punjab and Andhra Pradesh. *The Journal of Entrepreneurship,* 22(2), 161–180.

Smelser, Neil J. (1988). *The Sociology of Economic Life.* New Delhi: Prentice-Hall of India.

Smelser, Neil J. and Swedberg, Richard (2005). *Handbook of Economic Sociology*. Princeton and New York: Princeton University Press and Russell Sage Foundation.

Spencer, Herbert (1969). *Principles of Sociology* (Andreski Stanislav, ed.) London: Macmillan.

Stein, Kristiansen (2007). Entry barriers in Rural Business: The case of egg production in Eastern Indonesia. *The Journal of Entrepreneurship*. 16(1), 53–76.

Sullivan, Allan O', Munir, Kamal and Dougherty, Deborah (1998). Building organizational capacities for product innovation. In R.K. Kanungo (ed.) *Entrepreneurship and Innovation: Models for Development* (pp. 265–286). New Delhi: Sage Publications.

Suresh, R.R. (2010). *Economy and Society: Evolution of Capitalism*. New Delhi: Sage Publications.

Swedberg, R. (2000). The Social science view of entrepreneurship: Introduction and practical applications. In R. Swedberg (ed.) *Entrepreneurship: The Social Science Review* (pp. 7–44). New Delhi: Oxford University Press.

Swedberg, R. and Granovetter, M. (1992). Introduction. In M. Granvettor and R. Swedberg (eds), *The Sociology of Economic Life* (pp. 1–26). Oxford: Westview Press.

Tambs-Lyche, H. (1980). *London Patidars: A Case Study in Urban Ethnicity*. London: Routledge & Kegan Paul.

Tan, Luc Phan et al. (2021). Personality traits and social entrepreneurial intention: The mediating effect of perceived desirability and perceived feasibility, *The Journal of Entrepreneurship*, 30 (1), 56–80.

Thandi, Shinder S. (2010). Diaspora and development: Can Sikh diaspora finance and philanthropy contribute to human development in Punjab? In R.S. Ghuman, S. Singh and J.S. Brar (eds), *Globalization and Change: Perspectives from Punjab* (pp. 366–386) Jaipur: Rawat Publications.

Timberg, T.A. (1978). *The Marwaris: From Traders to Industrialists*. New Delhi: Vikas.

Timberg, T.A. (2014). *The Marwaris: From Jagatseth to the Birlas*. New Delhi: Penguin Books.

Tripathi, D. (1971). Indian entrepreneurship in historical perspective: A re-interpretation. *Economic & Political Weekly*, VI (22), M-59–M-66

Tripathi, D. (2004). *The Oxford History of Indian Business*. New Delhi: Oxford University Press.

Tripathi, D. and Jumani, J. (2007). *The Concise Oxford History of Indian Business*. New Delhi: Oxford University Press.

Tripathi, D. and Mehta, M. (1990). *Business Houses in Western India: A Study in Entrepreneurial Response, 1850–1956*. New Delhi: Manohar Publications.

Trivedi, Chitvan (2010). A social entrepreneurship bibliography. *The Journal of Entrepreneurship*, 19(1), 81–85.

Trivedi, Chitvan (2010). Towards a social ecological framework for social entrepreneurship. *The Journal of Entrepreneurship*, 19(1), 63–80.

Trivedi, Chitvan and Stokols, Daniel (2011). Social enterprises and corporate enterprises: Fundamental differences and defining features. *The Journal of Entrepreneurship*, 20(1), 1–32.

Trivedi, M. (1991). *Entrepreneurship among Tribals*. Jaipur: Printwell.

Trivedi, Mirdula (1983). *The Sindhi Entrepreneurs*. M.Phil thesis, Panjab University, Chandigarh.

Unni, Jeemol, Yadav, Vanita, Naik, Ravikiran and Dutta, Swati (2021). *Women Entrepreneurship in the Indian Middle Class: Interdisciplinary Perspectives*. Hyderabad: Orient BlackSwan.

Varma, Roli and Varma, Daya R. (2009). The making of Indian immigrant entrepreneurs in the US. *Economic & Political Weekly*, XLIV(3), 64–69.

Vasi, Ion Bogdan (2009). New heroes, Old theories? Toward a sociological perspective on social entrepreneurship. In Rafael Ziegler (ed.), *An Introduction to Social Entrepreneurship: Voices, Preconditions, Contexts*. Northampton, MA: Edward Elgar Press.

Verma, Archana B. (2002). *The Making of Little Punjab in Canada*. New Delhi: Sage Publications.

Vyas, Vijay (2005). Imitation, incremental innovation and climb down: A strategy for survival and growth of new ventures. *The Journal of Entrepreneurship*, 14(2): 103–116.

Wadhera, K. and Koreth, G. (2012). *Empowering Rural Women: Micro Enterprise through Achievement Motivation*. New Delhi: Sage Publications.

Watson, John (2003). Failure rates for female-controlled businesses: Are they any different? *Journal of Small Business Management*, 41(3), 262–77.

Weber, Max (1958). *The Religion of India* (Hans H. Gerth and Don Martindale Tr. and eds) New York: The Free Press.

Weber, Max (1976). *The Protestant Ethics and the Spirit of Capitalism* (Tr. by Talcott Parsons). London: Allen and Unwin.

Weber, Max (1978). *Economy and Society: An Outline of Interpretative Sociology*. Vol. 1. (Guenther Roth and Claus Wittich, eds) Berkeley: University of California Press (first published by Bedminster Press Inc. New York, 1968).

Weinberger, Katinka (2001). What role does bargaining power play in participation of women? A case study of rural Pakistan. *The Journal of Entrepreneurship*, 10(1), 75–85.

Weitzen, Harold Skip (1988). *Infopreneurs: Turing Data into Dollars*. New York: John Wiley and Sons.

Yunus, Muhammad (2006). *Creating a World Without Poverty: Social Business and the Future of Capitalism*. New York: Public Affairs.

Zeitlin, Irving M. (1969). *Ideology and the Development of Sociological Theory*. New Delhi: Prentice-Hall of India.

Zimmerer, T.W. and Scarborough, N.M. (2006). *Essentials of Entrepreneurship and Small Business Management*. New Delhi: Pearson Prentice Hall.

Reports

Annual Convention of CII on Family Business (2019). Users/HP/downloads/sectors.html

Asian Network Report (2006). Young and Minted, Broadcast on the BBC's Asian network at 1830 BST, Monday, 16 October.http://newsvote.bbc.co.uk/mpapps/pagetools/print/news.bbc.co.uk/2/hi/business/6054684) accessed on 5/15/2007.

Global Entrepreneurship Monitor 2014: India Report.

Global Entrepreneurship Monitor 2015–16: India Report.

Global Entrepreneurship Monitor 2016–17: India Report.

Global Entrepreneurship Monitor 2017–18: India Report.

Global Entrepreneurship Monitor 2018–19: India Report.

Global Entrepreneurship Monitor 2019–20: India Report.

Global Entrepreneurship Monitor 2020–21: India Report.

Reserve Bank of India, Annual Report, 2018.

Index